"The material and stories in this book are beautiful and riveting, rich in wisdom and compassion, at once healing and exciting. I think this book will fill you with the hope of having the life you were born to live and the life you've dreamed of, because this book is about our souls and hearts; about peace, gladness, and freedom."

Anne Lamott, *New York Times* bestselling author
of *Stitches, Traveling Mercies, Bird by Bird*, etc.

"Robyn's work and words are deeply beneficial and instructive to all who feel less than self-loving or caring.

You will find shelter and wings in the tender ferocity of these words that offer a sturdy platform of support and wisdom for people who wish to experience true self-love and care."

SARK, author and artist of *Succulent Wild Woman,*
Eat Mangoes Naked, etc.

"If your inner critic has been working overtime, if other people's opinions are more important to you than your own, if you would like to learn how to soothe yourself in times of stress and distress, pick up this book."

Nicole S. Urdang, M.S, NCC, DHM, LMHC
Holistic Psychotherapist, Buffalo, N.Y

"If you've been wanting the guidebook through the land of your truest self, you will LOVE, LOVE, LOVE this book!"

Julie A. Levin, MFT, Marriage and Family Therapist,
Pleasant Hill, CA

What reviewers have written about Robyn's journaling workbook,
Tenderly Embracing All the Ways that I Feel and Am: Journaling
to Kindle Gentleness and Compassion for Our Precious Selves

"This journal workbook could be one of the most important books you'll ever hold, because it will also hold you. Robyn Posin's words, unobtrusive thoughts and beautiful life-giving wisdom will be like a midwife for you, if you are anything like me, helping you gently bring forth your own truth, and being, and self. Take my advice—and a long deep breath—and begin the journey of a lifetime."

Anne Lamott, *New York Times* bestselling author of *Stitches,*
Traveling Mercies, Bird by Bird, etc.

"Robyn's wise and thoughtful words on the pages of this journal invite you to write your way to a deeper acceptance of yourself. Each page will take you to your core. Exploring the possibilities that Robyn offers here will help you to hear and embrace all of your self. This book could become your best friend."

Myrna Fleishman, Ph.D., Psychotherapist/artist. Santa Barbara, CA

"This journal is like your best friend inside, came out and made a book for you! Robyn's tender and soul nourishing wisdom weaves throughout and you will feel guided and supported to explore and discover all that you are and what you feel. Going inward with this book will lead you to develop even more exquisite self-care, self-acceptance and self-LOVE."

SARK, author and artist of *Succulent Wild Woman,*
Eat Mangoes Naked, Transformation Soup,
Glad No Matter What, etc.

"This journal is an exceptional tool to use for self-exploration. The quotes on the edge of each page are ideal for taking a simple idea and finding ways to apply it to our own lives. There is a love that comes through the pages that encourages you to take the time to be with yourself. It is gift that you give to yourself each time you sit down with the journal and write."

Caitlin J. Matthews, DC, Chiropractor, Ojai, CA

"This unique journal, with its generous space and nuggets of inspiring wisdom, encourages you to write, doodle, draw, scribble...whatever furthers your personal journey. No recipes here—just room to be the authentic you, in the company of Robyn's wise soul."

Vivian Sudhalter, Professional Wordsmith/Editor, Ojai, CA

What reviewers have written about Robyn's third book,
*Choosing Gentleness: Opening Our Hearts to All the Ways
We Feel and Are in Every Moment*

"This is a heart-singing book, filled with wisdom, tenderness, joy and humor about our soul and spirit, and the child inside. *Choosing Gentleness* is poetry and essays and artwork about healing, about accepting and even celebrating every aspect of our true beings, even the scary parts—yikes! Rich in truth and revelation and instruction, it is a song to the Self and it is a delightful way home, in the company of a singing, dancing woman of depth and quirk and general amazingness."

Anne Lamott, *New York Times* bestselling author
of *Stitches, Traveling Mercies, Bird by Bird*, etc.

"*Choosing Gentleness*—Let the wisdom within surround all the parts of you with uncommonly supportive love. It is not a normal book, which is a gift to us all."

SARK, bestselling author and artist of *Succulent Wild Woman,
Eat Mangoes Naked,* etc., Creativity Mentor

"A gift, literally and figuratively, the essays, poems and drawings in *Choosing Gentleness* persuasively whisper that gentleness is the needed foundation for self-awareness and transformation. As you gently, patiently coax the characters of your internal world to share their feelings and concerns with you—their ever-developing compassionate witness—deep self-acceptance melts long held patterns. With that, new strength and growth appear."

Carol H. Munter, co-author *Overcoming Overeating*
and *When Women Stop Hating Their Bodies*

"Our society is a supersaturated solution of experts, books and YouTube videos claiming to help you feel better about yourself and navigate your way through the labyrinth of thoughts, feelings and sensations that make up anyone's life.

What distinguishes Robyn's beautiful new book, *Choosing Gentleness*, from the rest of the pack is her ability to weave self-compassion into lives that have been inundated with unhelpful societal tropes."

Nicole S. Urdang, M.S, NCC, DHM, LMHC
Holistic Psychotherapist, Buffalo, NY

"This is a delicious book full of bite size nuggets of wisdom on how to be kind to yourself."

Caitlin E. Matthews, D.C., Chiropractor, Ojai, CA

For Harriet,
With love, hugs
& warmest
blessings,
always!

Go Only as Fast
as Your Slowest Part
Feels Safe to Go:

Tales to Kindle Gentleness and
Compassion for Our Exhausted Selves

Robyn L. Posin, Ph.D.

Compassionate Ink
Box 725
Ojai, CA 93024

Compassionate Ink
Box 725
Ojai, CA 93024

Some portions of this book have, in other forms, appeared previously in:
Encore: A Bi-Monthly Magazine Celebrating the Return of the Crone. Editor/Publisher: Joyce Cupps. Mariposa, CA
Venus Rising: A Bi-Monthly Magazine. Editor/Publisher: Dale Lewis. Santa Barbara, CA
AHP Perspective. Editor: Alexandra Hart. San Francisco, CA
The Overcoming Overeating Newsletter. Editors: Carol Grannick, Jane Hirschmann, Judith Matz, Carol Munter. Jade Publishing. Chicago, IL
New Dimensions: The Journal of New Dimensions Radio. Editor: Justine Toms. Publisher: Michael Toms. Ukiah, CA

Cover Photo and Cover Design by Steve Rossman
Book Design by Jacki Barineau with Robyn L. Posin and Barbara Fosbrink
Author Photo by Barbara Fosbrink

Publisher's Cataloging-in-Publication data

Posin, Robyn L.
    Go only as fast as your slowest part feels safe to go: tales to kindle gentleness and compassion for our exhausted selves / Robyn L. Posin, Ph.D.
        p. cm.
    ISBN 978-0-615-71700-5

1. Self-acceptance. 2. Self-esteem. 3. Self-actualization (Psychology). 4. Mind and body. 5. Happiness. 6. Peace of mind. I. Title.

BF697 .P685 2013
158/.1 --dc23   2012921869

PRINTED IN THE UNITED STATES OF AMERICA

For the Grandmothers: *The multi-racial, multi-ethnic, zany and outrageous band of ancient spirit beings that guided, nudged, whispered in my heart and protected me along the way of this extraordinary journey.*

It is long past time for us to be more gentle, tender, loving guardians for our emerging selves and for the wounded little ones inside of us...

- Robyn L. Posin

Contents

(The alphanumeric codes in parentheses are explained in Appendix I)

Acknowledgments

The emotionally abusive parenting of the damaged woman who birthed and raised me left a legacy of woundedness and self-hatred. Transforming that legacy has shaped my life and my work in the world. The woman I am today (a woman I love, respect and delight in) and the learning I share in this book exist because of that woman, Etta Rosenbaum Posin, and her failings.

The early, consistent love and cherishing from my dad: Zangwill Posin, my maternal grandparents: Simon and Fannie Rosenbaum, my aunts: Ruth Rossman and Toby Gottlieb and my uncle: Ben Rossman helped me to survive that mothering and kept alive the spark from which the me that I am has grown.

At the beginning of our deeply nourishing, 40+ year friendship, Carol Munter (www.overcomingovereating.com) shared with me her then-new approach for ending the tyranny of food/body size obsessions. The process (legalizing all foods and stopping the constant yelling at my self around what I was eating) resolved my craziness around food/body size. Inspired, I began extending those practices to dealing with all of my feelings, growing an inner Mommy/loving caretaker who helped me heal my life. The stories in this book describe that journey begun in 1971.

Without the gentle, determined persistence of my good friend Barbara Fosbrink this book would never exist. She nudged and mentored my crabby, resistant self into becoming both willing and computer literate enough to create and manage a website to share what she prodded me to see as my "body of work." The stories I've written for each of the Rememberings and Celebrations cards over the next several years combined with that earlier "body of work" to become this book. Barbara's been an invaluable technological mentor/collaborator, sister on the road and, most recently, an enormous help in getting me to see the myriad considerations that needed to be addressed/decided before the manuscript could be passed on to the person who would cast it into templates for publication.

Jodi O'Brien, Ph.D. gave me the amazing gift of organizing the sequencing of the four sections and the essays within them. In doing this she uncovered an organic flow I hadn't recognized. She edited the text with a commitment, as she described it, to preserving and clarifying its "Robyn voice" for "novice Robyn readers." Any awkwardness still present is entirely my own doing.

Deanne Jameson's loving support/cheerleading for getting this book out into the world included her careful editing that honored my often idiosyncratic use of language.

Annie Lamott's hilarious editorial commentary on an early version of the introduction trained my eye/ear to keep excising (most of) the excesses of adverbs, adjectives and repetitions that formerly weighed down my prose.

Steve Rossman, dear cousin and photographer extraordinaire (www.steverossman.com) six years ago took the altar photo that I knew then would become the cover of the book yet to be born. He did a lot of Photoshop work to prepare it for the cover he designed while also walking me through hours of Photoshop processes for casting drop shadows on the Rememberings card images.

Shelley Buonaiuto (www.alittlecompany.net) created the marvelous sculpture, Grandmother Nanima, which sits on my altar in Steve's photo. Shelley graciously gave me permission to use the photo of Nanima for the book's cover. Her amazing laughing grandmother sculptures are uncanny manifestations of the Grandmothers who live in my heart and to whom this book is dedicated.

Carol Munter, Myrna Fleishman, Faith Friedlander and Teri Mettala have been my emotional mainstays for more years than I care to count: sister-travelers on the road of living life deeply and authentically, keepers of each other's emotional archives, trustworthy mirrors in which we each see our selves reflected and loving allies with whom to laugh uproariously at the absurdities of life and our selves.

Marguerite Webster, Ellen Steininger, Sherry Price and Jonna Faulkner have been loving, affirming and celebrating cohorts as we've shared the intimate tales of our lives over so many years.

Special thanks to Vivian Sudhalter (vivians09@att.net), professional wordsmith and self-described OCD (obsessive-compulsive) pedant, for her eagle-eyed line editing and for her hilarious New York sense of humor.

With all my heart, my thanks to the wizardry and delightful collaboration of Jacki Barineau (jb@ourlittleplace.com) who put the final polish on the manuscript as she prepared it for the Amazon Create Space templates and publication.

And, finally, my profound gratitude to the hundreds of women who, while working with me as a therapist or in responding to the stories on my website, shared the stories of their lives, their struggles and their emergence with me as they, too, grew themselves beyond the limiting legacies of their pasts.

Introduction

My journey began one very hot and humid night in late August the summer just before my 23rd birthday. At the time, by all outward measures, I was enormously successful for my age and stage of development: at the top of my class in graduate school in psychology; the uncontested fair-haired darling of two distinguished faculty mentors – one male, one female; my intellect respected by both faculty and students in my department; National Science Foundation and National Institutes of Health Fellowships supporting my schooling and research; honored with a coveted position as departmental clinical teaching assistant; acknowledged for my Master's Thesis research paper presented at the Eastern Psychological Association convention; off to a smashing start on my Ph.D. dissertation research project and having recently extricated my self from a two-year relationship that had grown deadening.

However, none of these outward measures of success registered inside of me. None of them ever allowed me to feel good about my self for more than brief, passing moments. Most of the time I felt like a fraud, living in fear that the whole fabric of me would unravel if the right thread got snagged. Only those things that I had not yet done seemed to hold any promise of making me feel good about my self. Yet, once I'd accomplish any of these things, they immediately ceased to be of any value to me as something that could make me feel any better about my self. The more successes I accumulated, the more despairing I grew.

On that sweltering August night, I'd fallen deeper than ever into this despair that had plagued me for much of my life. My evening had been spent with a very caring man I'd known for some months. His kindness only deepened my sense of being cut off; frozen behind some invisible screen.

With a few sketchy words of apology, I fled his apartment on the Upper Westside of Manhattan. I got to my car and started on my way to the Westside Highway. I wasn't going home to my family's house in Brooklyn. Rather, I was intent on driving my car into the first concrete abutment I came to. I'd had it with life. I couldn't imagine how else I could ever escape from the pain and suffering I felt I couldn't bear for one more minute. I was filled with a sense of liberation, an anticipation of relief as I pulled out into the street.

Mort came flying, barefoot, out of his apartment building just as I was driving past it. He ran out into the street in front of my car to stop me. He cajoled me into pulling over and letting him in to talk with me. He'd grasped how at the edge I was feeling when I'd left and he wanted to try to reach out to me at that edge.

I don't remember what he said. I remember only how stunned I was that, without words, he'd known that I was at the end of my rope. I was equally amazed that he'd felt compelled to see if he could help me to reel my self back in. That reached through the frozenness.

I realized, as we talked, that since I was ready to finally check out anyway, I could postpone the moment long enough to see what therapy might have to offer me. Liberated, at last, from any hope or expectation that I could make my life better, I felt open to waiting a bit longer before actually letting go of it all. Until this moment, the possibility of trying therapy and having it not work was more risk than I could imagine taking.

It took a call to one of my mentors at graduate school to get a referral. And, it took another couple of weeks to get an appointment. August in New York is **not** a time to have an emotional crisis: all the therapists are off on vacation.

It was a watershed moment in my life. The choice to suicide stayed open as an option in me for many years after that night. Keeping the option to leave if things again became hopeless gave me the room to keep choosing to stay alive. That night marked the beginning of what, at this moment, has been a 49-year journey of finding my way home, of making peace with my self.

I started with a gentle bear of a male therapist whose support helped me to save my life. After some time on my own, I then worked with a woman therapist in whose presence I learned to listen in to the urgings of a voice from deep within me. That voice pressed me to "get to somewhere green." Though she feared for my choice to leave my complex, highly successful New York life behind and take to the road, that therapist supported my following the urging from within.

That voice led me, at 32, west to California in a van that I'd set up as a bed-sitting room. I went hoping to leave behind all the roles, achievements and intellectual accomplishments with which I had, till then, defined me to my self. I was filled with an aching, a hunger to uncover who I might be without all those trappings. I yearned for empty space in which I might be able to hear from and to tend the less developed parts of me.

Over the next ten years I both found and lost my self in ways I hadn't imagined possible: I learned how to play. I learned how to live in, to nurture and to value my body as something more than the thing that carried my head around. I discovered that I could actually feel like a worthwhile human being when doing nothing more than working on my tan. I found that whenever I got involved in working in the world, I would (sooner or later) fall into all the old self-damaging patterns of super-responsibility and super-achieving. I learned that I could withdraw from such projects as soon as I began to feel that suffocating pattern returning.

Despite many changes in my inner and outer life, the relentless voice of the critic continued to weave its web. Its litany would inevitably emerge to once again leave me feeling undermined, thrashed and unworthy. "You think you're getting so healthy," she might say, "but here you are again, caught in the same old shit, making your self crazy for a change. Anytime you get involved with something new, you do the same old routines again and again. I can't believe how stupid and ridiculous you are. All this so-called health is just a new line of crap you're telling your self."

Then, halfway through the decade, I was drawn into a relationship that recapitulated and made present all the awful pains and struggles of my childhood with a damaged, damaging mother. At nearly 43, I found my self yet again as undone and suicidal as I had been at nearly 23. The despair I felt was enormous: twenty years of exploration, of growing and transforming yet I seemed to be right back where I'd started from. My inner critic was apparently right about me.

In the midst of my confusion and despair I found my way to a creative arts therapist. My work with her radically changed my life. She offered me the permission that I had always been so able to give to everyone but my self: permission to embrace **all** of my self just exactly as I was.

With our work together, I began to listen more compassionately to my fears, upsets, yearnings and angers; to listen to and to trust my gut senses about people, situations and timing. I learned how to suspend judgment about any of the feelings that arose in me; feelings that I might before have ridiculed or dismissed. I learned to make room for my self to be however I might be.

From the earliest days, the learning process in this journey involved – and seemed to require – huge amounts of time out in the natural world: near trees, mountains, canyons, boulders, rivers and creeks. I was continually drawn away from so-called civilization. There was much comfort for my heart outside in nature where it's clear that growth is cyclical: perpetually sprouting, blossoming, decaying and rising anew. Being in nature kept reminding me (and reminds me still) that **all** life has value and has its own organic timing: one tree isn't better than another; a pock marked, lichen encrusted boulder is no less beautiful than a river-washed smooth one. Trees, boulders, streams don't worry themselves about why or whether they deserve to exist. And, they never rush themselves onto their next cycle of growth.

I began the practice of loving my self exactly as I might be in every moment. I was growing an inner caregiver: a strong, consistent, unconditionally loving inner voice that kept providing me with the simple acceptance for which I'd yearned all of my life. "Honey," she might say when I'd made a mistake of some sort or fallen short of some expectation I'd had of my self, "it's okay to make a mistake, to not do everything perfectly. You're always learning and growing, that's what mistakes are for. I love you just the same no matter what you do. You're a dear and wonderful being. You're enough, you're okay just as you are and I love you so much."

Over time, as this new voice grew and strengthened, I was finally able to de-fang the relentless negativity of my inner critic. In that process, my relationship with my self and with every aspect of my life was changed. Having this caregiver always with me has given me the capacity to love my self exactly as I am, with all my warts and imperfections, as a still stumbling work in progress.

As I was growing this caregiver, words, songs and images came through me. They spoke the truths that had long been drowned out inside me by the harsh noise and harried bustle of our civilized world. They reminded me that we do not **ever** need to prove our selves worthy of love: we are all lovable, all worthy simply for being.

From when they first began emerging in the mid 1980s, I translated the words and images into greeting cards that I sent each Winter Solstice/New Year's to my friends, clients and family. The cards were filled with messages that encouraged us to be kind and gentle with our selves no matter what challenging times we might be facing.

Some five years later, a series of 58 brief reminders emerged. They reflected much of what I had been learning and living into on the road to treating my self lovingly all of the time. These affirmations and a series of calligraphic drawings evolved into a deck of bookmark-sized cards that I called Rememberings and Celebrations: Loving Reminders of the Great Mother's Voice. Then, both the greeting cards and the bookmark deck became part of a mail-order catalog business that I called For the Little Ones Inside. Following wherever the muse led me, I went traveling with my wares through much of the mid 1990s, showing and selling them at various sorts of Women's Festivals along the West Coast and in New Mexico.

A new cycle began as the century came to a close. This time I went through a bit of kicking and screaming as I responded to being nudged by the muse. My resistance focused on having to become computer literate (something I'd not been inclined to do) so that I could build a website. I managed to do this under the dedicated mentoring of – and in collaboration with – a computer savvy friend.

After the site was launched that summer I began, most months, to write tales from my life. The tales were the back-stories for one or another of the 58 reminder cards. These tales, the affirmations themselves and some other stories written along the way are what you'll find in the pages ahead.

When, six months after launching the site I finally provided an e-mail address, I began receiving mail from readers all around the globe. It was wonderful to hear that people both recognized themselves in the tales of my struggles and felt supported by the learning that had come from those struggles. Their responses told me that permission to be loving and kind to our selves no matter what, support for going only as fast as the slowest parts of us feel safe to go, the affirming of rest as a sacred part of the journey and the acknowledgment of life as moving in cycles were the most deeply appreciated messages people took from the tales.

The tales are layered here in much the same way as they came to me. They weave back and forth through time, overlapping with several different perspectives on many of the same experiences. They are part of a spiral rather than sequential or linear. If you read the book straight through from cover to cover, you'll discover that there's a fair amount of repetition of details among the stories. This is the result of my decision to have each tale be complete in itself, able to stand alone rather than be pruned to fit into the usual progression of a conventional book. It's a format that lets you read randomly around in the spiral of the narratives, choosing only the tale(s) that speak to your particular interest in the moment. It also allows for using the book as an oracle: you can open it to a random page in response to some question or need you might have for help from Spirit/your deep self and then read just the tale to which you've been led.

On the simplest level this book is merely an autobiography-in-pieces. Yet, if you recognize a parallel with your own life in any tale, it becomes your opportunity to travel vicariously along the road that led to the lessons that have set me free. As you travel, you may uncover the lessons that are your own and may also be set free.

May these tales and affirmations support you to develop your own unconditionally loving inner caregiver, to expand your compassion for your self, to calm the clamor of your inner critical voice and to make peace with all the parts of your self.

Ojai, California
Summer 2012

The Little Ones Story

*(A tale written in 1993, when I was 53,
about a season of my life 10 years before.)*

At 43, washed up on the far shore of a complicated and challenging seven-year relationship that reawakened every part of my still unhealed childhood wounding, I found my self lost from any connection to the deep knowing places within me. Much of that disconnectedness came from seven years of contradicting their messages and cutting my self off from their truths as I talked my self out of recognizing the damage I was doing to me in that relationship. (It was nevertheless damage that, from this distance of time and growing, turned out to have been a necessary part of the process of healing my life.) Before that relationship, I had never lost my self nor known the source of the depression and self-hatred that frequently surfaced in my sometimes self-accepting and self-valuing life.

During these periodic descents into the pit of despair, my vicious inner critic, the Hatchet Lady, slashed away and struck down anything about my self that I might treasure or value. Each time I would be sunk in depression, convinced that my hard-won good opinion of my self was based on lies and distorted vision. At 43, there was no periodic-ness about it. I lived full-time in the middle of the deepest, darkest pit. I was immersed as well in more grief than I could have imagined possible: grieving the end of what had been, for both my partner and me, a love that had become a symbiosis that was killing both of us.

For a year we struggled, separately and together, to extricate our selves from that enmeshment; to let go of the relationship that, born in the most significant loving either of us had ever known, had become a prison and torment to both of us. Except for those hours that I worked (as a therapist helping other women in their journeys of self-healing), I spent my time in anguish: crying, feeling devastated and finding no hand holds with which to begin the climb up out of the black hole in which I found my self.

The magic that had frequently woven through my life seemed to have disappeared beyond any hope of reconnecting with it. Yet, during that transition year, a glimmer of the old enchantment returned. It brought me to a creative arts therapist whose work gave me the permission to begin to love and cherish my self just as I was, just for being.

In her workspace we played for two hours every week. I dreamed to music, drew, painted and sculpted images from those dreams; I moved and sounded, spontaneously creating movements and sounds my being needed for healing. We made music together on all sorts of percussion instruments. That music gave me an outlet for the intense, inchoate grief, rage and yearning that word therapy couldn't then (or in all the years before) touch or release.

I began spending most of my time, even when not in her studio, drawing, painting and creating sounds with my voice and my growing collection of percussion instruments. The images and sounds were helping me feel my way through the bleak underworld in which I was living.

In the most empowering experience of my work with her, I traveled back in fantasy to the time before the child in me began to be traumatized and damaged by the world she inhabited. In the drawings from that session, an exuberant, radiant little creature leaped and bounded through great fields and forests of green, growing things. She danced through skies, clouds, oceans and through fields of pure energy. I felt her aliveness with every cell of my being. My heart was filled to bursting with love for and connection to this joyful creature.

The Little One's emergence was a turning point in my healing. I began devoting my self to her as completely as I had typically devoted my self only to the hidden little ones in others. I listened for and to her through every moment of my days. She had so much to tell me, with and without words. She knew immediately where it was okay and not okay for us to be. She knew, as well, which people, situations and interactions were damaging or dangerous to our well-being. She had always been there, wailing from her prison beyond layers of soundproofing. Yet, I had never listened like this before. I'd never acted single mindedly to advocate for and protect her vulnerability. She'd won my heart completely, instantly. There was no way I would allow anything or anyone (even the Hatchet Lady) to bring harm to her.

I couldn't imagine not adoring and protecting her. I did nothing that wasn't safe and nourishing for her. My dedication to making the world safe for her and to loving her (even when she was being whiny, mean or angry) began to heal my life. I never expected of her things that were beyond her capacity, never demanded that she get over her fears, never demanded that she "stop crying before I give you something to cry about," never demanded that she "stop complaining," never forced her to stop having a tantrum or to be nice when she wasn't feeling nice.

As we went along, it became apparent that if I could make a safe space (away from my own past and anyone else's current judgments, away from situations in which she might hurt herself or someone else), she could be fully in the middle of her feelings. Being allowed to feel and vent her feelings, she would at some point come through to the other side of them, even the most rageful or most sorrowful or most terrified ones. It had to be okay for her to feel however she felt. We made an alliance that strengthened daily. She let me know what she needed; I listened and provided that as best I could. And, a fiercely protective, kind, gentle, unconditionally loving Mommy was developing inside of me, a Mommy that was committed to caring for the Little One, no matter what.

Over the years that followed, we have together visited and experienced long locked-away rages, terrors, grief, hates and feelings of helplessness. The more of these previously un-allowed feelings we could live through safely, the more fully the joyful, playful, creative, full-of-our-self self emerged. And, the new Mommy could make it safe for that full-of-selfness, too. At first, the process involved just the two of us. As I became a better and stronger protector and Mommy, we were gradually and in small steps able to include being around other people.

During the years of healing – even in the times we were just the two of us and not around people – we have never been alone. From the moment the Little One emerged, there has been a constant stream of whisperings in my heart, a powerful sense of being watched over and surrounded with the boundless love of a circle of ancient foremothers. These ancient feminine energies feel like Spirit Grandmothers whose whisperings bring rememberings from the time before woman and her woman-wisdom were denigrated and deposed from her central, enlivening place in all our lives.   These outrageous, zany and loving presences have guided and supported my journey home to my birthright of loving my self unconditionally in all my imperfectness. They have brought me gifts of words, messages, lullaby song-chants, magical amulets and images for courage along the way of this journey.

The Grandmothers' words and messages, the kindness to self that they continually urge, the acceptance of all feelings and all body knowing that they hold so crucial to all wisdom – these rememberings and celebrations of my woman-self have gradually transformed me. They've become, through practice, a part of my daily emotional vocabulary for talking with my self. They've transformed my relationship with my self, with my life and with the whole sacred circle of life. No longer whispers in the heart, these messages have become a bone and cell deep thrumming that keeps me alive, expanding and vitally aware of the never ending rivers of magic and wonder in every ordinary moment of my life: in my aging, temporarily able body and in all the richness of my feelings, joyous or painful. No matter what blunders or un-evolved feelings, no matter what upsetting images, body memories or painful feelings emerge, I am always surrendering into the middle of whatever it is that is coming up – even as I'm sometimes feeling furious that it's happening again.

To nourish my soul, the Grandmothers guided me then and still into the wild spaces near where I lived in the orange groves of Ojai's East End. In these canyons I found places where it was safe to go naked in the woods, to climb up boulders in the rivers and streams, to sit in the middle of little waterfalls, to hug trees. I walked almost every day, most often into the canyon just up the road from my house. I sat, and sit still, nightly at the stream's edge on my hug-me or my nap rock. I sat in trees on the property where I lived, began sleeping year round (except in the rains) on the ground in a four-windowed tent outside my house, under an ancient live oak. Every tree, boulder, stream and cloud brought me the energy of their fierce and abiding love. I felt (and still feel) it flowing into my body and my being. The further I am from the signs of human progress, the more strongly that energy flows into me.

Singing the lullaby song-chants the Grandmothers taught me and embracing their messages about bringing loving kindness to my self, I continued the process – begun a full twenty years before – of slowing my life and further simplifying my existence so that I could work less and spend more of my time immersed in the sacred play that has been helping me to heal the wounds of living in this crazy-making, woman-negative, out-of-balance world.

I spend lots of time walking in the canyons by day and through the groves and to the creeks at night – listening to hawks in their courting flights, to owls' calls and to the coyote conversations across the valley at night: drifting, dreaming, making art, puttering about my studio and garden. And, I keep in touch with the Little One's voice. Sometimes I find my self unaccountably full of rage, crankiness, sadness or aching of unknown origin. I yell and howl, beat on drums or a stuffed duffle bag, stomp my feet, roar, cuss, cry, wail, howl, curl up with the covers pulled over my head feeling sorry for my self, don't answer the phone and don't go out in the world.

Repeatedly and in cycles, more layers rise up into the open space: more old feelings to be felt and released. Unlike the me-of-the-past, I no longer need to make sense of the whys and where-froms of these torrents of emotion that overtake me. Sometimes images and memories come with the feelings; sometimes just the inchoate feelings by themselves. Each time, given the safe space to be in the midst of their storms, I come through to the other side. There the sun shines again, I feel cleansed and I have more of me from which to live and create. I feel the chest-full-to-bursting, heart-singing joy of being surrounded by so much beauty and wonder. And, even in the now less frequent hard times, I find my self (as my sister describes it) feeling wonderful about feeling awful – because, in the middle of it, I know I'm coming home to the all of me.

Between the rising up times, I continue to rest deeply for days and sometimes weeks or months on end. I read tons of women's detective mysteries and novels curled up by the fire or out under a walnut tree in my hammock and I take long and short voluptuous naps.

Because connecting with my Little One and the Mommy Inside has made such a profound difference both in how I live inside of my self and how I continue the ongoing process of healing my life, I try to share the wonder of it with the people who come to work with me. Over the years I've experimented with ways to help others create magical space for meeting their own inner Little One(s) and kindling their own loving inner Mommy. It's impossible to come up with some general recipe that will be just right for everyone, that won't feel stilted and formulaic. It's such a personal process. So, I've learned to use some concrete details to communicate a sketch of the possibility. Then, each person uses her own intuition and sensibilities to refine the sketch and tailor a process that feels exactly right for her self.

Here's the sketch. Remember none of it is meant as the-right-way-to-do-it, so consider using the sketch as a jumping off place from which to improvise and create what works for you. Keep tweaking till it feels like your very own way.

It helps to gather a photo or two or three of your self as a child. Try looking through old photo albums to see which pictures of your younger self catch your eye. Those are probably the age-selves who most need your attention at this time.

Choose a safe, quiet and private corner in your world where you can create a sacred space for you and your little one(s) to meet. A nice bit of cloth can define the space for you. Add the photo(s) and perhaps a candle that you can light each time you come to this meeting space. Lighting the candle can help you and your little one(s) mark the threshold between regular life and your special time together. Lighting some incense, burning some sage or ceremonially washing your hands are other ways that might appeal to you to help mark the transition. If there's not a place where you can safely leave this sacred altar space set up all the time, try arranging it in a special box that you can open when you're ready to visit your little one(s).

It can help to include in your sacred space any little toys or objects that remind you of things that you treasured and were comforted by as a little person. If you still have any of the original things you used, that can be especially wonderful.

It's important at the start to commit to only a very tiny bit of regular time. Five minutes twice a week that you keep to is much better than promising a half hour every day and then not showing up. The little one(s) have done without any attention for a very long time. In order for them to risk trusting that you really will be there for them if they show up, they need to know you'll keep your promises.

Having a pillow or a specially chosen stuffed animal or doll that you can cradle and hold while you talk with your little person(s) can be very comforting. You can imagine that your little one is inside whatever you're cradling. And, sometimes, you can imagine that you are inside the little being that the big you is holding so tenderly.

A good way to start each time is by apologizing to your little one(s) for treating her/them as harshly, neglectfully or uncaringly as she/they were treated by your original caregivers. It's helpful to keep letting her/them know that, even though you are feeling quite awkward and uneasy with all this, you are committed to learning to be an unconditionally loving, fiercely protective Mommy to your little person(s); to learning how to be there with and for her/them as much of the time as possible.

It may take many visits before you actually begin to hear from your little one(s). While you're there talking to them, singing favorite lullabies, reading favorite childhood books, telling made up stories or just rocking and humming can feel good. When they begin to communicate with you, you may hear or feel them in your heart. Sometimes words come, sometimes just a sense of their feelings. A blank drawing book or pad and some colored marking pens or big crayons are good to have for your little one(s) to use to draw pictures for you, scribble feeling-colors or even words when that feels right to her/them. It's good to place the pens or crayons in your non-dominant hand for this. It may feel weird or odd to see words/pictures emerge either inside of you or on the pages. Try not to dismiss them as just-your-mind, they really are coming from the little one(s) heart to you.

It helps each time to ask your little one(s) to let you know in words or feelings what she/they needs from you in order to feel safe to come out to visit/talk/play with you. And, too, to ask what your little one(s) might need or like from you in the middle of your ordinary day to day life.

If none of this feels right to do, don't bother your self with any of it. Just read the tales ahead.

Part One:
Taking More Gentle Care of Our Selves

Though we rarely get much support and encouragement for it in the so-called real world, taking the very best care of our selves **is** our first responsibility to all beings on this planet.

When we are being loving, tender, kind, gentle, forgiving and emotionally generous with our selves, we are filling our deepest selves with rich nourishment.

The more fully we nourish our selves, the more likely it is that we will have abundant, healthy energy with which to grow our selves; energy that we can then radiate and share with all the beings and creatures around us.

Finding time and ways to listen inward to our deep selves and learning to trust what we hear inside of us are at the beginning of this practice.

Talking lovingly to our selves, making time and safe space to be with all our feelings – happy, sad, grieving, confused, joyful, angry, rageful, goofy, bratty – are essential.

Treating our selves as lovingly as we would treat anyone else we truly cared about is the path.

1-1. Our First Responsibility

*Your first responsibility to all the beings on our planet
is to take the very best care of your very own self!*

I'm always moved by the safety instruction programs at the beginning of airline flights. The ones emphasizing that adults (always pictured as female) traveling with small children should adjust and secure their own oxygen mask before tending to the child's mask. I feel moved because these programs are the only place in all of ordinary life where women are encouraged, in any way, to put taking care of our selves ahead of taking care of anyone else.

For many years of my life I, like most well acculturated women, felt responsible for the emotional and physical well being of everyone around me. I'd need to feel that everyone else was taken care of - feeling comfortable, happy, entertained, engrossed in something enjoyable, etc. - before I could begin to think or feel my way into what I might need or want for my self. It was only rarely that I got to my self. Even more rarely that I got to my self with enough energy to actually explore me. And, since I'd neither birthed nor raised children (toward whom some of this kind of responsibility might be appropriate), everyone-else was most often a reasonably competent being of at least my own age.

Many times I'd remain in conscious oblivion about needs I know that I had in order not to have them get in the way of my caretaking commitment. I lived in fear of being seen as selfish. That is, as wanting to do or not do something, to be or not be some way that, while it might please my self, wouldn't also please whoever was around me.

Your First

Responsibility

To All The Beings

On Our Planet Is

To Take The Very

Best Care Of

Your Very Own

Self!

o1

My devotion to this impossible agenda left me quite depleted, often frustrated and, as well, resentful if my efforts seemed to no avail. More often than not, I was uncomfortable, unhappy, un-engrossed in anything other than trying – with varying degrees of success – to take care of everyone else. Or, I'd be trying, at the very least, not to displease anyone else.

In my early thirties, I felt a welling up of despair, a fear that I might never feel good about or at peace with my self. This, despite all I was doing and being for and with the others about whom I cared and despite all the external trappings of my outward successes. It was a critical time of turning inward, the beginning of a conscious journey to both uncover and discover my own self: What I might think, feel, need or want at any given moment.

In the almost forty years since that turning, I've chosen more and more to risk exploring my self instead of trying to disappear my self into the selflessness I was taught was praiseworthy in women. I've gone inward to listen to and come to know my own self. As I've traveled inward, I've gradually become quite adept at taking good care of my self. I discover that I am quite capable of providing comfort, happiness, entertainment and engrossing enjoyment for my self. And, what I can provide for my self is deeper and more lasting nourishment than either that which I could provide for someone else or that which they could provide for me.

As I do better at this, I understand how much of it **is** something we can do best for our selves. Much of comfort, happiness and feeling enlivened, entertained or engrossed enjoyably is basically an inside job: Not something you can create in someone outside of your self or that someone outside of you can create in you.

As we get better at knowing and taking good care of our selves, there is an overflowing of our well-nourished energy that spreads out into the world. Our giving comes from fullness rather than our need to feel okay about our selves. This brings loving support to other beings as they themselves do their own work of becoming responsible for knowing and taking exquisitely good care of themselves.

Consider spending some time turning the light of your finely tuned sensitivity toward your very own self. Then, practice taking the very best care of your very own self. It's the greatest gift you can give to all beings on this planet.

1-2. Giving That Depletes You

Giving that depletes you can never truly be nourishing to another...
When you give more than you can, you come to need more than you
can find anywhere outside of your now depleted self...
Practice taking better care of you!

Growing up in a Judeo-Christian tradition, I've been subject to the pervading notion that it's nobler to give than to receive. Growing up female, I've also been subject to our culture's cell-deep indoctrination that a woman's role is, as writer Anne Lamott would call it, emotional Sherpa – primary nurturer to others, trained to serve her self last and only with what is left over after everyone else in need is replete.

Giving That Depletes
You
Can Never Truly Be
Nourishing To
Another...
When You Give More
Than You Can, You
Come To Need More
Than You Can Find
Anywhere Outside Of
Your Now Depleted
Self...
Practice Taking
Better Care Of You!
c7

A very damaged woman who needed much more mothering than she could ever provide to a child, my mother didn't fit this mold. My early survival depended on being attuned to the nuances of this disturbed woman's generally unpredictable psychic state. My safety depended on sensing and accommodating to her needs. To need anything from her was to seriously endanger my self. My job was to do whatever I could to lighten her load without ever appearing to be doing any such thing. Failing in either aspect of this assignment brought her rage, shaming verbal abuse and/or disparagement of anything I'd done for her.

Trained, as I was, to deny or ignore her needs, my inner child languished, an unnourished starveling. Still alertly sensitive to those around me, she/I resonated with the unexpressed needs of similarly denied inner starvelings in anyone and everyone else. I was, by my culture and personal history, encouraged and permitted to try to nourish these starvelings in others (even as I continued to feel the imperative to do that covertly).

This awareness of others' unacknowledged neediness carried with it a grave sense of responsibility. If I could perceive someone's unexpressed hunger, I felt compelled to do something for or about it. It never mattered if I was spent or at the edge of my own endurance. My responsibility was to covertly tend to those or any other needs that were, however indirectly, revealed to me. And, it was essential that my help be given in ways that did not force the person to become conscious either of their need for help or of my ministrations to that need.

I was forever being psychically grabbed-by-the-collar by the unacknowledged waifs inside others. Most often these others were people like me. They were outwardly highly functional. They appeared (and had a stake in appearing) self-sufficient. As I involved my self in covertly responding to the waif inside of these other people, my own starveling would sort of jump into the person I was tending. By vicariously identifying with that person she could feel as if she, too, were receiving some of my caring bounty.

My attempts to help others move toward their own wholeness usually proved insufficient and never-ending. After devoting some considerable time to this thankless and ineffective giving, I (and my inner starveling) would feel depleted, frustrated and despairing.

Sometimes, I'd secretly be furious with the recipient of my bounty: "if someone gave me what I was giving you I would have done so much more with it. I would have appreciated it, used it to help heal my self." I'd feel angry that nothing I did ever seemed to fill them up or to be enough to heal them. If I had slipped and they'd noticed my giving at all, I'd feel angry that they were disparaging or dismissing the value of whatever I was giving to them.

These cycles were a continuing, though less than conscious, replay of my early unsuccessful attempts to covertly nourish my own mother into enough wholeness that she might then mother me. I repeatedly and automatically gave away that for which I longed.

What I didn't understand then was that, had someone actually offered me what I was longing for, I would have felt threatened by it. Given my early training, it would have been very hard to allow it in. I would have felt bad and wrong. I would have felt both shamed and indignantly offended at being seen as needing anything at all.

In those years of my life, I also didn't understand that feeding the little starveling is for every one of us always an inside job. When others are trying to nourish her directly it doesn't work: nothing can reach across the time warp to her. She feels badly. What is given doesn't get inside of her to the empty place. She may see this as hateful evidence of her own insatiability. Or, she may see it as infuriating evidence either of the giver's incompetence at giving or of the giver's malevolent manipulation of her neediness.

Only we our selves can re-mother the self that wasn't properly nourished in the time that she was a physical child. Only when we our selves have opened a conscious connection with that little one within can others' gifts work to help support our own loving ministrations to her.

In my early forties I gradually understood these truths. I began to give my self permission to recognize and to care for the needy child inside of me. Not having that permission had set me up for the awful, fruitless subterfuge of trying secretly and vicariously to get for her some of the nourishment I was always offering to others (whether they wanted it or not). Till then, I'd felt shamed by being a vulnerable human being, by having any needs at all.

As I began to focus on giving to my self, to my Little One inside, I saw how much my giving to others had been freighted with hidden expectations and agendas. I expected people to use what I offered to make them selves better. I expected them, once better, to be able to give back to me what I had given to them. Much of my supposedly selfless giving to others was convoluted, a less than conscious (and doomed to failure) attempt to get nourishment for my self.

When we give because we believe that everyone else's needs are more compelling or important than our own, when we give to get, when we give to others what we really (often less than consciously) need and want for our selves, we are depleting our selves. Because we are giving with secret agendas, what we give is tainted, therefore toxic for its recipient. All too often, what we are giving is what both that person and we our selves each need to be giving to our own selves.

When we do the work to develop and then act on the permission to give that devoted caring to our own selves, we are doing the work of nourishing our inner starvelings. When we deepen our practice and hone our skills at loving and nurturing our needful selves, we become at last capable of filling the emptiness inside of our long abandoned little inner selves. We become less vulnerable to being grabbed-by-the-collar by disowned neediness in others.

Becoming adept at feeding and filling our selves, we also become able to truly gift others out of our inner abundance. This kind of giving often feels the same as just being our selves: no effort, no agendas, no needing anything in return. The joy we feel in sharing our selves, our overflow is complete in itself. We offer our love, our energy, our caring and our being as giveaway rather than as give-to-get or give-to-fix. In this offering, it is possible for all of us to be nourished in appropriate, effective ways.

Releasing my self from my convoluted giving, I learned that the hardest piece of the work was giving up the belief/hope that anyone other than I could or would ever be the Mommy for whom my starveling ached and yearned. So much of my Mommy-ing of others had been my way of creating and sustaining the illusion that it might really be possible for one person to Mommy another person into wholeness. Sustaining that illusion allowed me to keep on hoping and believing that one day someone would at last appear to Mommy me into wholeness.

Giving up that hope/belief was for me and is for each of us extraordinarily challenging. We are forced to come to terms with the fact that if we didn't get the mothering we needed when it would have been age appropriate, we can never get it from anyone outside of our selves. We are filled with inconsolable grief and intense rage. Yet, it's only when we can give up the hope that we reach the threshold from which we can at last begin to do the work to grow an inner Mommy who can finally provide us with what we've so been longing for.

Consider giving your self permission to take exquisitely loving care of your very own self.

1-3. Loving Your Self Unconditionally

Loving your self unconditionally is a revolutionary act!

There are times that my heart fills with sadness for the me that I was for much of the first half of my life. Often I feel that same heart-hurting sadness while witnessing the struggles of many of the dear people with whom I've worked during the more than 47 years that I've been a therapist.

The level of self-loathing and self-criticism with which I and so many of us have lived (or still live) is staggering in both its overt and its more obscured versions. The depth and breadth of what we suffer in our anguished yearning to be seen – and to see our selves – as worthy, lovable beings is astounding.

I was such an odd little creature, quite different from my peers, an outsider from my earliest years. Yet, my own company sustained and nourished me. I could delight in my own imaginings and creative play. In relations with others, however, I usually felt quite at a loss: confused and of no value. I never seemed to fit in; never seemed to get-it-right.

Loving Your Self

Unconditionally

Is A

Revolutionary

Act!

b1

This experience echoed my daily experience with my cold, critical and dismissive mother. With her, too, I never seemed to get anything right. Nothing I did brought any warmth or approval from her. This filled me with despair. Early on, my little heart began believing that, if I could figure out how to be better, different, a **good-er** girl, less needy, more something-other-than-I-was, then my mother would magically be transformed. She would be warm and loving with me. Others, too, would see me as a worthy being.

This belief led to more than thirty years of laboring at the Herculean task of trying to be exceptional and perfect at everything I did. I felt compelled to bend, twist and re-form my self to fit the images of what I imagined she and others would hold as valuable. It was a desperate search for recognition, for the outside acknowledgement that I thought would help me to love and value my self. None of this ever worked. My mother was never transformed. No amount of recognition for my specialness made me feel more worthy or lovable.

Then, not long after my 32nd birthday, some deep wordless knowing within me began urging me to let go of this way of being me in the world. (See **Pirouettes**, page 125 for more about this.) I felt pushed from within to give up the futile attempts to achieve the perfection, the outside recognition that I had believed would transform my crippling self-criticism and self-loathing. I felt moved to leave behind all the trappings of my compulsively super-achieving lifestyle, the geography in which I'd lived that lifestyle and, with just a few exceptions, the relationships that had been part of that lifestyle.

In the ongoing (if sporadic) journal I kept during that first year of travel and transitioning, my belief that doings lead to feelings of worthiness fell away. In its place, a yearning emerged, revealed in a poem that speaks of the longing for someone who might love me into loving my self. In that poem, *I Want a Momma*, there is a poignant call for someone to "love me to pieces, just how I am…till I have no choice but…to revel in the joys of being me."

And there were, indeed, many people that I met in the early years of my new life who responded with lavish appreciation for the person I was at the time. None of them knew anything about who I'd been in my super-achieving, pirouetting former life. Their valuing of me had only to do with the just-me-ness of me, without any credentials-of-value earned by doings. Yet, none of this lessened the intensity of my recurrent self-loathing. It did little to transform my self-criticism or to nurture me into loving my self.

I discovered an awful irony in that season: When someone actually does show delight or appreciation for this self that we hate, that person is instantly devalued in our eyes. We see them as deranged, lacking in judgment or, at the very least, quite misguided. We are convinced that only a very poor judge of character/value could love and accept someone like us just the way we are – inadequate, flawed creatures that we see our selves to be.

When, for some reason, we're unable to discredit the judgment of the person who holds positive visions of our loathed selves, their good opinion of us is likely to further exaggerate the intensity of our self-hatred. Their good opinion contributes to our feeling that we are imposters. We're likely to rip into our selves for pulling the wool over their eyes. We're certain that, if we would stop inadvertently bamboozling them, they would see who we really are behind our subterfuge. Then, they would surely agree with our terrible opinion of our selves.

The child, the young woman and the thirty- early forty-something woman of me were all dreadfully tangled in this terrible catch-22. Starved for loving reflections, I longed for acceptance from other(s). Yet, the more I was surrounded by such reflections, the more antsy and loathing of my self I would become.

Despite this baffling experience with loving reflection, I was dedicated to being as sensitive, compassionate and unconditionally accepting as I could be to the broken, self-critical, self-loathing selves of others. Relentlessly, I committed my self to giving to others just what I felt most desperate to find for my self; exactly what I continued (despite the mounting experiential evidence to the contrary) to believe would heal my own similar brokenness, were it given to me.

Through all this effort and confusion, I gradually began to understand that no amount of others' loving could actually dismantle our self-loathing. Until and unless we develop at least a kernel of self-acceptance, their good energy has no opening through which to enter into us. There is no question that being surrounded by a loving environment is more supportive to our growing into self-love than being surrounded by a demoralizing, critical one. (Even as the loving environment brings some real challenges with it.) Yet, the job of actually transforming the self-hatred into self-love is something only we, our selves, can do – from the inside out.

The transformation from self-loathing into unconditionally embracing my self began with my discovering the Little One inside of me. (See **The Little Ones Story**, page 9 for more about this part of the journey.) When I met this little creature in a guided fantasy, I couldn't help but feel beguiled by her. She was captivating: exuberant, vulnerable and outspoken. I fell instantly in love with her. She inspired fierce protectiveness in me.

I was working with a creative arts therapist at the time. She had been able to give me just what I needed at that moment: the permission and encouragement for me to give to that little one all the love and acceptance I had till then felt allowed only to give away to others. (Never mind how ultimately useless it was to the others to whom I gave it.)

Over the more than 29 years since that remarkable day when I was 43 years old, I have opened my arms and my heart to various little selves inside of me, devoting my self to hearing and tending to their separate voices, their stories, their sorrows, their needs, their frustrations, their fears, their joys and their silliness. My life has been a daily practice of re-mothering all these little one parts of me.

Though I'd intentionally chosen never to birth or mother a physical child, I certainly had an extensive, well-honed repertoire of mothering skills to bring to my practice. These were the skills that I had used responding to the broken little ones I saw in other grown-ups. Now I was directing those skills to the task of re-mothering my self. In this journey I have become the Momma I was yearning for in that long ago journal poem.

(Note: In me, as in most of us, these inner little ones are not fully developed multiple personalities. They are merely the usually unattended internal parts of a complex self. Were these parts true child-multiples, though, I would be doing the very same practice with them.)

The care I keep giving to all the parts of my self has and has had an amazing effect on my life. The whole emotional vocabulary with which I talk to my self has changed. Though it has taken time and dedicated practice, I no longer have to contend with the heinous self-derogating of the Hatchet Lady (my formerly ferocious inner critic).

These days, no one (inside or outside of me) has permission to verbally beat me up or to tell me that there's something wrong with how I am. I can hear that someone (outside or inside of me) doesn't like how I am being. I'm equally willing to hear how they find me problematic. Or, how they wish that I were able to be different. I can listen sympathetically to these kinds of feedback. Yet, as soon as someone is suggesting that how I am is categorically not okay (rather than not-okay-for-them) the Mommy interferes so that I do not have to listen to such harmful messages.

Her unconditional acceptance helps me to no longer be subject to other people's ideas of how I should be or act or feel or think. I understand that their ideas about and for me reveal much more about them than about me. Rarely, these days, am I available to be seduced by their good opinions or devastated by their bad opinions of me.

I don't necessarily like every way that I am. But, I can and do embrace all the ways that I am. I know, in a cell-deep way, that accepting where and how I am is the only way I have a prayer of ever moving beyond that place. (This, the opposite of conventional wisdom that would have us abhor and repudiate whatever in our selves we wish to change.) The Mommy Inside is calmly patient with me when I am stuck in such places, no matter how long the stuckness lasts. This gives me a gentle spaciousness in which to grow my self.

As we each work to develop and expand the practice of becoming unconditionally loving mothers to our selves, we are part of a revolution in consciousness. We are freeing our selves from the countless undermining torments that our pasts and our culture can visit upon our impressionable selves. We are becoming more solidly grounded in our precious evolving selves. We are becoming consistently more gentle, more kind and more tender with our vulnerable and empowered selves.

The more we practice unconditionally and compassionately embracing our selves, the more fully we can bring compassion and unconditional acceptance to others in our lives. We grow our capacity to be spacious witnesses rather than impatient interferers in the processes of others. We give up the misguided notion that we can fix anyone but our selves.

Imagine the possibilities in bringing your unconditional loving to your own self.

1-4. Love Your Self as You Are Now

You are entitled to love your self just exactly as you are right now!

Although I occasionally do stretch to attend milestone celebrations with my family or my friends, I generally avoid settings that involve groups of people or parties. Though this quirk of mine is sometimes hard for my friends and family to embrace, they've all come to accept that this is just what's so about me. Typically, they'll let me know about their events so that I can send my good wishes and my spirit-self to join them there. Then, because they know that I love celebrating their special moments with them one-to-one, we usually make such a plan close in time to the event.

I rarely go to any workshops – even when their plans seem tempting. Being in workshops listening to people (who are neither my close friends nor my clients) as they process even their richest personal material exhausts me.

You Are

Entitled To

Love Your Self

Just Exactly

As You Are

Right Now!

j2

Though I sometimes think about taking a class (tai chi, yoga, dance, Pilates), being plugged into time or having to be in synch with any outside schedule feels so noxious, I rarely make such a contract. Appointments with my clients, scheduled semi-monthly massages and my occasional acupuncture, chiropractic, doctor, dentist, and hair appointments are about all the being-plugged-into-time with which I can cope without irritation. For that very reason, any plans made with any of my women friends are always, and up to the last minutes, subject to change by either of us. That way we each can honor where and how we actually are on the day for which we've made the tentative plan.

Except for the solitary sort-of-traditional Thanksgiving meal and practice of giving gratitude that are part of my yearly birthday retreat, I don't celebrate the calendar holidays. Yet, I often do seem to be led into private spontaneous rituals in the weeks around the solstices and equinoxes. These rituals usually include cleansings: down-to-the-bone cleaning of my cottage, going through my stuff and my space and passing on or pitching out whatever is no longer actively a part of my life. Long solo hikes in the mountains usually figure in these rituals as well.

My celebrations of the Jewish holidays are typically limited to sending loving cards to my family and to my Jewish friends. Except for Passover. Then, I join a gathering of lesbian-feminists and their children for an annual Seder that has a 22-year history. (I've been a part of this somewhat non-traditional tradition for many of those years.) There, every year during our Seder, we each take a turn responding intimately and personally to that year's reflective question about our lives. Though I see most of these women only that once each year, we've become a tribe, an extended family-of-choice rather than a group. That makes this particular being-together feel nourishing to me.

For many years now, I've gone on silent retreat (in my own space) for my actual birthday, choosing not to share that day with anyone but my own various inner selves. Still, I love getting cards and phone messages celebrating me on my birthday on that day. So, I do go out to the post office to gather the cards. And, I do turn up the volume on the answering machine to hear birthday messages in the middle of my otherwise silent time. I love hearing what my friends wish for me and how they feel about me. I love being able to hear all that without having to engage, **that** day, in **any** conversations that are focused on anything or anyone **but me**.

Being given gifts is not my thing either (much to the consternation of some of my friends). I already have just about all the stuff in my little cottage that I can manage to care for, to keep track of or that I might want. Still, some of my friends won't be restrained by my preferences. They offer me presents knowing that I may not accept them or that I may quickly pass them on. Some of my friends even manage to find things that surprisingly delight me, after all. Some of them tell me what they **would** have gotten for me if they didn't know about my feeling that presents are often added burdens. I love when they do that.

For more than 27 years, I've consciously chosen neither to be involved romantically nor sexually with anyone but my self. As the years have gone by, I've grown even more confirmed in these choices than I was when I first made them. I've come home to my truest self, finally honoring my nature as a solitary. I find solitude enchanting, nourishing, voluptuous, rich and delicious. I love the freedom and the open possibilities of having only my own energies around me on a daily basis.

I neither miss nor yearn for a sexual, romantic or daily relationship. Rather, I love and revel in the intimate, nurturing, ongoing sharing I do with my five or six closest women friends often by phone and when in person, usually out in the wild places. All of these luscious women are committed to their own deepening journeys. Much that challenges and stretches me/us happens in these intense and often giggle-filled sharings, these relationships of radical honesty. I'm grown by these relationships in ways that others seem to grow in partnering relationships.

For me, these days, the thought of partnering or living with anyone but my self feels claustrophobic and stifling. Some of my friends talk about the comfort they feel in having someone else around even when they're not directly engaging with that person. This kind of being by oneself with another is completely unappealing to me. If I'm spending time with someone, I want to be engaged with her (or him). If I'm not actually engaging with them, I'd much rather be by my self, **by my self** without someone in the background.

Over this past year, in several of my closest relationships, my women-friends and I have had to deal with a discovery that has proven somewhat challenging on both sides. In this season of my life, it seems that while my capacity for emotional support is still dependable and unwavering, my capacity for physical presence can no longer be counted upon in crisis times. This is different from how it's been with me in the past. And, it's taken some getting used to by all of us. It's not been easy, but it's been doable.

My most passionately politically and environmentally activist friend has struggled a lot, particularly since September 11 (2001), with my general disengagement from emotional or actual involvement with what's happening in the world. I am enormously grateful that others – like this dear friend who is so viscerally affected – are called from within themselves to respond consciously, actively and politically in meaningful ways. I know this needs doing. Yet political activism, an active engagement with the larger world, seems beyond me at this moment, not my path. I do what I'm able to help move us toward the paradigm shift. I offer prayers. And, I do my website: sharing there about living out-loud with permission to live from our truest selves, from the Sacred Feminine, the new (ancient, returning) paradigm.

Though I worry seriously about the escalating degradation of our environment, I seem unable, at this moment in my life, to find any authentic place in me from which to engage actively with the larger issues. I'm committed to recycling and composting. I garden organically and avoid the use of environmentally toxic or damaging products in and around my house. I try to be as conscious and conservative in my consumption of energy and resources as I'm able. So, although I continue to make my trips to Northern California by car rather than air (in order to provide the safety of a mobile home base for my Little Ones), I do accumulate and plan my local and next-big-town errands for the most gas-efficient use of my car. And, though my hot tub is not on solar power, I use no bromine or chlorine products in it.

I don't know whether or to what degree these odd and often inconsistent ways that I am (and am not) are born from what is healthy or from what is wounded within me. I discover that, the longer I live with my self, the clearer it becomes that this distinction is essentially meaningless to me.

How I am (inconsistencies and all) is just how I am right now. For all I know, it may even be how I am forever more. And, in just this moment, these ways that I am seem as so for me as that I have blue eyes. So, I work daily and assiduously on assuring my self of my own permission to be just who and how I am right now. And, I'm committed to the practice of entitling my self to cherish and value me just as I am right now – warts, imperfections, inconsistencies and all.

Years ago, supported by my friend Carol Munter's work (now available in the books *Overcoming Overeating* and *When Women Stop Hating Their Bodies*) I learned a very powerful lesson around body-size and self-hatred. We have to develop the practice of loving, cherishing, pleasuring and honoring our selves at just exactly the weight that we **are** (never mind how undesirable it might seem to us at the time). Unless we practice and learn how to do this at the weight we are and are starting from, we will never be able to love, cherish, honor and pleasure our selves at **any** weight, no matter what our when-I'm-thin fantasies might be.

Once we believe there are some more pounds/more pirouettes/ more things about our selves that we **have** to lose or do or fix before we can feel entitled to feel okay about or to love our selves, we are lost in a repeating loop. These beliefs are the **symptom**, not the cure for our experience of our selves as unworthy, unlovable. We won't feel more lovable after accomplishing these mores than we did before. So, there will **always** feel like there's another and another more after each set is accomplished.

There is a simpler (though far from easy), more direct path to healing our sense of our selves as not okay or as unlovable. The real cure, the only magical solution is simply and immediately to begin to practice treating our selves, exactly as we are in this moment, **as if** we already are entitled to be loved. If you're unsure how to proceed, just pretend, as you're talking to your self, that you're talking to one of your most beloved friends.

It's hard to do this practice. Still, it does get easier over time. And, the reason it works (eventually) is that it's the truth. We **all** are worthy and lovable, just for being; and, just-for-being includes **exactly** where and as we are in any moment. This is the birthright out of which we've been swindled and which we actually can begin to reclaim. (See **Pirouettes**, page 125 for more about this.)

Re-membering and reclaiming this birthright, this knowing of our essential okayness, of our unquestionable lovability is an empowering and powerful process. It opens the door to liberation. It creates miracles in our lives. I wish you courage for the first baby steps.

Consider treasuring your dear and quirky selves.

1-5. Feeling Not Safe

It's not safe to move ahead into anything you don't feel ready for... Taking breaks and taking all the time you need to get ready is what's really going on when you think you're "avoiding," "escaping" or "running away"!

From May of 1992 through December of 1995, my friend B and I had been traveling almost once monthly to sell our wares at women's, goddess and pride festivals. We improvised from these experiences to create three women's craft festivals of our own. These festivals, held in Ojai, were experiments in creating sacred communal space with other crafts women. We put together a single issue of a newsletter/journal for women exploring the Sacred Feminine. And, during 1996, we also coordinated several women's drumming events for the solstices, equinoxes and a couple of the cross-quarters.

It's Not Safe To Move Ahead Into Anything You Don't Feel Ready For... Taking Breaks And Taking All The Time You Need To Get Ready Is What's Really Going On When You Think You're "Avoiding," "Escaping," Or "Running Away"!

r5

It was quite a departure from what had, before then, become my usual life. For many years, I (a recovering super-achiever) had been working only two days every other week as a therapist. After those two days I'd be free to loll through long stretches of open time that I spent drifting, dreaming, resting, meandering in the mountains and aimlessly puttering around my little cottage and its tiny gardens as I journeyed deep within.

Those four and a half years of travel and doings were about taking my work out into a larger field, about being available to interact with lots of people from the center of the me-that-I-had-become during the seasons of my slowing and inward journeying. It had felt right to answer the urging from Spirit/my inner self to move out into the world. Still, I often missed my slowed down, non-achieving, resting life. Often I found my self wondering, "Whose life am I leading, anyhow?"

At the end of the year-long cycle of drumming events, I was feeling exhausted, more than ready to go back into my solitude. I looked forward to a well-earned return to hibernation, to space for resting and assimilating all the new experiences I'd been through.

Just a couple of months (to the day) into my yearned-for rest period, I received a call from a delightful young woman, a writers' agent specializing in women's and spirituality books and connected with one of the largest, most well-known creative talent agencies in the country. She'd been given a deck of my Rememberings Cards a year before and grown very attached to their supporting comfort. Just that week, one of her authors had been visiting her (someone who also knew my work). After they'd talked about their shared delight in the cards, she acted on her almost year-old intention to call me. She wanted to see if I might be interested in having her represent me.

It was exciting. She was warm, vital and juicy. She was eager to help me get my work out into the world. We had several conversations. I sent her a huge packet: copies of the many articles I'd written along the way, photographs of my house, my artwork, me. We talked about book ideas, the process of publishing, the ways she might mentor and coach me along the way. I felt truly seen and heard by her. She appreciated my need to move slowly, to move from the inside out so that anything that grew would be growing in harmony with what I believed and how I lived.

We agreed that I would open my self to whatever might come to me over a period of some weeks. I was clear that anything that felt like work wouldn't be right for me to do. The timing seemed right in some way: I was at last finished with my four and half year cycle of busyness. But, I wondered, was I ready to take such a big new step without first having a long space of empty, folding inward time.

The weeks stretched into months during which I felt pushed and pulled inside my self. Other writers I knew were engaged in long, frustrating struggles to find representation. Here I was being given an amazing gift of possibility with none of that effort. I felt that the gift was from Spirit. I definitely did want, someday, to put something together from my writings. Still, the days would go by and I would find my self napping, reading more novels and detective mysteries, wandering in the mountains, puttering in my little gardens or finding sorting/winnowing projects inside my little cottage – everything but writing.

I struggled with feelings I hadn't had since college paper-writing days. I was beset with vague feelings of unease and almost-guilt for procrastinating and avoiding the blank page. I'd find countless self-nurturing things to do with the open space I'd carved for writing to happen: manicures, pedicures, clay masques, etc. I kept having the painful sense that I might be running away from or squandering this gift from Spirit.

In the middle of all this stressing, I would remember to talk kindly and lovingly to my self. I'd remind my self that, if I wasn't getting to the writing, it was most likely because, for whatever reason(s), I wasn't yet ready for it. I would remind my self that following where my energy led me was the best guide; that it was important not to allow my own or anyone else's ideas of what-might-be-better to undermine that inner, natural flow. I'd remind my self that I had learned that my inside self was a completely trustworthy guide: when I listened to that voice, I was certain to be in and acting from my own center.

I'd remind my self how I had come to trust and believe in the healing power of going only as fast as the slowest part of me felt safe to go. I'd remind my self of how I'd been unfairly tyrannized most of my life by the inner imperative to live up to my potential. Then I could feel (for longer and longer stretches of time) that I was fine just as I was in all my resting-timeout glory. I could embrace the reality that it was okay for me not to take this gift that I wasn't yet ready to accept. I could know that this would not be the only such magical opportunity I'd ever be offered for going forward. And, I could recognize that all this needed resting time was surely a part of my process of getting ready for the future.

I called the agent to thank her and tell her I wasn't yet ready for working together. I promised that if and when I were ever up for such an enterprise I'd definitely be in touch.

A website and tales about the individual Rememberings and Celebrations Cards that began coming almost monthly some three years later turned out to be the next step that I was getting ready to take.

Remember to be really gentle with your self, not to ask your self to move ahead into anything that you're not ready for and not to harass your self for taking all the time you need to become ready.

1-6. Feeling Frightened

Be kind and gentle with your self when you're feeling frightened...
Especially when your own mind, or anyone else, thinks there's
"really" nothing to be afraid of!

In the winter of 1982 my (now former) partner and I had just returned to California after two draining, emotionally undermining years in the heartland of Indiana. We had been living in relative isolation near my partner's family in South Bend. We'd moved there to help cope with the serious illness and then the death of my partner's closest sister.

Our relationship had been sorely challenged during those two years. Except for one 10-day visit from a close California friend, both of us had been without viable support systems as we each struggled with our selves, a very difficult family situation and with each other. The return to California was a welcome relief for both of us. It was a coming home of sorts even as, at first, we lacked a physical home base. We each had friends here. And, we had couple friends here. There was hope of re-grounding our selves and, perhaps, the relationship.

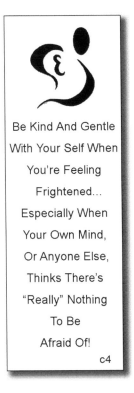

Be Kind And Gentle
With Your Self When
You're Feeling
Frightened...
Especially When
Your Own Mind,
Or Anyone Else,
Thinks There's
"Really" Nothing
To Be
Afraid Of!

c4

During our first three months back, I began the work of building a psychotherapy practice for the fourth time in my almost twenty years as a therapist. Not ready to rent office space and not comfortable working out of our shared house, I chose to have a mobile practice. I made my self available both to do house calls and to work with people in their most nourishing outdoor spaces.

Since my work and I were known in Santa Barbara, I began to advertise and reconnect there despite the fact that we were living in Ojai. As I began to face traveling to Santa Barbara to meet with people (both to build a referral base and to work with as clients), I found my self feeling very frightened. I was terrified about driving the beautiful 25-mile mountain road between Ojai and Santa Barbara alone.

I couldn't make any sense of my fears. I would be driving the same van in which I had, alone, lived as well as traveled both across country and all through California several years before. The van, though 9 years old, was in excellent mechanical condition. The road was one I'd traveled, alone, many times in those earlier years as I'd moved between camping places in Santa Barbara and Ojai.

I thought it was ridiculous that I was feeling so much anxiety and fear about something so inconsequential. I felt embarrassed by the unfamiliar feelings of helplessness. My partner was equally unsympathetic, suggesting that I was "making a big deal out of nothing."

Those were the days before I had begun the work of lovingly re-mothering my self. My response to my fears was self-condemnation and self-ridicule since there-wasn't-really-anything-to-be-afraid-of. Of course, there was no question that I would have been kind and caring with anyone else (friend or client) that might have been feeling such seemingly groundless fears. In those days, however, I still excluded my self from such sympathetic concern.

I pushed and badgered my self into getting over it. I shamed my self mercilessly into just doing it. I remember trembling and hyperventilating as I drove as slowly as I could, pulling over several times along the way. After many such awful trips, I gradually did become less frightened and more secure about being able to make it through the ride. After many more less-awful-but-still-scary trips, the fears ultimately dissipated.

I ache now for the battered Little One I treated so abusively way back then. I was as mean, impatient and condemning of her as my own biological mother had always been when the Little One needed any help or support. And, I was treating her fear just as our culture encouraged me to: push through the fear/there's nothing to fear but fear itself/get over it/just do it, etc.

It's true that the harsh treatment did ultimately lead to the dissipation of my fears. Yet, the way I treated my self robbed me of any opportunity, at the time, to discover what the fear was about inside of me.

On the road to lovingly re-mothering my self, I have learned that it's never okay to be harsh and abusive with my self, especially when some part of me is feeling fearful; and, even more especially when there seems to be no reason to be fearful.

When any part of me feels afraid, I listen carefully to her. I trust that there is something really scary for that part even if she and the most advanced part of me (or anyone else around me) doesn't understand what it might be. I explore the fear with her. I hold and comfort her. Metaphorically, I put all the lights on. We check in the closet, behind the doors and under the bed to confirm that there isn't any bogeyman hiding there.

Then, instead of impatiently making her sleep in her own bed by herself, I stay with her. I let her know that even though there isn't a bogeyman around, I hear that she's still feeling scared. I let her know that I will stay and snuggle with her while she feels frightened. I let her know that she doesn't have to be alone with her fear anymore, even when we don't know what she's afraid of. I let her know that it's okay to feel scared even when there doesn't seem to be something out there to be afraid of. I let her know that sometimes things just feel scary to us – without our quite knowing why they do. I let her know that, in those times, it can be that something inside of us is feeling scary.

In this tender space the fear usually melts away. Often, it seems to have been her fear of being completely alone with her experience. With the loving Mommy there, she is no longer alone with her fear. Other times, having the assurance that she doesn't need to know what she's afraid of in order to receive comfort allows her to gradually become aware of what inside her is creating the fear.

She learns not to feel afraid of feeling afraid. This allows her to have room to explore her fear and discover what she needs from herself or from the Mommy to help her feel safe again. She learns she needn't feel embarrassed or shamed about her fears, no matter where they come from. She learns that her fear is a signal to listen to and to explore. She learns that listening to her fear will help her to know herself more fully.

Being tender and gentle with our frightened selves allows our fear to become our teacher. With the Mommy to make the space safe to feel the fear, the fear can deepen and grow our understanding of all of our selves, big and little and in between.

Remember to be as compassionate as possible with your fearful selves.

1-7. Accepting Who You Are

When you can let your self really accept who and how you are...
No one else will have much problem with it.
Practice letting your self just be!

The neighborhood children my age (7, 8, 9) played together: either active, physical outdoor games or indoor games of dolls-and-house. I, on the other hand, spent much of my childhood alone. I'd curl up in a fan-back chair in our living room reading fairytales and myths, fantasizing, writing poems or stories and drawing pictures. When I wasn't in the gold chair, I was in the children's section of the public library sitting on the floor and reading in the fairytale, myths and legends section. On rare occasions, I'd be on the front stoop stairs at our apartment building playing school with the younger children in our building (and always being the teacher).

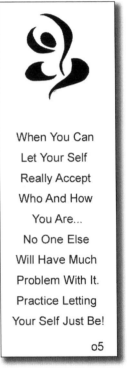

When You Can
Let Your Self
Really Accept
Who And How
You Are...
No One Else
Will Have Much
Problem With It.
Practice Letting
Your Self Just Be!

o5

My Aunt Toby, a secretary and office manager in a small legal firm, brought me regular gifts of small and medium white pads, index cards, pink phone message pads, yellow lined legal pads, Ticonderoga pencils and wheel-shaped typewriter erasers with green bristles attached to brush away the eraser shavings. My grandpa contributed small and large cigar boxes in which I could cache all but the big legal pads. All these sensuous treasures and my Crayola crayons were neatly arranged on the bottom shelf of a glass-doored bookcase right next to my special chair in our living room. It was a rich universe in which I found much delight.

Sometime around the third or fourth grade, my (often critical, judgmental) Grandma Posin, who'd been visiting with us said to me, "What's wrong with you? Why don't the other children want to play with you?" I remember being startled and confused by her question. I'd never been particularly interested in playing with the other children. It hadn't, till then, occurred to me to think that that was either odd or something wrong with/about me. Nor had it occurred to me to think that **they** didn't want to play with me. I don't remember ever thinking about how I spent my time at all: I just did what I pleased, enjoying my self – mostly with my self.

My grandmother's comment triggered a season in my life of moving from **inside** to **outside** eyes, of beginning to look questioningly at my place among my peers. My first conscious memory of feeling different was in the fourth grade. At the wall-length coat closet, listening to classmates joking, chattering and laughing with each other, I realized I hadn't a clue about what was so funny or of how to participate in their easy chatter. They seemed to inhabit a world about which I knew nothing.

In the years of my feeling uneasy about my way of being, I would sometimes try to pass, to act like others of my cohort. It was very difficult. By trying to be other than how I was, I was thrown off-center, unmoored from my own foundation. And, I had no inner compass to guide me into their sort of normalcy. I felt confused and disoriented.

The seeming impossibility for me to pass as normal left me with no choice but to follow my own meandering path. I turned back to my inner world: reading books, writing, daydreaming and, in the summers at rented bungalows in the Catskill Mountains of New York, creating fantasies in the woods. My inwardness, my fascination with introspection and reflection grew me in ways that continued to move me further and further away from the world of my age peers.

After the loss-of-innocence about my way of being I found that, by judging the ways of my peers as inferior to my own, I could regain a feeling of okay-ness about my choices. It wasn't until years later that I was able to give up the inferior-superior frame and still feel okay about my own different ways of being. (See **Judging Difference**, page 145 for more of that part of the story.)

Over the years of growing into adulthood, I did learn to function more adequately in the world of interpersonal connections. I looked to find others with whom I could connect in a deep, intimate way. Inevitably, these would be people who were also reflective, with a decidedly inward focus.

The easy flow of casual social chat has remained forever beyond my reach (and, truly, beyond my interest). Having more than one or two people in my home at one time, attending parties or social gatherings and participating in groups of any sort, all continue – for the most part – to be unappealing prospects. Since any of these occasions require more effort than I would choose for my self, I rarely consider any of them.

My delight in the voluptuousness of solitude with its timeless drifting and my joy in the lushness of sharing intimately with just one person at a time have been at the center of my life all of my life. It doesn't seem to matter whether this way of being comes from my damage – my unhealed woundedness – or from my wholeness. It's just what's so for me. The longer I live, the more at peace I am with this different way that I am. I notice that as I've grown more accepting about this aspect of me, others in my life seem to struggle less with it. Friends no longer try to coax or cajole me into group gatherings. Instead, they call to tell me of their celebrations-to-be "so that you can be here with us in spirit."

Directly naming how I am, without defense or justification seems, in fact, to work as well with just about anyone with whom I deal. Over and over again, as I take the risk of being my self, of simply speaking what's so for me – as if I believe it's perfectly okay with me to be as I am – people seem to get it. If they criticize at all, my willingness to acknowledge that this is just how I am (rather than to defend or to counter-argue) usually ends the discussion.

Choosing to see our way of being as okay with us (since it's the only way we're able to be in the moment) allows us to discover an amazing truth. When we accept and feel okay about how we are, there is no Velcro on us to attract others' judgments about how we are.

Consider letting your self **just be** exactly as you are, right now – as if it's okay with you to be your very own unfinished work-in-progress self.

1-8. Being with Your Self

Take time just to be with your very own self...
Explore ways to find pleasure in your own company... When you learn
how to delight and thrive with just your self, you can make much
better choices in friends, lovers, work and activities... Practice
spending small regular bits of time alone treating your self lovingly!

The summer before my tenth birthday was both one of the most difficult and one of the most life-changing summers I can remember as a child. Each of my first 12 summers, my parents would rent a bungalow in one of the scores of bungalow colonies in the Catskill Mountains north of New York City. Usually at least one other family we knew (friends or relatives) would rent a similar cottage in the same colony. The women and children spent all week there, from the time school let out through the Labor Day weekend. The husbands came for weekends after they'd finished a week of working in The City. Arriving for late suppers on Friday, they'd leave after dinner on Sundays. Each of the men came, as well, for his week of vacation, whenever that might fall.

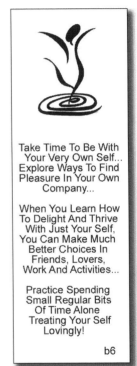

Take Time To Be With
Your Very Own Self...
Explore Ways To Find
Pleasure In Your Own
Company...

When You Learn How
To Delight And Thrive
With Just Your Self,
You Can Make Much
Better Choices In
Friends, Lovers,
Work And Activities...

Practice Spending
Small Regular Bits
Of Time Alone
Treating Your Self
Lovingly!

b6

That summer we were in a tiny cottage (a kitchen and a bedroom) that was half of a duplex. Next door were some old friends of my parents and their two children, each a couple of years older than my sister and I. At almost 12, Cynthia (the neighbor girl) was gorgeous: slender with budding breasts, a waistline, hips and glossy, naturally wavy black hair. At almost 10, I was feeling at my homeliest: chubby, shapeless, my dirty-blonde hair frizzy and dull with a permanent wave that I hated.

Cynthia was very much a girly-girl. I was rather awkward both physically and socially, totally mystified by girly-stuff. Cynthia went off to the colony's day camp with most of the other pre-teen kids. I wasn't sent to join the camp. Though my mother told me that it was because I "wouldn't like it," I suspect it was more a matter of her decision that camp "wasn't necessary" as an additional expenditure.

After the day at camp, Cynthia was part of the gang of colony kids that ran around teasing and laughing uproariously with each other all late afternoon and evening. I was only a watcher-from-the-distance. I felt excluded: a social misfit, friendless. I had no idea of how to become a part of the community of kids.

My mother was particularly irritable and cold with me that summer. My sister at two and a half was adorable, sparkling and, it seemed to me at the time, the center of my mother's otherwise limited attention. I was filled with envy. My mother made it apparent repeatedly – in ways both verbal and not – that she couldn't stand having me hanging around the cottage or around her. I had no idea of what to do with my self during the long beautiful days and evenings in the country. There were not enough books, no place to curl up safely and no library around for me to explore. I remember feeling sad and despairing.

Lonnie, Cynthia's brother, at almost six, was very much a loner. With a half loaf of white bread and a makeshift fishing pole, he disappeared early each morning to be gone all day. I suspect it was his behavior that raised a possibility for me. I noticed the woods that were less than 50 yards from our cottage door. (We were at the furthest boundary of the colony.)

Early one dew-wet morning while my mother and sister still slept, I put a bagel and cream cheese in a paper napkin into my pocket. In rubber boots, layers of warm clothes and my rain slicker, I set off to wander in the trees.

The misty wetness, the pungent smell of pine, the moist springy bed of browning needles under foot, the brilliant green humps of furry moss, the vibrant flashes of darting orange-red salamanders, the mysterious stillness of the little rooms among the trees – I was awe-struck and bewitched. I felt, more than ever before in my young life, a sense of belonging, of rightness, of what I'd now call "home." (As I write this today, tears spill down my face; my body and being remembering that first experience of fitting within the natural world; that relief from my sense of being alien.)

I started waking early every day during the week, wandering off to my fairyland while everyone else was asleep. I stayed hidden and lost in fantasy play in my green and fragrant rooms all day. As the air warmed and dried, I'd slip out of layers of clothing that I'd pile for taking home later. I'd explore barefoot, loving the textures, soft and prickly under my toes. I'd catch and release the beautiful salamanders wondering at their iridescent freckles. I'd stretch out on the bed of needles, lean up against and hug the trees. I felt enfolded, surrounded with loving presences. I felt joy and comfort there, no longer a homely misfit.

Before that summer, my refuge, both from my mother and from the world (see **Accepting Who You Are**, page 47 for more about this) had been with my books, with writing poems or stories and drawing pictures curled up in the gold brocade chair in our city living room. Now, when life was feeling too hard or lonely back in the city, I learned to take buses and trains to get to Prospect Park and the Brooklyn Botanical Gardens. I found magical nooks and crannies in those green worlds. I could go barefoot in the grasses, lie down and roll on the warm, fragrant earth, lean against and hug tress, put my feet in little ponds and feel comforted, feel that I fit somewhere.

Like so many of the obstacles in life, the deprivations and ordinary miseries of my childhood became doorways. Without the warmth or acceptance of traditional mothering, I had to find other ways to soothe my self. The depth of shaming and humiliation to which I had been subjected for having needs of any sort made it impossible for me to turn (knowingly) to anyone other than my self. The wounds of my relationship with my mother were, in the end, a great gift she gave me. Her emotional absence forced me to develop an independence that was neither expected nor experienced by most of the young women with whom I grew up.

So much the outsider, both in my own home and in the world at large I, very early in my growing years, had learned to tend to and to be content with just my self. I didn't (till much later in my life) understand what powerful and empowering skills these were for a person, especially a woman.

I've continued, through the years, to bring to the time I spend with my self the same curiosity and devotion we're all much more likely to bring to the time we spend with others we care about. This practice has kept expanding my capacity to be fascinated with my own inner process, to delight in my own company and to find rich solace in the world of nature, books, fantasy and solitary creativity.

Though as I've grown up I've become more socially adept, the capacity to enjoy my own company has made me very picky about where, how and with whom I spend my time. Despite how particular I've been, I actually have found a few kindred spirits. Not surprisingly, they're people who have a similar capacity to be fascinated by their own inner life and to delight in being just with their selves. These delicious beings are friends with whom I share fully and intimately.

Nevertheless, I'm rarely willing to do something/go somewhere that doesn't interest me just to have someone's company. I find it easy to give up the possibility of company in order to be doing something/going somewhere that feels right to me. I'm unlikely to settle for any activity, endeavor or company that doesn't, at the very least, promise to feel as nourishing or compelling as does time with my self.

Over the years of spending so much time with my self, I've also been expanding my ability to embrace and nurture all the different parts of my everyday self. This capacity has grown out of consciously experimenting with the practice of treating my self the same way I'd treat anyone else that I truly care about. (And, from considerable work transforming the inner critical voice. See **Criticizing Your Self**, page 137, **Loving Acceptance**, page 159 and **Doing Better**, page 157 for more about that work.) The more I've developed this unconditional acceptance of my self, the less tolerance I have for being around people or in situations that treat me less than kindly. It's an amazing liberation. I give thanks daily for the help from Spirit that has supported and guided me on this path.

May you consider exploring the practice of spending small bits of time alone, treating your self lovingly. May you consider honoring that practice if you're already doing it. And, may you remember to be tender with your dear and precious self.

1-9. Too Much Work

If it feels like "too much work" it's probably not what you need to be engaged with right now. The struggles that are truly enlivening never feel like "too much work" even when they're intense, persistent and exhausting!

In the early mid-eighties I was renting a magical, beautifully converted two-car garage on a sweet piece of property. The area around my little cottage, though, was a mess. Excavated boulders, rocks and an assortment of construction debris littered the back and side yards.

I spent the first two years there focused on healing from the devastating end of a troubled and troubling relationship, tending the wounded Little One inside of me. When not working my two days a week or wandering in the mountains and canyons of Ojai, I was also slowly transforming the cottage into a cozy home for the Little One and me.

When the inside space felt right, I began considering the messy, neglected outside yards. At first, I simply wanted to create a place for a hot tub and an area to lie comfortably out in the sun or moonlight. I started by gathering up the construction debris and hauling it away. Then, I rearranged some of the rocks and boulders to make a terrace for the hot tub and a clear space for lying about.

Each bit that I did filled me an exhilarating sense of satisfaction. I was hooked. I continued rearranging more of the rocks and boulders. I formed rock gardens, low meandering rock walls, little terraces and then a sacred space of concentric circles with a central fire pit.

For almost two years, I worked long hours at the rock piles, often well into the star- or moon-lit nights. I dug and levered and pried up

If It Feels Like "Too Much Work" It's Probably Not What You Need To Be Engaged With Right Now.

The Struggles That Are Truly Enlivening Never Feel Like "Too Much Work" Even When They're Intense, Persistent And Exhausting!

j4

huge boulders, often sitting down in the dirt with my back against a huge rock, digging in my heels and using my back to push it where I wanted it to go. In my struggles to free the really deeply embedded ones, I'd use a thick and pointed six-foot long stake that I'd raise and drop repeatedly to loosen the earth around them. Then I'd use the flat end of the stake to lever the boulders out of the loosened earth. Often it felt as though the Grandmothers or the spirits of the place were helping me, pushing the boulders up from underneath.

Some weeks I worked at the rocks from early morning till well after dark, day after day. Often food seemed irrelevant. Water to replenish what I'd sweat away was all I needed or wanted. I loved hurling small and midsize rocks over the hill into the wild chaparral. Cursing or breathing fiercely as I hurled made it an unbeatable way of releasing the anger, frustration and rage that sometimes rose up in me those days.

When I'd run out of steam, I'd take a break and spend several days wandering around the mountains and canyons of Ojai's backcountry. I'd lie naked on rocks in the river watching the clouds, the water, the leaves and the birds, mindlessly drifting and dreaming.

Then I'd come back to the rock pile or to digging fertilizer and soil amendments into newly created flowerbeds. Or, I'd head to the nursery to find flowers and bushes to experimentally plant in all these beds. The work was strenuous, unremitting and exhausting. At the same time it was exciting and deeply gratifying.

My friends shook their heads and joked about my days with the rocks. I was fascinated by the pull the rocks exerted on my being; intrigued by the way that, rock by rock, boulder by boulder I was transforming what had been mess and debris into something of beauty and wonder. All this just by rearranging what I found around me: a fitting metaphor for that season of my healing.

It was a daily exercise in patience. No expectations. No goals. No rushing. Just moving one rock at a time. Never thinking about how long it would take to finish or where it was leading or how much there was to do: just rock after rock in timelessness.

Several years later, in the nineties, I was drawn in and similarly captivated by something quite other than rocks. After I'd spent almost six years immersed in inner work, Spirit began nudging me back out into the world, into sharing the harvest of this inward cycle and interacting with more than just my small circle of friends and clients.

The Rememberings and Celebrations Cards had begun emerging. At first a few at a time and then, quite remarkably, a whole deck of 64. A catalog took shape. New versions of all the cards and amulet-gifts I'd created over the past many years for friends and clients got printed and assembled. I started being invited to speak at Women's Councils (on aging, on power, on the Sacred Feminine). Each time, I'd bring along a few catalogs and a small stash of my growing collection of treasures to offer for sale.

A woman I was just getting to know in those days was creating drums and rattles for women's ceremonial use. Spirit had been nudging her into traveling to sell her creations at various women's gatherings in California and New Mexico. She started taking along the overruns of my Rememberings and Celebrations Cards to give away to women who stopped at her booth. And, she sometimes also took along samples of an emerging line of T-shirts with my words and images on them. She brought back intriguing anecdotes about the responses women had to my words/work.

Before long, her tales had gently seduced me into toting my goodies off to many of the same gatherings. There were Women's Music and Comedy Festivals, Goddess Festivals, Women's Spirituality Festivals, Art Festivals and Gay Pride Festivals. Sometimes I'd present small workshops at these events.

We started caravanning to the events, renting adjacent booths, hanging out with each other between customers. As we got to know each other better, we moved on to exploring sharing a single booth and together creating Sacred Feminine space into which women could come to explore our wares.

It was an exciting and often challenging time. Collaboration was a revolutionary notion for me, especially when it involved my otherwise quite solitary creative life. Taking my words and work out into the world and becoming accessible to numbers of people was equally revolutionary for my reclusive self.

The coordinating of space, esthetics, personal styles and rhythms was a stretch for me. Some of it flowed surprisingly easily. Some of it was pretty bumpy. As with the rock moving, everything we did seemed to open the door to something more to do. Being in a collaboration meant adjusting to having the next steps sometimes come through someone else's intuitions rather than through my own. This required a good bit of internal rearranging, an increase in radical trust and, sometimes, a lot of reciprocal articulation of needs and feelings as we processed together. (See **The Sacred Feminine**, page 361 for more about this.)

In the earliest days I'd been hauling around a few boxes of inventory, a couple of tables, some portable folding display panels I'd designed and built and display boards that could be hung on those panels. There were always fresh flowers, velour tablecloths, objects for an altar and a shade tent along as well.

Including an adjacent sacred-play tent in our traveling show was an idea that came through my colleague. It meant carting additional boxes of art materials, face paints, goddess coloring books, portfolios of my own and other women's writings and a collection of my large fiber masks, the Spirit Mother Totems: a lot more hauling, but all for what proved a very lively addition.

Our experiences at these shows run by others inspired us to create a series of Women's Fine Craft shows in Ojai. These collectively designed Sacred Feminine spaces where participating crafts women worked as an ensemble involved us in lots more processing and work: press releases, flyers, and the coordination of intricate lines of communication with all our crafts women.

The excitement generated by these shows birthed a vision of creating sacred space for women's drumming gatherings. This venture brought more stretching as we wove together the separate, sometimes similar, sometimes very different threads of our visions for the happenings.

We produced a series of women's drumming nights at the solstices, equinoxes and a couple of the cross quarters in 1995 and into 1996. For each evening we hauled all we'd been hauling for the other shows along with a collection of miscellaneous percussion instruments I had been gathering at my cottage.

Each month we came together for composing the images and intentions on the invitations, getting them and the flyers printed, getting out our mailing and press releases and posting our flyers. The day of the drumming involved the elaborate setting up of either the indoor or outdoor space we'd rented: masks, art materials, wares for sale, percussion instruments, arranging a large communal altar, a communal food table and a threshold altar at which the entering women would receive a water blessing as they moved into sacred space and time. There was Oshu, the 48" in diameter ceremonial drum my friend and colleague had built, four five-foot tall hand carved redwood goddess totems from which Oshu hung and a large collection of hand-made beaters for women to use when drumming on the big drum.

Over the year, more and more women came to these drumming nights – with or without their own drums or instruments. Many were local but increasingly, as word spread, women drove considerable distances to join us. The joyful noise we raised together, the chanting, the dancing and the food we brought to share, the creation of Sacred Feminine Community – it was quite phenomenal.

As with the solitary rockwork, there was in all of this collaborative process an organic progression: one step unfolding into the next, nowhere to get, a timelessness, a sense of being in just the right place at just the right moment. It was growing me into a person who could work-and-play-well-with-other(s), something I had never before been able to do with much equanimity or skill. It was intense and sometimes exhausting, just as the rocks had been. It was also as exhilarating and as deeply gratifying as the rockwork had been. Until, one day it wasn't. Suddenly, it all felt like too much work.

Holding a safe container for the increasingly larger number of women who showed up was a big strain, especially after we had had to deal with some serious intrusions. This degree of responsibility made it much less possible for the two of us to feel free to simply be in the container that we were creating/holding. It felt to me like being the Mommy for everyone else. Repetitive, draining cycles of packing and hauling and setting up and dismantling and cleaning and packing up and hauling for us – while everyone else got to have fun playing with our toys.

As I shared these feelings with my friend/collaborator, we saw that hints of my growing disenchantment had begun creeping in some time before the day when it finally became too much work for me: We had recently asked some of our dedicated regulars to help us with the setting up and blessing as well as with the dismantling and cleaning up because it had started feeling like too much to handle by our selves.

The moment when none of it felt enlivening for me was a difficult one for us. There was a whole community of women who had come together around these drummings. All along, it felt that Spirit/the Grandmothers had been leading us, stepwise in a process of expansion that brought us to the creation of the Sacred Feminine space in which the drummings unfolded. It was unclear where Spirit was moving us now.

As we explored this shift in me, my friend/collaborator began to see that it had become more responsibility than she, too, felt comfortable holding. Finding our way to letting go of it all with skillful means was daunting. Reaching agreement about the how and when of announcing the end of our tenure was perhaps the greatest test yet in our collaboration. Here, our different styles and needs were the most discrepant.

The work of reaching consensus without violating what each of us needed to have happen in the closing ceremony took us both through a good deal of anguish and tears. We stayed committed to the belief that, if we could tolerate sitting in the middle of that pain without pushing, a resolution would emerge that would give each of us 100% of the essence of what we needed. We did, and it did. Our last evening was a bittersweet celebration as we gracefully gave and received thanks to the whole community and invited other women to step forward to continue the tradition.

I've learned that it's not okay for me to do things or to be in relationships or situations that feel like too much work. There are still **many** things that I do, many relationships and situations that I am in that **do** involve me in considerable amounts of concentrated work and energy. When that to which I'm devoting so much of my self is **truly nourishing** and **really right** for me, it doesn't ever feel like too much work.

Again and again, when how it feels to me changes into – or when how it feels to me at the start is – the too much work feeling, I practice giving my self permission to stop or to decline from participating. This uncompromising permission for my self allows me to find my way out of whatever it is honestly and care-fully no matter what my earlier agreements may have been. Repeatedly, and with less surprise each time, I see that others survive my openly named and self-caring withdrawals – intact and without rancor. Sometimes I can see that my willingness to withdraw when I need to helps inspire others to give themselves the same option.

Consider exploring the possibility of giving your self permission to stop (or not to start) doing things that feel like too much work.

1-10. Not Berating Your Self

No matter what you have or haven't done, or how you are or aren't being... You never deserve to be berated or "beat-up-on" by your self or anyone else! If that's happening, remember to remind your self, and anyone else, that you are a tender, delicate being truly doing everything you can in this moment to grow your self into sanity and realness in the midst of this crazy-making world!

I can remember the earliest days of my conscious sensual awakening in my fourteenth year. My body recalls the lush feelings that rose up and blossomed in me whenever I was being touched, the eddies and ripples of delight set in motion by the sensitivity of every inch of my skin's surface.

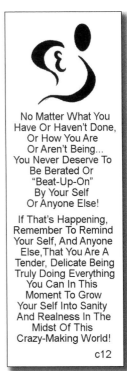

No Matter What You Have Or Haven't Done, Or How You Are Or Aren't Being... You Never Deserve To Be Berated Or "Beat-Up-On" By Your Self Or Anyone Else!

If That's Happening, Remember To Remind Your Self, And Anyone Else, That You Are A Tender, Delicate Being Truly Doing Everything You Can In This Moment To Grow Your Self Into Sanity And Realness In The Midst Of This Crazy-Making World!

c12

I remember, too, repeated dialogues with my 20-year-old boyfriend about not yet feeling ready to go all the way to intercourse. I felt too young to handle the sensory overload I imagined would come with going beyond the erotic intensity of our necking, petting and oral sex.

And, I remember the summer weekend when, at fifteen and a half, I finally agreed we could go ahead and have intercourse. I gave up my virginity in my own bed while my parents were out of town and my younger sister was staying at her friend's house. It was **such** a ho-hum crasher for me. Despite my anticipation of over-the-top arousal, I actually felt very little sensation, pleasurable or otherwise during penetration. I seemed not to have a hymen: there was no pain, no bleeding. I remember feeling quite disappointed afterward, asking him "Is that really all there is to it?" Of course, in the way of such things in the middle 1950s (and perhaps in every era), once intercourse became part of the agenda, my young man became less available for all the sensual touching in which, before then, I had reveled. Penetration was now always his focus. There seemed to be nothing I could do or say to bring back the earlier, slower, more interesting (to me) flow.

I wondered why intercourse was so unexciting to me. I began to worry that there might be something wrong with me. Already more sexually precocious than my peers and unwilling to reveal this new secret, I had only the book hidden in my parents' dresser to consult. Unlike the later (1980s) *Hite Report* that reported the prevalence of this experience in women, *Love Without Fear* offered little to dissuade me from my sense that there was something awry with me. What I read there led me to start pretending that intercourse was more pleasurable to me than it was.

When I went off to college a year later, (the avant-garde, notoriously sexually liberated Bennington College) a rather insidious process took shape in me. Hating what I saw as the disempowerment of the traditional woman's role as the one seduced, I chose to seduce-before-I-was-seduced. Adopting the persona of a sexually aggressive and sophisticated woman, I readily began engaging with many different male partners. An avid observer/learner, I quickly became adept at pleasing men sexually. I fancied my self a courtesan.

My sexuality became a mental game of power and control. There was little in what I did that had any of the embodied sensuality of my earliest experiences. My pleasure, such as it was, came from the sense of being in control of the sexual program; from feeling superior to the sex-hungry, unaware young men with whom I toyed.

This focus eclipsed my earlier concern that there was something wrong with me. Though my sexual experiences were (for me) disembodied and devoid of any physical pleasure, I continued this repetitive, unhealthy behavior with men through most of my years in college and graduate school.

In graduate school my horizons expanded to include many senior professors in my field. With only two exceptions (both of them adjunct professors), these men were from universities other than the one in which I was enrolled. Most of these were brief, short-lived encounters. Most were, as body experiences for me, joyless. Rather, I enjoyed the power I felt over these men who were so unaware (of anything but their own need) that they never realized how absent I was from the experience.

In my last year of graduate school, I did meet a special man with whom I actually developed a personal relationship. As we dated, then lived together and later married for a time, my sexual life became for a while more embodied, more sensual – no longer a power/control game.

We had married in the early days of the era of open marriage: the then new wave of non-monogamy and swinging (intentional, episodic partner swapping). Not long after we began our brief marriage, I agreed to his wish to become involved in sexual adventuring. For me, it was yet another season of disembodied sexuality. (This, even as our dialogues about the adventuring seemed, uncannily, to deepen our emotional intimacy with each other.)

The adventures were mentally rather than physically stimulating. Again I was living out a persona that was far from what was real inside of me. Sometimes we wound up in scary, unpleasant or vaguely unsavory situations. In the end, I opted out, first of the adventuring, then of the marriage.

In the years that followed, I dedicated my self to reclaiming and re-inhabiting my body. The work I did brought me to healing experiences with two different men, each of them able to love a woman and delight in making slow, voluptuous love to her. The work also brought me to claiming my identity first as a bisexual woman then, later, as a woman-identified woman. Ultimately, the path has led me, for the past more than 27 years, to honoring the comfort my being-in-a-body experiences from choosing to be partner-celibate, to be in sensual/erotic relationship only with my self and the natural world.

Some dozen or so years ago, after long ignoring those earlier painful eras of my sexual history, my inner travels brought me to looking back on all of this from my now embodied, more conscious self. I was mortified and devastated to realize how terribly I had misused my being-in-a-body. I could barely take in the extent to which I had violated and degraded my precious self. I was flooded with memories that filled me with disgust and self-loathing.

All my practice of being loving and tender with my self went out the window. I raged at my self: "How could you do such unconscionable, disgusting things to/with your self?" "What on earth were you thinking?" "How could you give those people permission to use and abuse you?" "How could you even believe that you were in control?"

I would feel nauseated, filled with revulsion. I could hardly tolerate the remembering, the flashbacks. I couldn't stop hating the me I had been that had let all of that happen. I felt flayed. It was so awful to feel it all, I had to push it back and away, had to try to close the door on it. Of course, the door wouldn't stay closed: visual or body memories continued to pop out periodically and swamp me with despair and disgust.

Slowly, as I continued deepening my practice of embracing my self all the ways that I might be, I could bring the loving Mommy into those awful moments of remembering. The Mommy-Inside held me compassionately in the midst of the memories. She reminded me that I had done the best I could with the consciousness available to me in those difficult times; that what I did then – regardless of how it felt to my now-embodied self, regardless of how misguided it was – I had done in an effort to help my self heal the woundedness in me.

The Mommy-Inside helped me to feel how confused and damaged that poor young woman had been, how much pain she had lived with for so long. I could begin to feel how much she needed my caring and compassion to help her heal from her terrible wounds; how alone and abandoned she had been for so long. Gradually I opened my heart to that broken me, feeling sorrow for her pain, forgiving her for what she did, reminding her and my self that we truly did the best we could at those earlier times.

As I could hold my younger self caringly, I found room to consider what the source of her woundedness and self-wounding behaviors might be. There is certainly a lot in all of the particulars that speaks to my having had sexual abuse in my history. The one vivid conscious memory I do have of being molested is of being finger-penetrated by a stranger in the back hallway of our apartment building when I was between 4 and 5 years old. Remembering how I dealt with it at the time (first crossing my legs then pushing him away, telling him "Don't do that!" and walking away from him) leaves me uncertain that it in itself was enough to account for what followed. Still, no other memories have surfaced. So perhaps it was enough.

I hold that brave, strong and smart little 4 1/2-year-old close to my heart. I wrap her in all the love, celebration of her feisty courage and protection that she didn't have back then when she needed it.

And, these days when those painful flashes of remembering occasionally come up again, I'm able to soothe and gentle my self. I acknowledge how terribly hurtful and sad it was to have subjected my self to such dishonoring of my precious body. I remind my self that I won't ever do that to me again.

As always, I find the power in opening our hearts to our selves awesome and compelling. It is in finding the generosity to embrace our less than perfect selves that we grow our selves; that we open our selves to deeper knowing; that we begin to heal our selves.

Closing our hearts to our selves – hating, disowning and distancing our selves from that which offends us about our selves (the generally accepted cultural prescription) – only stunts us, deepens our woundedness and stifles all opportunity to heal.

Consider being more loving, generous and compassionate with your delicate, less than perfect self.

1-11. Feeling Confused

When you feel confused or in doubt...
Stop: doing, figuring, thinking, talking.
Take: a breath, a break, a nap, a walk.
Listen inward to your "belly" feelings!

It was 1973, my first year as a 32-year-old dropout from my former life as a feminist activist clinical psychologist in private practice in New York City. I spent the year being on the road. Living in the off-the-showroom-floor empty shell of a commercial van that I'd bought and set up as a cozy bed-sitting room, I was a roving vagabond. Like a turtle, I traveled around with my house on my back. In this safe womb-like space I was self-sufficient, surrounded with the few important-to-me possessions that I had taken from my last life and some bare bones, improvised kitchen and bathroom facilities. (See **Pirouettes**, page 125 for more about how this unfolded.)

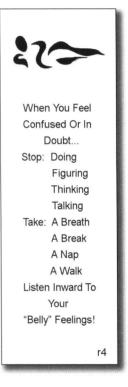

When You Feel
Confused Or In
Doubt...
Stop: Doing
    Figuring
    Thinking
    Talking
Take: A Breath
    A Break
    A Nap
    A Walk
Listen Inward To
    Your
    "Belly" Feelings!

r4

First and quickly that chilly March, I drove the southernmost route across the country to California. Then I wandered up and down the California and Oregon coasts, exploring and drifting. I spent my time working on my tan and listening to the – till then – unheard parts of my self. Lazing and napping in the sun, I sometimes crocheted cotton bikinis, silly hats and later chunky sweaters. For some part of every day, I rode the racing bike that I'd hung on a rack on my van. I walked on the beaches, sometimes on trails and, in Big Sur, along endless miles on the side of the Pacific Coast Highway.

Over time I narrowed my roving range, moving back and forth between campgrounds and safe roadside nooks in Santa Barbara and Big Sur. From the first time I'd seen them on a solo vacation in 1967, these two geographies had felt, in some indefinable way, like home to me. Though at first I kept very much to my self, I felt a sense of belonging and an inner peace in each of these places.

Sometimes I took breaks from my footloose, solitary life and went north to San Francisco. There I had a kind of family base. I'd park my van outside the home of my oldest college best friend. Each night I'd retreat to my van-womb to sleep and ground my self. During most days, I'd become part of the family's complex, busy world. As an eccentric quasi-aunt, I slipped easily and seamlessly into the fabric of life with my friend, her husband and their three amazing young children.

Some months into that first year on the road, I began experimenting with being a little more plugged-in and connected in both of my geographical home-places. For a while, I shop-sat a couple of days a week at a small boutique booth in a 1970s style indoor marketplace in downtown Santa Barbara. There I sold my growing collection of hand crocheted bikinis, hats and ski sweaters along with the fabric creations of the two other women with whom I collectively rented the space. In the marketplace I met several alternative artisans. Occasionally, I spent time outside the marketplace getting to know a few of these lively women.

A while later, I signed on for a couple of early mornings a week as baker's helper at an organic bakery collective in Santa Barbara. Acting as the bakery's sales rep bringing samples to the local health food store on my frequent jaunts to Big Sur, I began meeting some of the previously invisible to me locals. They were yet another community of alternative/drop-out folks.

As I got to know people in both places, I began to sometimes park my van in their driveways rather than on the streets of Santa Barbara or the pullouts on Pacific Coast Highway in Big Sur. And, I started being less solitary.

For nine months I lived mostly on the roads in Big Sur. I got to use the mineral baths at Esalen during the nighttime hours they, in those years, set aside for local residents' access. I explored the local trails, hung out occasionally with some fascinating women and some very odd men. Sometimes I did stints as a guest-baker in Esalen's kitchen. I picked miners' lettuce, mustard and horseradish greens and even some watercress growing wild in the mountains and creeks for wild-salad-picnics alone or with friends. I did odd jobs as a carpenter's apprentice.

After a time, I started feeling disenchanted with life as I was living it in Big Sur. The social/sexual scene, when I plugged into it, felt way too incestuous and weird. Coming from the East Coast's high feminist consciousness, it was upsetting to watch the same-old same-old tired sexual politics playing out between the strong, otherwise independent women and the generally adolescent men in that tiny enclave. I was interested in exploring becoming part of a community again and Big Sur no longer felt like the right place for me to be doing that.

With little inner turmoil, I pulled up the tentative roots I'd put down there. (I actually kept just one friendship from that time.) After a trip to San Francisco to regroup, I headed south to explore life in the feminist/activist community in Santa Barbara.

When I came back to town that late November of 1974 – at 34 and after almost two years of my transient, van-lady existence – I checked in with two women I'd met and gotten particularly close to earlier on in my travels. These women had been willing to develop open, intimate friendships with me despite my peripatetic habits and non-reciprocal accessibility (no phone, only an occasionally visited post box and periodic, unpredictable departures for indeterminate sojourns in Big Sur or San Francisco).

Both of them were active in the alternative/feminist healthcare community. (Those were the still early days of legal abortion/birth control clinics.) The afternoon I arrived, they colluded to present me with a high-pressured proposal that I apply for the opening as Health Education Coordinator at one of the three local free clinics. The position was part of an existing five-woman collective in which one of these two friends was already a functioning member. I'd arrived in Santa Barbara the day before the deadline for applications closed, so they were **very** pushy. It seemed an intriguing possibility.

I stayed up that night handwriting a letter of intention/ application by the light of the battery lantern in my van. On my way back from submitting the application the next morning, using a friend's address, I signed up for a Santa Barbara library card. It was an act of prayer and a commitment to putting down firm new roots.

Within three days I had been interviewed and offered the job. The same day the offer came, I found an ad for a small affordable furnished apartment down near the beach, just a block away from one of my safe overnight van-parking places. I moved in two days later. After adding some plants and rearranging the furniture (covering the worst of it with Indian print bedspreads from the thrift store), I was suddenly a quasi-normal, locatable person again. For two or three months, as I transitioned from having been in total charge of my accessibility (or inaccessibility as the case might be), I chose not to have a phone. I coped, instead, with unpredictable arrivals on my doorstep, learning to say a face-to-face "no" when I wasn't feeling available for contact.

Two weeks after I'd accepted the offer, I began my first real job in almost two years. It was exciting, challenging, hilarious fun and crazy; high-pressured, contentious some of the time, operating in crisis mode most of the time: the so-called full catastrophe. Oddly, the transition from full-time drifting-freedom into 5-day weeks and full-on people contact doing free health care education at the Freedom Clinic went smoothly. I loved it. It felt exactly right for where I was at that particular moment.

Under the banner of "Health care for people not for profits!" the clinic was a radical health care delivery system dedicated to educating people about their rights as patients/consumers of medical services. The clinic was committed to demystifying illness and medical treatment, to providing people with useful, user-friendly preventive mental and physical health care information and to providing essentially cost-free health care services. Our support staff of patient advocates, counselors and clinic receptionists were trained volunteers. All of our services and much of the medication prescribed were provided without cost or by donation. County funds, foundation grants and private donations paid the salaries of our coordinating and medical staff.

As the job took shape, my primary responsibilities involved giving talks as well as developing recruiting/training/coordinating procedures for staffing a speakers' bureau for presentations at public high schools and junior highs. We offered talks on contraception, sexually transmitted diseases, alternative lifestyles (usually a lesbian and gay speakers' panel) and preventive mental/physical health care.

There were also countless meetings with the coordinating staffs of all three free clinics in town. There were various trainings coordinated or participated in by all of us that addressed preventive mental and physical health care. For the three of us who were not directly involved in running the medical clinics, there were pamphlets to write and a weekly public radio talk show to produce on similar topics. There were columns for our newsletters, fund appeals letters and letters to lobby our County Supervisors for the governmental funding necessary for our projects and programs. There were peer counselors and patient advocates to oversee. And, too, there was a training program to be developed and implemented to provide trained peer mental health counselors for the three Santa Barbara free clinics. All five of us paid coordinators regularly rotated staffing what were then called "bummer squads." At local concert venues, we "bummer squad" staffers were available to talk people down from bad drugs and bad psychedelic trips.

In addition to our own weekly coordinating meetings and the interminable grant writing, all of us in the collective shared the grunt work of secretarial support, janitoring, go-foring, mimeographing (those were pre-computer days) and preparing mailings. It was a lot of dedicated, socially conscious work that kept on growing and expanding week by week.

In the earliest days, it was exhilarating to be in the middle of such a radical agenda for helping build a healthy community. It was exciting to be both engaged with these activist women colleagues and part of the extended family of the staffs at all three free clinics.

After a few months though, things began to slip. Everyone who'd been there before I came had already been running on overload for a very long time. Two of the co-coordinators were financially struggling single moms who were also going to school part-time. The other two were RNs who carried the major clinical responsibility while also working toward nurse practitioner degrees. I was fresh blood: rested, with no other commitments, excellent verbal skills and some credible amount of political savvy.

While I wanted to share my skills and support their process, they wanted and needed desperately to offload some of their tremendous burdens. "It would be so much more efficient/faster/easier if you just would do it rather than walk me through it" was the more and more familiar drill. It proved nearly impossible for me to say no to these requests despite my having worked so hard to become adept at saying no in all other contexts.

It was a slippery slope right back into the kind of super-responsible, super-achieving, perfectionist and exhausting life I'd dropped out of in New York City just a little more than two years before. I felt lost, confused, paralyzed. I kept trying to talk about it with my colleagues.

They tried to hear me but they were immersed in that same over-doing way of being as if it were the natural and reasonable way to be.

I spent many hours trying to think the situation through, trying to figure out how I might redirect the flow, drop some of what seemed too much for me. Every strategy I'd start to design foundered when I recognized the burnout everyone else had been dealing with and enduring for so much longer than my own short few months.

I cried a lot while walking along the beach or curled up at night in my little apartment. I was feeling frustrated with my predicament. I couldn't believe that I had locked my self into something like this all over again, after all the work I'd done with my self in my two years alone. Feeling hopelessly muddled, I tried, without any success, to figure out ways to go part time, ways to divest at least some of the burdens.

Finally, my back went out and I was reduced to a quivering puddle of pain. Sleeping on the floor in my bedroom, barely able to care for my self and no longer able to think at all, I gave up the struggle. My body forced me to take a complete break.

As I slept and rested and hurt and cried and breathed through all the pain, both physical and emotional, I began at last to simply listen to my belly-feelings. I gave up trying to figure anything out. I gave up trying to make the whole thing work. I gave up feeling bad and wrong for needing desperately to say no to all of this important political work. I gave up feeling bad and wrong for not being willing to sacrifice my well-being in the same ways my colleagues had been doing for so much longer. I gave up feeling like a failure because what I'd worked out in my by-my-self space hadn't readily translated into the working-with-people space.

Listening to the truths of my belly-feelings, I could refuse to feel bad and wrong because I needed to drop out yet again. I could refuse to feel defeated because I now understood that I needed to go inward, back to the drawing board. I knew that I needed to learn from this devastating experience, to learn about how to support my not sliding into these old habits whenever I might again engage in a committed way with work and other people.

Listening to and trusting my belly-feelings, it became apparent that there wasn't a way I could make it okay both for my colleagues and for me; that I had to exit as quickly and cleanly as possible. Listening to my belly-feelings, I was able to craft a care-full and careful letter of resignation in which, from outside their system, I promised to support the collective in its transition and its search for my replacement.

The whole excruciating process taught me an unforgettable lesson: most often, when we're frozen, paralyzed or stymied by confusion and doubt, our minds are the least likely source for getting clarity. In these moments and the moments when we feel trapped in predicaments where there seem to be no acceptable choices, the only possible path is to listen inward for the truths and knowing in our bellies. Listening to those truths gives us the courage to move forward in ways that take the best care of us.

And, the only way to be able to hear those feelings is to stop the noise of all the thinking, figuring, talking and doing. Taking a break, a solitary walk, a nap if we can (for dreaming) or just slowing down to breath deeply and to watch our breath – any of these can be a doorways into that deep knowing place. That place is always there inside of us. If we can focus to listen to it, it will **always** show us the way that's right for us.

Consider listening inward to your belly-feelings when you feel confused or any other time you remember that they're a source of knowing that is constantly available to you.

1-12. Making Room for Feelings

It's important to let your self make room for you to feel whatever you're feeling... Particularly when your own mind, or anyone else, thinks what you're feeling is unreasonable, extreme, immature, ridiculous, silly or "not like you!"

I grew up with a mother who consistently invalidated and ridiculed my feelings. One of her favorite messages was "you're **always** making such a big deal out of **nothing**!" Others were "you've got nothing to cry/be so depressed about!" and, "if you don't stop that, I'll really give you something to cry/be depressed about!" Or, she'd tell me to "Stop with the Miss Sarah Heartburn, already!" Implying (with this parody of Sarah Bernhardt's name) that I was being overly dramatic. Not a wonder that I learned to be critical of the intensity of my feelings and to stuff or hide them as best as I could from the outside world or even, at times, from my self. This early conditioning from my mother was reinforced by messages from our emotion-phobic culture that devalues all strong feelings (with the exception perhaps of men's anger and occasionally, over-idealized romantic love).

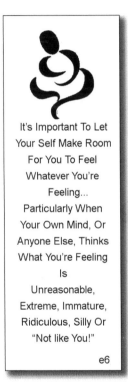

It's Important To Let Your Self Make Room For You To Feel Whatever You're Feeling... Particularly When Your Own Mind, Or Anyone Else, Thinks What You're Feeling Is Unreasonable, Extreme, Immature, Ridiculous, Silly Or "Not like You!"

e6

At times, my sadness and grief were so overwhelming I'd feel as though I could die from the pain. Other times I wished that I **would** die rather than have to go on suffering so much. I wished I could be less sensitive so that I could live more comfortably in the world. Nevertheless, I usually made space for my self to feel my despair, no matter how extreme it might seem.

On the other hand, until my mother's death when I was 30, anger was not a part of my emotional repertoire. Devastated by my mother's sarcastic anger toward me, I couldn't imagine feeling or acting in such terrifying and hurtful ways toward another human being. The closest I'd come to experiencing or expressing anger would be screaming my hate into my pillow after some particularly mind-twisting interchange with my mother.

When someone was undermining me or being gratuitously nasty to me (as she had so often been) I would feel hurt rather than angry. I'd turn my energy to figuring out what damage or sense of personal inadequacy in the other person underlay their behavior toward me. (Just as I had tried for so many years with my mother.) Deciphering their motivation would defuse in me what might otherwise have blossomed into anger. It felt safer to understand the why of a person's meanness than it did to feel even the slightest indignation toward them.

This focus produced in me a substantial capacity for tolerance and patience with people who were treating me badly. I typically missed reading (on a conscious level) the hostility in the energies that were being directed toward me. Instead, I'd be likely to come away from the interactions feeling vaguely anxious or crabby, without a clue about what had provoked those feelings. Some hours later, if sharing a meal had been part of the interaction, I'd wind up sick to my stomach. Only vomiting up all the still-totally-undigested contents of my stomach would reduce the searing pain in my gut.

My mother's death freed me to begin to become consciously aware of the depth of my anger with her and her treatment of me. Yet, it wasn't till my mid-forties that I learned I could feel and release anger in ways that would be safe; that I wouldn't have to fear that experiencing/ expressing such emotions could demolish someone in the ways I'd felt demolished by my mother's rage.

Learning to separate the **energy** of my anger from the **content** of the behavior/circumstances by which it had been triggered was a major first step. Finding safe, effective ways then to move and release that energy – by my self, in private, not on someone – was both a scary and a remarkable process. Yelling, cursing, stomping, kicking at pillows and pounding on my bed were terrifying and at the same time thrilling.

After each time I'd feel and release the energy of my anger, I'd find words and ways to calmly and effectively communicate what I was angry about, what was unacceptable to me. With safe ways to be with my anger and my rage when they arose, I was able to risk becoming consciously aware of those emotions in the situations that provoked them. While I've continued to be curious about what leads people to be mean or nasty toward me, I now can also feel the hostility in their behavior. I can feel my own anger rising and choose to be with it. When I share about it, even when the other person thinks I'm being unreasonable or too sensitive, I now have my own permission to feel and express just exactly what's so for me. (See **Safe Space to Scream**, page 211 and **Safe for Feelings**, page 203, as well as the later parts of **Coming Home**, page 287 for more detail about all of this.)

As I've become more accepting of and comfortable with my own rage and anger a very strange thing has happened. There are moments when, alone with my self and in response to the most inconsequential seeming incidents, I erupt into towering rage. Coming in from a peaceful night of sleeping in my womb-tent, I might spill some water, stub my toe or drop something and suddenly find my self wild with rage: cursing, roaring and slamming around my little sanctuary. Most often I'm screaming "I can't take this anymore!" Or, "I can't stand this!" Or, "I hate this!" Or, "Stop it, stop it, stop it!" Or, "Leave her alone!"

The ferocity astonishes me. Yet, I am no longer frightened by these episodes. I know that making space to let them just play through me is important. I know that these eruptions end as abruptly as they've begun. I know how to blow without harming my self physically. And, since I told them about this propensity of mine when we first began sharing the space with each other, my neighbors on the property know that there's nothing to worry about when they hear me storming.

Sometimes, there is a tiny background voice that reverberates with the old critical, stopper messages about how ridiculous, extreme and not like me these outbursts are. Yet, the stronger witness/Mommy voice inside fiercely defends and holds the space for me to have them. There is an inner knowing that these experiences are essential to my healing process.

There's rarely any content or context to these flare-ups. No memories rise; no images of what this might be about. I know it's pointless to try to figure out any whys for these episodes. They are long bottled up and fermented unexpressed rage that it is, in this moment, finally safe to release. After each such outpouring, I feel exhausted and cleansed, complete for the moment, more spacious inside my self.

Recently, after I'd had several days of draining rages over thwarting problems with my computer, I was feeling a need for lots of rest. On the way into a non-work/unscheduled week in which I hoped to have the room for that kind of stillness, my Feldenkrais healer and I did some powerful releasing work on my stomach area. We were addressing the sporadic stomach pain/pressure that results in my needing to vomit out swallowed toxicity.

As my resting week began, each day was filled with lolling about reading and napping my way through the hours till it was cool enough to take a long walk. For some brief part of that cooling time, I would also feel the urge to do a bit of something. Unfortunately, whatever little something I did seemed to lead me quickly into a raging uproar.

Each eruption was triggered by some frustration or feeling of being thwarted. One day it was no-see-ums that kept biting me while I was washing away a spider web disease from the trees and plants around the cottage. Another day it was knots that kept breaking or unraveling spilling beads all over the place as I was restringing several old bracelets that needed fixing. Another day it was the streaks left everywhere by the guaranteed non-streaking, biodegradable window cleaner I was using to clean all the windows I'd spotted with hard water as I'd washed the trees.

I went from placid to hysterical rage in seconds each time. The Mommy voice came immediately to talk tenderly to the distraught Little One. She soothingly reminded the Little One that when things go so badly and she gets so frustrated, the best thing to do is to stop whatever we're doing. She reminded the Little One that it's okay to leave it for another time or day when she might be feeling less raw.

Usually, the Little One feeling comforted, listens to the permission and stops. But, on these few awful days, no one inside me was willing to stop. The Little One wanted it done, **now**. So each day I responded to the irresistible push from inside, kept going and kept on screaming and tantruming. After a while I'd be done. With both the tasks and the exploding/falling apart. I'd calmly go back to reading and drowsing. I didn't bother wondering about it all. I just let it go. From past experiences, I know that if there is something I need to know about what's just been happening, it will – unbidden – reveal itself to me at some point.

On the day I was transitioning back into work-mode, it occurred to me that, in this intense succession of days, the old rage, grief, frustration that I'd been releasing had been a layer that had been locked in my body rather than my psyche. I suspected that the energy work on my stomach had loosened all this and freed it to find its way out. I felt pleased and amazed with all the work I'd just done.

Growing and healing inevitably involve upheavals of painful feelings, strong emotions that often seem out of proportion to what is currently happening. When there is such a disproportion, it's almost always because some earlier un-experienced/stuffed feelings are piggybacking out on the emotions that have been stirred in this situation. The psyche or the body is taking this opportunity to release what it hasn't been safe to feel before now.

It's often difficult to allow this process to take its natural course. We can feel crazy by the measure of our culture's yardstick of appropriateness. So, it's important to be gentle and care-full with our selves when this is happening. It's important to make room to feel all that wants to come up without judging it; without allowing others to judge it. It's important to provide safe, private space for moving through these times.

It helps to remind our selves that such times have a natural trajectory. At some point, all that can be released at this moment will have been released. We get to a more balanced place where we then have more of our selves available to us than ever before. We get to have the energy that had been holding all those feelings locked inside and to use it to go forward. We also have more open space inside of our selves for newness to come in.

Consider tenderly making safe space to feel whatever you're feeling.

1-13. Letting Go of Goals

When you "set goals" rather than framing more open-ended intentions, the you-that-you-are-becoming may be constrained by the limited understanding and vision of the you-that-you-are-at-this-moment. You are always expanding and deepening. What looks like a detour to the goal-setter-in-you might well be a rich and enlivening direction for the you-that-is-emerging!

When I was 16 and a half, I went off to Bennington College as a drama major intending to train for acting and directing in legitimate theater. In Vermont, Bennington was then a very small (360 students) avant-garde women's school with an excellent reputation in the arts as well as academics. A substantial scholarship made it possible for me, from a working-class background, to afford this very expensive school.

By mid-way into my second year I'd become disenchanted with the Drama Department: weird students I couldn't relate to, flaky faculty and nutty, claustrophobic sexual politics. After a fraught confrontation with both my academic counselor and the department chair, I made a choice that we all agreed would require my resigning from the Theater Arts Division.

When You "Set Goals" Rather Than Framing More Open-Ended Intentions, The You-That-You-Are-Becoming May Be Constrained By The Limited Understanding And Vision Of The You-That-You-Are-At-This-Moment.

You Are Always Expanding And Deepening. What Looks Like a Detour To The Goal-Setter-In-You Might Well Be A Rich And Enlivening Direction For The You-That-Is-Emerging!

j5

At the time, the only other course I was taking that interested me was a lively abnormal psychology class. In what was an arbitrary and expedient decision, I switched my major to Psychology/Social Science. As far as I knew then, I was simply shelving my plans for acting training until I'd finished my BA and could enroll at one of the professional drama schools in New York City or London.

Semester by semester, as I progressed through abnormal psychology into experimental psychology coursework and research seminars, I discovered that I was enjoying my rather accidental major. The faculty and my classmates were interesting and inspiring; the material, often fascinating. The sexual politics that had been such an irritating part of most of the Arts Divisions were either invisible or absent in the Social Science Division. By junior year I was passionately involved in the research project for my senior thesis.

During our yearly winter non-resident terms and our summers, we generally tried to find temporary work in fields related to our majors. The professor who was both my academic counselor and major advisor found me a placement with one of his colleagues for the summer after my junior year. I worked as research assistant to a well-known, highly respected researcher in the same field as the one in which I was writing my thesis. For ten weeks this dedicated, kind man – also the Chair of the Graduate Program in Psychology at his university – was a mentor to me.

I returned to the job during the winter non-resident term of my senior year. Then, I stayed on working with him throughout the spring as I completed my last semester for Bennington in-absentia by taking a couple of graduate classes at the New School for Social Research. My plans were still to try studying at a professional acting school as soon as I'd completed my degree from Bennington.

Late that spring, my boss and mentor invited me to meet with him and two other faculty members from the graduate program. They praised my resourcefulness and creativity as both thinker and researcher and offered me a guaranteed place in their incoming class if I would consider it.

I was surprised and disoriented. I had never considered going to graduate school, much less graduate school in psychology. While working at the lab, I had been gathering and comparing information about drama schools. Psychology had been just what I was doing till I could get on with my real life in the theater. But, oddly enough, their offer and their respect for my talents in the field set me to wondering.

I started thinking about whether the people or the process in professional drama schools would be any different from what I'd found in Bennington's Theater Arts Division. I suspected it could easily be the same and maybe even more so. I thought about how much I'd been enjoying my work and my colleagues in this graduate psychology department. Being invited in by faculty that I already knew and that already knew me – not having to go through the usual rigmarole of applications and interviews – would mean that I could come into the program without any pressure to prove my self. I would be free, if I chose it, to explore the possibilities of this path for a while with nothing at stake. I decided I would approach it as a one-year experiment; if it didn't feel right I would drop out and go on with my theater training plans.

So, I began life as a graduate student in the doctoral program in psychology at Yeshiva University/Albert Einstein Medical School. Faculty recommendations helped garner substantial fellowship support for my schooling. The first year was a mixture of fascination with the material and frustration with the arrogant snobbery of the great-name professors who, as distinguished visiting lecturers, came to teach us. There was space to engage in frank dialogue with my mentor about this frustration. That he acknowledged the validity of my perceptions and promised me intermediate and advanced seminars with more inspiring professors made it possible for me to consider staying and continuing to explore.

I started out in the experimental psychology program, a logical progression from my absorption with research process. But, as one year led into the next, I drifted into taking all the clinical psychology coursework as well. Without ever having it as a goal and in a year-by-year curious-to-see-what-happens-next fashion, I went all the way to getting my Ph.D. Although my doctoral dissertation was in experimental psychology, I came to the end of the joint program certain that I wanted to work as a clinical psychologist doing psychotherapy not research. Professional acting school no longer held any interest for me.

Although I loved the whole process of doing psychotherapy, it was often difficult in my early days to keep from feeling exhausted by the intensity of being witness to other people's struggles. Doing psychotherapy has continued to become even more fulfilling as, during these past almost 48 years, it's kept being informed and transformed both by what I learn from my own ongoing inner healing and what I learn from just the doing of the work itself. I've found ways to navigate and balance the intensity so that it no longer exhausts me. Not only do I love what I do, I believe that it's exactly what I was meant to do this time around on the planet. That I got to this place in such serendipitous and seemingly accidental ways has been a powerful lesson/teaching for me about goals.

My early commitment to becoming an actor/director was born of the life experiences and yearnings I had as a young adult. I started out at college certain that I was on the right path for me. Yet, in a series of random steps, life kept moving me away from that track. Had I, out of single-minded dedication to my original goal, resisted this nudging, I wouldn't have found my way to this work that so richly feeds my soul.

There is strong pressure from our culture to have and strive toward actualizing particular goals in every aspect of our lives. From early on we are pushed to choose a major, to channel our energies toward particular careers, to define our direction, to articulate 5-year and 10-year-from-now pictures of where we want to see our selves. The implication is that these defined goals determine the shape of our futures.

For those on a spiritual journey there is a different cast to this pressure. The New Age prescriptions/directives for manifesting: the process by which we are meant to create and move dreams/visions of our selves and our lives into reality. The counsel: to precisely articulate the images of what we want to draw into our lives. Then, to repeatedly write our affirmations – or repeatedly re-energize our visualizations – of those sought-after outcomes as if they were already existing in reality.

Committing to these affirmations, visualizations or goal-settings assumes that the person we are in this moment can choose fittingly for the person we will be in the future. This supposes that who we'll be down the road is pretty much the same as who we are in this moment, as if the experiences we'll have between now and then might not change us, as if the goals this self sets might not later be experienced as outdated, too limiting or even completely irrelevant by the who-we-are-becoming.

Along with this (to me ridiculous) idea that our vision of our selves at any moment will be valid and appropriate for all time to come, there is implicit a vision of our beings that seems undermining of our true nature: the assumption in both the dominant and spiritual cultures that only by our mind focusing in this very structured, narrow way will we ever move forward in our lives/journeys.

None of this feels so to me. I trust that we are changing and growing in every moment, even (and perhaps especially) during the times when on the face of it we appear to be doing nothing of any redeeming value. I believe that change/evolution continues to unfold in us whether or not we consciously effort to make it happen: it is part of our very nature as beings. Sometimes it seems to me that consciously efforting actually interferes with the natural, organic flow of our evolving selves.

I **do** believe there is value in having open-ended intentions of a broad sort. Here intentions like "I am ready and available for my next step to reveal itself to me" or "I am needing this process to slow down for a while so that I can better assimilate/incorporate all the changing" seem like good examples. These consciously but loosely articulated requests/prayers to Spirit/our deepest selves have a way of framing the **essence** of what we feel we need.

When we get very specific and detailed about what it is we want that next step to look like or to be, we run the risk of being too narrowly focused on the appearance of only that specific thing or outcome. This restricting vision can leave us blind to the arrival of something that answers the **essence** of our request if not the concrete detail of it. Focused on and invested in rehearsing the menu (as it were) we may fail to notice that a perfectly delectable dinner is arriving at our table.

As I continue my journey, I am taught almost daily and in the most minute ways to give up any thinking that might be goal-like. I learn that having a plan or agenda usually means having to work to disengage from this menu so that I can show up for what is arriving unbidden as a gift from Spirit/my inmost self. I learn to open my self to what comes into my life from that place: to trust where the energy pulls or leads me, rather than where my mind might have me go. This allows me to live in the center of what is right for the me I am in each moment.

The more I help my mind not to argue or interfere with where I'm being led by the energy/Spirit/my inmost self, the more my faith in this authentic, organic process grows. Then, my mind is a valuable resource I call upon to support my belly-led unfolding.

Consider exploring how life feels and unfolds when you frame broad open-ended intentions instead of investing in detailed goals, highly specific affirmations and very carefully articulated visualizations.

1-14. Celebrating Our Selves

*Celebrate and acknowledge your self for having the courage
to risk being in the process of healing and growing your self
in a world that makes it difficult to claim your birthright:
truly loving, accepting, enjoying and knowing your inmost self!*

When I walked away from my outwardly successful life just a few months past my 32nd birthday (see **Pirouettes**, page 125 for more about this), people were incredulous, baffled by my decision. In those early days of the second wave of feminism, it seemed profligate for a woman who had made it in the male-dominated world to be turning her back on that success rather than using her position to mentor other women into that world.

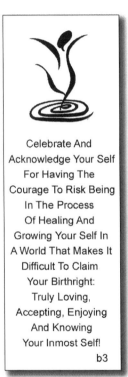

Celebrate And
Acknowledge Your Self
For Having The
Courage To Risk Being
In The Process
Of Healing And
Growing Your Self In
A World That Makes It
Difficult To Claim
Your Birthright:
Truly Loving,
Accepting, Enjoying
And Knowing
Your Inmost Self!

b3

It didn't matter to me then what anyone else thought or felt about my choice. I left that life – both my work as a feminist psychotherapist and my open marriage to a feminist man – because I felt compelled to.

I was heeding a call from deep within me. I couldn't any longer bear living in the middle of the contradiction that was my life: an abundance of external success, achievements and accolades, yet never a sense in my self of being okay, a worthy human being. My inner critic attacked me mercilessly. Her lacerating barbs undermined everything I did or accomplished. The self-loathing with which I lived was extreme and pervading.

At the time, I didn't see this leave-taking as an act of courage. I didn't even see it as a choice that I was making. It was simply what I **had** to do, no matter what. Leaving almost everything and everyone behind wasn't hard; it was the irresistible unfolding of the necessary next step.

For all the remarkable experiences I've been through in the now more than 39 years since that turning point, it remains the most powerful watershed moment in my journey. That decision set me on the road to a life that has been very different from the sort to which I, before then, had aspired. There was a particular refrain repeated by my mother whenever I took exception to being told that I wouldn't be allowed to do or have something I wanted to do or have. "When you're rich and famous you'll be able to do/have whatever **you** want!" I took that flip message to heart and set about becoming rich and famous so that I might escape from feeling unhappy and deprived for the rest of my life.

By 32, I knew I was probably as rich and famous as I'd ever get to be. My income was above the 98th percentile for professional women at the time. It was already more money than I could find ways to use once I'd bought all the shoes and matching purses for the walk-in closet full of all my specially chosen or hand-crocheted (by me) clothes. (This, my reaction to years of being told by my mother that more than one pair of shoes or one purse or any clothing of particular quality was "not necessary," even when there was money available and she had a considerable closet-full herself.) I'd also by then had my small share of fame: being interviewed for radio, TV, and modest newspaper and magazine stories about my work and life as a feminist/feminist therapist.

It was painfully apparent that being rich and famous was not, after all, going to change anything that felt wrong either about me or about my life. I finally got it. Nothing I'd been doing was of any use in my struggle: excesses of outward accomplishment would never put an end to my feelings of deprivation or bring me to feeling happy or at peace with who I was. I hadn't a clue what a new and different path might look like but that didn't feel daunting at the time.

The journey that began with this understanding and with walking out of my old life has been an amazing one. It started me on the way to living from the inside out. My path became one of uncovering (and sometimes recovering) who I was underneath all the socially valued but personally meaningless trappings. The work involved learning to accept, nurture and celebrate **all** of who I am in every moment of my days, just **exactly** as I am in these moments. This, even when how I am is less than I might hope someday to be; even when those around me may be less generous with me than I am being with my self; even when other people may find my dedication and life style unforgivably self-indulgent.

Nothing in the media or the culture's generally touted version of the good life honors this way of being. The good life we're swindled into valuing involves climbing to ever more important career positions, acquiring ever more – and more costly – possessions, traveling to ever more exotic places, having ever more extreme adventures and amassing ever more excessive amounts of money. It also involves, particularly for women, considerable attention (and money) devoted to maintaining our physical appearance as thin and free from signs of aging.

The socially/environmentally/politically conscious good life calls us to values and awarenesses that are clearly much healthier for the planet and for all living beings. Yet, its insistent calls to action-for-the-greater-good also tend to marginalize the significance of a sustained commitment to self-knowledge, self-acceptance and self-nurture.

Many of the currently popular Spiritual paths are also less than supportive of claiming our birthright of knowing, embracing and taking good care of our inmost selves. Rather, these paths encourage us to find peace by way of transcending our particular self or by the practice of immediately turning any of our (normally occurring) so-called negative thoughts or feeling into positive ones. I have a lot of trouble with any versions of the good life that inspire devaluing all emotions that are less than grateful or serene.

Coming to know and compassionately embrace and care for our selves is our most basic right and our most essential responsibility to our selves, the planet and all beings on the planet. As we each take this inward journey, the energy we put forth into the planetary field becomes one of healing and wholeness. We do not seek to fill our emptiness or create a sense of our value by aggrandizing our selves at the expense of others or at the expense of the planet itself.

When we take the risk of living from this inside place: claiming our own healing as a focal part of our journey in this life and resisting the pressure to conform to more socially valued, more culturally acceptable paths, we are being courageous spirit-warrior goddesses (or spirit-warriors). This is so even if we feel there isn't a choice involved in our taking this path.

It is important to honor and celebrate our selves for this courage; for taking this course in a world that rather than acknowledging its worth, more often mocks and devalues it.

Consider how courageous and brave you are to be engaged in this revolutionary process of growing, healing and nourishing your self.

1-15. Not Pushing Our Selves

It's never okay to "push through" your fear...
Instead, listen to what the frightened part needs
from you in order to feel safe to go ahead,
act on that information!

My dear friend Faith and I found our selves simultaneously at turning points in our lives, moments that we each felt the need to mark with some meaningful ceremony or ritual. We'd opened our selves to whatever possibilities Spirit might bring to us. We both were listening inward while looking around for something that would feel right. A flyer on the local health food store bulletin board announcing a Women's Vision Quest caught my attention.

It's Never Okay To
"Push Through"
Your Fear...
Instead,
Listen To
What The
Frightened Part
Needs From You
In Order To Feel
Safe To Go Ahead,
Act On That
Information!

e5

The Quest was to be led, under the auspices of The Ojai Foundation, by two local women who'd been trained as Vision Quest guides. There would be four days of camping out in the Ojai wilderness. In the middle of those days, we would each spend a 30-hour period of camping by our selves. During this solo time – in separate spaces that we'd each have a chance to scout for – we would fast, meditate and offer prayers to Spirit for the blessing of a vision to take back into our ordinary lives. We would move into this time from, and return out of it into, a base camp community. The days before and after our solo would be spent learning about wilderness safety, doing ceremony and building community with the dozen or so women going on the trip.

Though Faith was more drawn to the communal ceremony part and I more to the solo part, the mix sounded promising to both of us. So in April of 1986, several months past my 45th birthday, I was planning to be in the wilderness, camping both alone and with a group of women I'd (except for Faith) yet to meet.

As we prepared for the trip, Faith was feeling anticipatory anxiety about the physical challenges of camping alone. We agreed that she had permission to bail – at any point up to the very last moment – if she decided it was more than she felt up to handling.

Eager for the opportunity experienced guides in the background would provide for me to be alone in a wild place, I was unconcerned about physical challenges. Instead, I was feeling irritable about the amount of time we'd be spending with the other women building community. So much was moving and shifting inside of me during those early days of re-mothering my self, I felt skinless and frequently too permeable to be around other people's energies. More often I was into being reclusive.

When the departure day came, I felt crazed: slamming and raging around the house, alternately cursing or crying. The morning was filled with a series of minor but aggravating mishaps: spilling things; not being able to find things that I'd suddenly decide I had to have with me; having to repack my backpack again and again as I tried to fit in these last minute things and still leave room for a share of the cooking utensils and food that would be distributed among us when we gathered. There was cleaning up cat vomit; having a **really** bad hair day; insane interactions with my new, intrusive landlord and worries about an injured knee that had only recently stopped getting swollen whenever I walked more than a little ways.

Faith arrived at my door excited with her courage and readiness for the adventure she had thought might be too much for her. She found me in emotional disarray: ranting and in tears. She reminded me that I had the same permission she had had: even at this last moment, I didn't have to go if it didn't feel right to me. Of course, in my state, I got irritated with her for thinking I needed **her** permission in order to give my self permission not to go. Yet, the truth was that her reminding me actually **did** help me give my self more space in which to make my choice. It released me from concern that I'd be letting her down if I decided I couldn't go.

Because she knows and loves me so well, she stopped trying to be helpful and quietly sat down to see where I'd get to on my own. I raved on and on about the miseries of my morning and my worst-case scenarios about how it might be for me around the women with whom we'd be Questing. Faith was her gentle and generous self, patiently sitting in witness to my process.

In the end, I decided to try going. We took two cars to the meeting place (some six miles from my house) so that I could keep my options open until after I'd had a chance to feel out the group. I groused my way up the hill to the Ojai Foundation then sat through the opening circle ceremonies feeling crabby and sour. In the end, the lure of the alone time outweighed my reluctance to be in this community so I chose to risk staying for the whole adventure.

We wagon-trained (in three vans) out to a canyon I know and love. We hiked in – further than I'd ever gone on my own – to a wilderness campground on the river. There were some wonderful moments those first hours as we cleaned up the trashed campsites, built a stone altar, dug latrine trenches, learned about low-impact wilderness camping and then prepared a communal dinner. I got as hilariously excited as any potty-training two-year old when I pooped outdoors for the first time in my grown-up life.

After dinner we sat in a formal circle with the intention to tell the stories of what had brought each of us to the Quest. We were also to name the greatest uneasinesses/fears we were bringing with us and to speak to what our plans were for caring for our selves in the face of these uneasinesses/fears. Attending to everyone's heartful self-revelations was agitating.

My cranky thoughts: "I spend my work time listening to the details of the lives of the women who are my clients and about whom I care deeply. In my private time I listen to the details of the lives of my intimate women friends whom I love dearly. That's all the listening and caring I have room for. I can't bear to listen to you. I don't care or want to care about you. I have **no room** for this. I just want to wrap my self in the stillness of this wild place, **alone**."

Some of the women talked on at length, the circle being one of the few places where a woman, trusting that she will be witnessed from the heart, can feel free take all the time she needs. Despite wanting to scream and run away, I made my self honor my commitment to the sacredness of the circle. I stayed and listened as best I could, struggling to open my heart as I was meant to do. I felt intense emotional claustrophobia. I felt like vomiting.

When my turn came, I did speak my truth – in more graceful words than I was experiencing it, but only barely. I acknowledged that to take better care of my currently skinless self, I would keep to the fringes of the group much of the time. Giving voice to what was so inside me helped quell some of the noxious feelings I was having. (Giving voice to what's going on inside of me usually does that.)

When the circle ended for the evening, the social, get-to-know-each-other-better chat began. I thought I'd go out of my mind. I started having an anxiety attack. After checking in with Faith for a hug, I went off to sit alone on the bank of the river. Listening to the wind in the trees and the rush of the water over the rocks, I sat breathing slowly into my belly.

As my anxiety loosened, I could listen to the frightened parts of me. They let me know how betrayed they'd felt by my forcing my self to sit in circle opening to the women and their stories when I was so desperate for stillness and solitude. They let me know it was upsetting and scary for them to have me overriding what they/my belly feelings were trying to tell me. They helped me to see that once again in my life I had been violating my vulnerable self: pushing to do what was expected of me so that I could get to what I really needed.

By going along with the conventions of the Vision Quest and honoring what I had implicitly agreed to do when I signed on for it, I was dishonoring my own distress in the moment. That betrayal of my inner self had moved me from edgy discomfort into an anxiety attack.

I promised my big and little overwhelmed selves that I would listen in and do whatever they needed me to do (or not do) so that they could feel safe on the Quest (and anywhere else). I promised that I wouldn't again make us do anything that felt emotionally claustrophobic or too much for us to bear. I promised that I would commit to putting what they needed ahead of the demands of any external agendas, rules or expectations; that I would do this regardless of any agreements I – explicitly or implicitly – might have made with others beforehand.

With this powerful reassurance that I would listen to and act on what I heard from them, the distressed parts of me were willing to return to where the group was gathered. Over the rest of the time bookending the solo journey, I wove in and out of the circle. Knowing that I would have my own support to withdraw immediately whenever things felt too much for us allowed me to stay in contact more of the time than I would have imagined possible. Refusing to force my self to stay in the circle gave me the freedom to more often **choose** to stay connected and connecting. This was the most empowering gift of the Quest, the vision that I brought back with me into my ordinary life.

Later that same year, I chose to go on a longer Quest with older, more experienced women leaders in order to have four days of solo time in Death Valley (see **Our Slowest Parts**, page 99 for more about that journey). On this second trip, I spoke with the leaders in advance to explain what I'd learned about making it safe for my self to travel with a group, I advocated successfully for the freedom, as needed, to move in and out of the circle.

Much of current self-help rhetoric promotes the path of feel-the-fear-and-do-it-anyway. The sub-text: that giving in to one's fears leads to an escalation of those fears and increased incapacitation. I find this approach harsh and the sub-text an outright distortion of what's so.

When we listen compassionately and protectively to our fearful selves, they can let us know what they need from us in order to feel safe to move forward into and through what feels frightening to them. When those parts of us experience the steadfastness of our sympathetic concern and our willingness to attend immediately to their needs for safety, they become more trusting of our caring.

When we can promise to instantly remove our selves from any circumstance that feels too scary or overwhelming, these parts can then tolerate pushing the edges of their envelope. When they have to put up with argument and negotiation from us, they start working to get us to leave long before the moment beyond which they'd not feel safe to go.

New Age and recovery talk frequently focuses on the importance of honoring commitments and keeping promises. Yet, most often the focus is on the commitments or promises we make to others rather than on those we make to our selves. As I continue my dedication to lovingly re-parenting my self, I understand that whenever conflict emerges between promises I've made to others and those I've made to my self (in order to take the best possible care of me), the ones made to my self have priority.

I've learned to be more gentle with and responsive to others' feelings when I need to break my commitments to them because of this priority. And, I've learned to be more careful about the ways in which I initially commit my self to others. I let people know, up front, that keeping any agreement with them will be conditional on it continuing to be okay with my inner self.

Acknowledging and acting from the awareness that we are constantly growing and changing allows us to be more realistic and considerate in how we commit to each other. We can act in ways that violate neither our selves nor the others about whom we care.

Consider being more tender, protective and attentive to the frightened parts of you.

1-16. Our Slowest Parts

Go only as fast as the slowest part of you feels safe to go!

At 45, a year and a half out of the difficult relationship that was to mark the end of my interest in partnering (see **Others' Views**, page 259 for more about this) and a year and a half into the process of becoming an unconditionally loving, fiercely protective mother to my self (see **The Little Ones Story**, page 9 for more about this) I was at a threshold moment in my life. I asked Spirit for help in finding some ceremonious way to mark this crossing place.

In early spring of that year (1986), Spirit answered. I saw a flyer describing a 3-day Vision Quest experience for women in the Ojai wilderness. The trip called to me and, with a close woman friend, I signed up for it. (For the story of that trip, see **Not Pushing Our Selves**, page 93.) It was a deeply moving experience that set me searching for a longer Quest somewhere further from home.

Go Only As

Fast

As The Slowest

Part Of You

Feels Safe

To Go!

e3

Shortly after starting the search, while browsing through a Shaman's Drum magazine that someone had left at the library, I found an ad for a 10-day Vision Quest for women in Death Valley that winter. The leaders for this Quest were older and more experienced than the dedicated young women who had led the Ojai trip. That earlier trip had been a tantalizing appetizer and this one sounded like it would be an exciting full course dinner.

As soon as I'd registered, just as the brochure predicted, the Quest began for me. Everything that happened between that day and the day of the physical trip to the meeting place in Sebastopol seemed charged with meaning and portent. I felt that I was living in an altered state of consciousness, readying my self for something momentous.

I moved slowly and carefully through the so-called severance stage of my preparations for the Quest. It was the first time that leaving home for a trip involved me in consciously completing every project in which I had been investing my energies. I cleansed and tended my physical and psychic spaces as if I were never coming back to them. It was as though I were preparing for my own death. The process felt exhilarating rather than frightening.

I felt hungry for the four days that we would each spend alone with our selves in the desert. I was intoxicated by the idea of being so far from the civilized world, alone and yet protected by wilderness-experienced women leaders who would hold a safe container for us.

The three days before and after the solo time – days that would be devoted to meeting, traveling and developing a questing community with the rest of the dozen women questors, two leaders and three assistants – were of **much** less interest to me. Still, I could feel threads of magic weaving me into this web as the departure day approached.

My uneasiness about the not-alone time settled quickly once we gathered in our primary leader's home. As we arrived, we were asked to commit to being together in sacred silence through that late afternoon and evening as well as through the next day of travel. Except for the time each of us would meet separately with the leaders to set our intentions for the journey, the silence was to be broken only for instructions or emergencies. It seemed a perfect way to build spiritual community as we caravanned and kept trading places among the three vehicles that carried us across California and into the heart of the desert. It was a relief to know there'd be no irritating social chitchat surrounding me.

At the end of that travel day, in the desert though not yet at our base camp, we slept out under the stars. The following morning we drove to our entry point and carried our personal gear in on foot for the last couple of miles. Then we made several trips back out to the vans for kitchen gear, food supplies and the innumerable gallons of water we'd brought for our selves and for cooking. After the hauling, we spent the rest of the day learning about desert safety and the formal structure we were meant to use during our quest for vision in our solo time.

In my individual intention-setting interview, I'd experienced some uneasiness with Sedonia's (our primary leader) general approach. My disquiet increased through the teachings she gave those first and second days in base camp. Her style of leading felt uncomfortably male-model-of-authority: kind of imperious, top-down and somewhat impervious to the innate wisdom that each of us questors might be bringing to the circle. There definitely was **a right way** everything was to be done, particularly when we were out on solo. The gist seemed to be that since we were adopting this Native American tradition, we were to follow its form precisely. There was no room for any modifications to better fit it to our different context as Anglo women or to our personal styles/needs.

Since this was Sedonia's show that Spirit had brought me to experience and since no one else seemed at all bothered by the constraints I chafed at in the rigid rules-for-proper-behavior, I kept my concerns to my self. Certainly, once off in the desert, I could (proper form be damned) do only what felt right for me.

Part of Sedonia's instruction was a very strong message for us each to "really push your envelope," to move out of our comfort zones to our farthest edges and then beyond. This, too, felt very male-model and at odds with where I was in my own process of learning to be more gentle and less demanding with my recovering super-achiever self. I wasn't sure how well I could resist getting swept up again by this pressure that I'd lived with all of my life and from which I'd only recently begun to break free.

The second day we were sent further out into the desert to find a sacred spot for our solo. Once we'd found it, we'd be going back and forth to ferry our four days stock (nine gallons) of water out to it. Returning, we'd gather in circle and, with something we'd brought back from our spot, mark our locations on the leaders' rough map of the area. We'd be paired with the geographically closest other questor as rock-pile-buddies. On our way to our solo, we'd establish a rock pile together in a place between our secluded spots. Each of the four days of solo time, both buddies would separately come to the pile to leave evidence for the other that they were ambulatory and doing okay: drawings, rock arrangements, desert flowers and such served us.

Some of my cohorts went way out to the back of beyond to find their sacred places. One of the women actually wandered for hours before finding her bedraggled way back to base from her far away spot.

When I headed out on my search, I was feeling agitated by Sedonia's instruction to "push [my] envelope." I'd already spent too much of my life pushing my envelope, trying to do whatever it might be way ahead of schedule, way beyond what might be reasonable to expect of my self and way faster than the slowest part of me ever felt either safe or capable of going. (See **Going 75 mph**, page 321 for more about this.)

Stewing as I walked out into the desert, I noticed that a small mesa just ahead was beckoning me. It was within easy walking distance. From it I could see the chaparral surrounding the base camp but not the staff people moving around inside of it. The mesa was the closest in that I could be while remaining invisible to base and having base remain invisible to me.

It was the perfect spot for my solo. Seriously pushing **my** envelope meant daring **not** to force my self into some super-achievement or over some more literal edge. Being this gentle and solicitous with my vulnerable self was the most powerful edge-walk for me. It was a blessing, having that sweet little close-in mesa calling me home to my slowing down self.

The following morning we were, in beautiful ceremony, birthed out of the womb of our base community and sent, with prayers, off to do our solo questing. I arranged a shade shelter by tying down my tarp as a lean-to at the bottom of the mesa, laid out my sleeping bag, water jugs, pens and journal and began the next phase of the journey: Four days of fasting on water while paying keen attention to everything around me, absorbing this wild place. Listening within for the voice of Spirit. Writing and drawing in my journal and trundling daily to the rock pile.

It was, as well, four days of being laid low, wrenchingly sick with nausea. At the time, I thought the nausea was a reaction to the heat leeching chemicals from the cloudy plastic of the containers into the water and making it so I could barely drink without gagging and vomiting.

Yet, when I told the tale of my questing time during the re-incorporation circle after the solo ended, I understood that the retching and nausea were also full of symbolic significance: Through the four days alone, I had been recognizing and experiencing the toxicity of the internalized societal standards with which I had mercilessly pushed and punished my self for most of my life. I had been retching and vomiting all of that out of my being.

The wind and heat of the desert had stripped away the forms I had come in with: my own life-long internalizations and all of what Sedonia's teachings had added to that package. Had I followed the form she set for us, I might well have learned something of value. Yet, in the cauldron of my nauseated sickness, I saw that my lesson was to listen only to the guidance from my own core – the part of me beyond all the toxic internalizations. This I did with fierce gentleness, aching and in tears for all the past years of breaking my own heart and spirit with those terrible incorporated shoulds.

At the close of our solo time, we were to spend the entire last night awake in the middle of the circle of stones we had arranged in our sacred place. There we were to sit in prayer for our own vision and for the psychic community of people and concerns represented by those stones. Earlier on that day, I had made my last trip to the rock pile. I felt hollowed out, exhausted. At the same time I felt filled by the undemanding love and grace with which I had tended my ailing self and my inner Little One(s) during this transformational desert sojourn.

On my way to the rock pile, I noticed something oddly out of place in the beige and pale gray landscape of my daily route: a small bubble gum pink lump with a trailing strand of paler pink fiber. I picked up what turned out to be a deflated balloon with printing on it. When I stretched it out to read what was written, I roared with laughter. The message? "**Childcare is everybody's business**!" A powerful **yes** from Spirit to all the work I'd been doing at the foot of my little mesa in the womb of my lean-to. I felt affirmed in the life path I'd chosen and affirmed for choosing to stay on that path in the desert despite the directions that would have had me act less caringly to my little selves. I had received my vision; an all-night vigil in my stone circle was unnecessary.

When we returned to base camp exhausted and radiant, we were ready to begin the re-incorporation phase of the process. Ceremonially welcomed, we were fed some mild fruit soup to break our fast and called to meet in the sacred circle of our desert-born community. We began the almost three-day cycle of sharing the stories of our solo quests. Sitting in solemn (and sometimes hilarious) witness to one another, we wove the mythic tales of our individual Heroine's Journeys.

Of course, as is often the case in my life, my experience was out at the far end of the continuum from the rest of my desert tribe. I sobbed my way through the telling of how my solo time repeated yet again my life long fight for the right to be and value how I am even while how I am leaves me as outsider, the odd one out struggling with the pressures to conform.

And, at the end of my tale, the epiphany. The pink balloon and its message from Spirit affirming my path, honoring the thread I weave into the fabric of the world: going slowly, caring for the little ones inside, recognizing the power of vulnerability. There was joy in that coming home to my self, feeling welcomed and seen as part of the community even as I lived in my differentness. Afterward there was the gift of being given my questing name: "She Who Walks Her Truth In Beauty."

Once we all had shared and been witnessed in our Heroine's tales, we began what I felt was the most enlivening ritual of the whole Quest: the Sacred Theater experience Sedonia herself had created as the final ceremony. With her orchestration of this amazing ritual I got to see and be touched by all of whom else she was as a teacher/facilitator, a woman holding power from the Sacred Feminine.

The staff disappeared at dusk leaving us questors to prepare our selves for this as yet unknown next step. Luminaria (votive candles in paper bags filled with sand) glowing orange against the night's blackness and the sounds of drumming and chanting guided us out into the further depths of the desert. There each of us – bedecked in ceremonial garb we'd been asked to include in our gear and wearing body paint we had been given to decorate our selves – processed into a candle lit circle/arena. There we each celebrated our selves with words, movement and song creating the dance of our journey and joyfully celebrating one another's beauty and power.

The gifts of that Quest were substantial. Sedonia and I (with one sick and sleeping questor in the back of her camper-pickup) drove the 9-hour journey back to Sebastopol deeply engaged with each other in a far-reaching and exuberant dialogue. I reflected on my experience of her two different styles of teaching/leading during the quest: from the masculine in the early instruction phase and from the Feminine in the Sacred Theater ritual. That sharing opened into talking and dreaming together about the possibility of holding power from the Sacred Feminine; about building new images of empowerment that went beyond the hierarchic forms we'd learned in patriarchal culture. We talked about form and formlessness. We talked about the power of vulnerability, the challenge of gentleness and moving slowly.

We birthed a soul-nourishing friendship on that drive that fed us both for the many years until her death. Our connection spawned a Women's Lodge that brought together ten powerful, empowered women who, for several years, gathered seasonally in circle with the intention to explore and experience how power looks and feels when held from the Field of the Sacred Feminine.

So much of power and empowerment in our world is conceived as connected with moving fast, doing more – always accelerating and expanding into bigger, more and finish-it-yesterday. It takes great faith and courage to break away from the relentless, pounding rhythm of that trance. It takes great trust and willingness to move differently, to listen for the quieter voice of the soul: the voice that asks for us to slow down, to listen inward; that asks for us to savor the stillness in which magic can be born; that asks us to be cherishing and gentle with our delicate selves.

May you find the courage to go only as fast as the slowest part of you feels safe to go.

1-17. Be Gentle with Your Self

*Remember to be really gentle with your self
as much of the time as you can!*

For most of the first thirty-odd years of my life, I was a harsh taskmaster to my self, mercilessly pushing me through any endeavor in which I engaged. If I were tired or sick, rather than backing off, I'd be more likely to up the pressure to which I subjected my chronically super-achieving self. I had to be the best at whatever I was doing in order to feel worthwhile. (My father tells me that even when I was very young I would abandon any undertaking in which I didn't immediately see that I might excel.)

Remember To

Be

Really Gentle

With Your Self

As Much Of

The Time

As You Can!

c1

When, at 23 – and in suicidal despair – I began working with my first therapist, I brought that same striving to the work with my emotional self. I was as relentless in the pursuit of healing as I was in **everything**. As a consequence, my life was highly charged and productive (in our culture's terms). It was also exhausting – though I would never have admitted to that then.

At 32, responding to the urging of a different sort of inner voice, I dropped out of my super-achieving existence (see **Pirouettes**, page 125 for more about that time) and took to the road West in a van that I'd set up as my traveling home. For the first time in memory, I began questioning the ways that I had been treating my self. I started paying attention to the body that I had persistently flogged in order to get me to wherever it was I thought I'd needed to go. Every fiber of my body and my being called to me to slow down, to go more gently both in the world and with my self. Paying attention to this call from within, I began the long, sometimes arduous journey to becoming a kinder caretaker of me.

My new choices went against everything I had learned in trying to survive my critical, undermining mother. (See **Speak Kindly to Your Self**, page 193 for more about these beginnings.) This made the road quite edgy. These choices also went against the grain of mainstream culture. This added to my general experience of being other, an outsider wherever I found my self. Neither challenge deterred me.

That I was moving into this new way of being in the world without putting on it any of my usual pressure to excel was pretty amazing. Without yet having a vocabulary for what I was doing, the path I took was to begin to observe my self. I became a curious, non-judgmental witness to my own life. Anything I did and any way I thought or felt or acted became something for me to examine and try to understand in its own terms. My focus shifted away from achieving any specific outcome. Instead, I was drawn to simply observing the processes by which I moved and was moved.

I stopped seeing the twists and turns of my thinking, feelings and doings as acceptable/good or unacceptable/bad; they just were what they were. If I wasn't busily evaluating them, they became opportunities to explore my own convolutions. Being just with me, wandering along the West Coast childless and now without partner or work to call my attention away from these meanderings, I had the emotional and physical space I needed to devote to this research. The approach moved me from harsh, demanding-of-self ways toward a growing gentleness in my treatment of me.

Though in my forties, as I began the work of uncovering and re-mothering the Little Ones inside me (see **The Little Ones Story**, page 9 for more about this), my capacity to treat my self tenderly was much expanded and fine-tuned, it all started here with this shift in perspective.

I've watched many of the women with whom I've been privileged to work – women with lives even more complex and contextually embedded than I had had – begin on the path to treating themselves with greater gentleness. Almost always the gateway lies in the willingness to become cultural anthropologists, ethnographers exploring the terrain of their own beings. In choosing to observe, we let go of being outcome-focused. We become witnesses gathering understanding of the ways in which we function in our selves and in the world. Engaged in investigating how we are wired, we can allow our selves to be exactly as we are, without our usual judgments or expectations.

Openhearted curiosity about our selves expands the capacity for kindness and generosity toward our own beings; ways of treating our selves that our upbringings and our culture rarely teach us. In conventional life, goal-directed and outcome-oriented behaviors are valued and rewarded. This valuing leads us to measure our lives against other people's accomplishments and/or against accepted norms. In that measuring we are constantly judging our selves. The judging is rarely gentle. Contrary to popular belief, criticism does not encourage or sustain the flourishing of the best in us. Only when we treat our selves with compassion and generosity of spirit can we live into our fullness.

Consider remembering to approach all that you do and all the ways that you are with curiosity: interest in how you are wired; see how much more gentle you become with your self and watch how you thrive.

1-18. Beginnings and Endings

Beginnings are times of joy and, also, times of ending...
Even endings that feel "right" inside are times of grieving.
Beginnings are times for both celebration and grieving.
Allowing the grief to flow allows the joy to blossom more fully!

It was late August of 1984, just a couple of months before my 44th birthday. I had finally thrown in the towel after an abortive four-month attempt to reconcile with the former partner with whom I had struggled painfully over the preceding seven and a half years. (See **Others' Views**, page 259 for more about this challenging, fraught relationship.) I was emotionally exhausted. Ojai was in the midst of a heat wave: over a week of above 100-degree days and I was trying to move into a wonderful rental house that was to be for me alone.

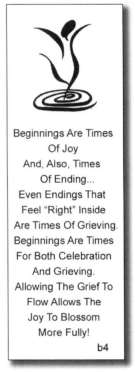

Beginnings Are Times
Of Joy
And, Also, Times
Of Ending...
Even Endings That
Feel "Right" Inside
Are Times Of Grieving.
Beginnings Are Times
For Both Celebration
And Grieving.
Allowing The Grief To
Flow Allows The
Joy To Blossom
More Fully!
b4

I was feeling both excited and miserable. The guys I'd hired had moved all my things into the new house, stacking furniture and boxes against one wall of the large, A-framed main room. There was lots of cleaning to be dealt with before I could begin to arrange furniture or to unpack my stuff. But, it was too hot to do anything and I was too disoriented by the ending of the living-together relationship to contemplate beginning to nest in a place of my own.

Instead, I'd drive to the beach in Santa Barbara. After hours of walking at the tide line I'd be irresistibly drawn to the current doorstep of my ex-partner. Though relieved to have finally extricated my self from what had been an emotionally abusive relationship, I couldn't stay away from her long enough to roost in my new life. At night, I camped out on the floor of my Ojai house or the floor in her Santa Barbara house. Either way, I spent my days in Santa Barbara not in Ojai. Nothing got done at my waiting house.

I felt crazed by this strange dance I was doing but couldn't cajole my self into any different or healthier feeling behavior. It went on for ten days. Then the heat wave broke and so did my paralysis. I began staying in Ojai. And, baby step by baby step, I started to claim the lovely space that Spirit had brought to me.

As I cleaned, moved furniture and unpacked boxes I'd feel devastated, sobbing uncontrollably. I ached with grief over what I was giving up: the hope that I could find a way to be all of me with this person that I was leaving. I mourned what felt to be the final severing of the enmeshment between my now-ex-partner and me. Then, when I kept finding ways that my things fit perfectly into the spaces available, I'd get excited and do little dances of joy. The new house was wrapping me in its comforting arms, welcoming me to the threshold of the next chapter of my life. I'd feel a billowing up of promise, of the freedom once again to be all of my self, uncontained. It was a confusing and paradoxical time.

I knew that separating out from the love-turned-deadly-symbiosis was the best thing I'd been able to do in many years. I felt brave and strong and courageous. I felt proud of me, grateful to Spirit and the Grandmothers for their help in this process of releasing my self. I felt equally grateful to them for their help in bringing me the gift of this sweet living space. At the same time I felt abandoned, bereft and suffocated by my anguish.

I went on like this for several months, feeling the joy and the grief braiding together: sometimes alternating between them and sometimes feeling them simultaneously. I often felt like I was going crazy in the middle of it. Other times, I understood that I was getting sane.

Slowly, as I rode with whatever feelings came up, I found that I was spending more and more of my time in the joyful spaces. The sieges of overpowering grief came less and less often. They lasted less and less long each time they came. The times of being with the joy and celebration came more and more often. They gradually lasted longer and longer. All the while, the grief, when it hit, continued to be as take-your-breath-away fresh as it had been from the first. Only with the passage of considerable time did that intensity begin to diminish.

We've been taught so little about the complex emotional whirl of beginnings and endings. We are ill prepared for the inevitable both-and of exhilaration and anguish. We are confused by the sorrow that fills us even when the ending is one we've chosen, one that feels totally right for us. The emotional reality often stuns us: the beginnings we embrace enthusiastically are simultaneously (and inevitably) the endings of what had been before and even righteous endings bring sadness and feelings of loss.

We (and others around us) can think we're crazy when, in the midst of celebrating some wonderful newness, we fall into what feels like an inexplicably blue space. "Why are you feeling unhappy, this is such a wonderful beginning?" we, or others, ask our selves. And, "Why are you acting so mope-y, I thought you'd be so thrilled to be done with that situation, that relationship, that challenge?"

The voices of our own inner critics and those of other people's undermining commentaries often push us to close our selves off from the shadow side of the complex mix of feelings. We squelch and see as unreasonable the normal flow of sorrow over the endings that are part of these beginnings. As we relax our censorship and allow the grief to flow, we open our selves more fully for the blossoming of the joy.

Remember that beginnings are also times of endings, that beginnings are times for both celebration and grieving – consider giving your self permission to feel all the seemingly contradictory feelings.

1-19. Feeling Not Ready

If you don't feel ready yet to move with an opportunity that presents itself in the moment, let it pass! There will always be another one... And, another one and another one – until you are truly ready to take it! Trust in that, despite all you've wrongly been led to believe!

My friend B and I had just ended a long season of doing Spirit work out in the world. It was Winter Solstice 1996, the end of a year of coordinating women's drumming circles and almost three and a half years of mounting local and geographically distant road shows selling her handcrafted drums and rattles and my For the Little Ones wares. We were exhausted, done with being around large crowds – even if they were of wonderful women. (See **Too Much Work**, page 55 for more about that whole experience.)

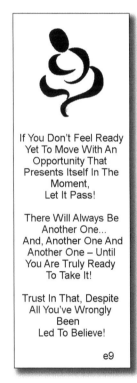

If You Don't Feel Ready Yet To Move With An Opportunity That Presents Itself In The Moment, Let It Pass!

There Will Always Be Another One... And, Another One And Another One – Until You Are Truly Ready To Take It!

Trust In That, Despite All You've Wrongly Been Led To Believe!

e9

B was on a sabbatical from her ordinary professional life, in a season of exploring new possibilities. With this more open time, she began to lobby me about creating a website. It was, she suggested, a way to put my work, my way of looking at life and growth out into the larger world without me having to actually **be** out in that world. I listened without much enthusiasm. I was too worn out to consider any new undertaking, even if it didn't involve people contact.

I was neither ready nor willing to engage with the world of computers. Though not techno-phobic, I had no interest in incorporating the fast track of technological progress into my slow lane life of no cell phone, no FAX, no microwave, no TV, no using ATM cards, no computers, and no email. Cordless phones and a small word processor were my concessions to technology. The word processor had come only when the limited 17 character erasing capacity of my 16-year-old electronic typewriter started driving me nuts. Too many experiences of (painful) frustrated desk pounding and rageful yanking and ripping of error-riddled pages had prompted my capitulation.

Had we started building a website at that time, we would have had to learn to write HTML: an interesting stretch for computer literate B, an impossible prospect for me. Since it was a perfect time for B to launch such a project, she gently pressed her case. In the face of my continued resistance, she backed off.

When web-authoring software became generally available a year or so later, she again broached the possibility with me. I responded as grumpily as before. Though I was more rested this time around, I still wasn't interested in anything that would feel like work and this project certainly did. I had no investment in getting my way of looking at life and growth further out into the world. I was happy sharing what I'd been learning with my clients and friends. That they in turn shared with their own friends whatever in my sharing was of value to them – this was enough for me. And, too, the Rememberings and Celebrations Cards were finding their way out into the world even though we weren't any longer traveling to fairs and festivals to get them seen and known.

B kept nudging me. I kept crabbily opposing her website idea. After a while, she again gave up.

Another year later, at the end of 1998, B – amazingly persistent – re-opened the topic. This time she presented a less ambitious framing of the undertaking: She would scan the texts of some of my earlier writings. She would help me adapt my word processing skills to the Microsoft Word program on her computer so that I could copy edit the scanning errors in those texts. Then, together, we would put up a bare bones site. No bells and whistles, no re-framing or reorganizing of all the material I had been creating over the years: just a few selected pieces. Later, if and as I felt moved to, I could occasionally write columns about one or another of the cards from the Rememberings and Celebrations Deck.

This time – with the simplified conception and her promise to go as slowly as I needed to go – I finally, though grudgingly, agreed. The challenging and often incredibly tedious process of creating the first For the Little Ones Inside website began. I spent days word processing in her study, yelling for help when I got stuck or in trouble. As she learned the web-authoring software, with me watching – riding shotgun as it were – we'd spend long hours putting it all together and test mounting it on-line.

There were computer glitches of one sort or another almost every time we got together to work on the project. It inevitably took longer to do anything than we thought it might. From the beginning, we understood the need to set sacred space with candles and smudging, reading oracles and asking the Grandmothers for their help and guidance. We learned (as we had before with the drumming project) that we needed to be impeccable in our processing with each other about the work. New to collaboration as a creative field, I often hated it and wanted to give up. I had zero frustration tolerance with computer misbehavior, usually ready to either take a hammer to it or shut it down and go back home to my un-computerized little cottage. Nevertheless, I knew in my bones that this was a right thing to be doing and a right time to be doing it.

B, unlike cranky me, was an old hand at creative collaboration, an enterprise she found rewarding. She was adept at processing the interpersonal difficulties that came up as we tried to integrate our different styles of working. She had limitless patience with computer/software problems, taking much pleasure in finding routes under, around or over the obstacles that littered our path. She'd always find a way to the other side. How long that took was another matter. I'd fidget, grumble and get bleary-eyed. I'd want to bail many times along the bumpy road to that other side.

Over time we learned to listen better to Spirit and to stop persisting when things got tangled between us or with the computer. We started seeing the obstacles as opportunities to take a break, a walk, get a bite to eat, stretch or talk about other things. We found a balance between B's dedication to staying with the difficulties and my inclination to walk away from them. (As the work continued, we noticed our selves sometimes actually switching these roles.)

I grappled with anxiety around allowing someone to give this much time and energy to a project that was all about me/my work. Finding a way to feel comfortable receiving this from someone who wouldn't accept payment for her time was very difficult. I had a hard time trusting her take on the collaboration as a gift to her, her Spirit work – especially since she had to deal with **a lot** of my grouchiness.

It was a powerful and transforming process. I was delighted with the site that we launched in July of 1999. Even more, I was thrilled to be done with a project that had taken eight months from scanning texts to being fully functional on-line. I wanted to enjoy the relief of having finally made it through to launching. The Grandmothers, however, were nudging B into nudging me onto the next threshold. She and they were relentless as they pushed me to see my writings as a body of work with a form that was trying to reveal itself. The idea of building a second website from this framework dismayed me. Again I resisted. Then, there was an unaccountable moment in which I suddenly got what B and the Grandmothers were trying to get me to see.

That moment propelled me wholeheartedly into the new, more complex undertaking. I was amazed, as we began building the second (current) incarnation of the website, by how much the collaborative process had opened in me. We designed the site together, with some consultation from a young woman computer expert much of whose input I could, surprisingly, understand. We got a lot of inspiration and support from the *Non-Designers Web Book* (by Williams and Tollett). In the early stages of the venture, as B's professional life shifted into high gear, I got to discover just how much computer technology I had osmosed during those long hours of riding shotgun as she tried to get around obstacles. In the end, I astonished my self as, for the most part by my self with only occasional coaching or technical input from B and our consultant, I built, rebuilt and refined the more than 60 pages that comprised the earliest version of the current website.

I was soaring with the exhilaration of developing a new set of competencies, stretching my envelope as I began using the computer as just another creative medium – like the pen and ink, paint, yarn and hand-written word with which I was more familiar and comfortable. I was giddy with the excitement of using my mind in ways I hadn't in years as I problem-solved computer, software and design glitches. I was doing this on my own a good deal of the time and becoming a more technologically creditable collaborator with B for the rest of it.

B had been (and continues to be) an awesome mentor/collaborator through the entire process. Quite amazingly – given my past experiences with academic mentors (see **The Power of Vulnerability**, page 163 and **The Vulnerability of Power**, page 171 for more about that history) – she's also been as delighted as I've been with my growing competencies and my fledging independence from her help.

As I worked on the pages for the current website, and with B's encouragement, I began to see her little Mac power book as my own. It had been living at my house through all the months of constructing the second website. I'd become attached to it. Though claiming ownership of a computer was a huge step, it became truly mine when she (reluctantly) let me replace it with a Titanium power book for her.

Over the more than eleven years that the second site has been on-line, we've marveled at all the magic and slogging that's gone into it. We're both proud of how easily you can navigate through it and go out to links and back again. Each month as first we and now I ceremoniously upload my columns, we grin at how beautiful it is and how readily it accommodates expansion.

The website journey has provided a powerful lesson about **not** taking advantage of what feels like an opportunity-coming-at-the-wrong-time, about **not** doing whatever one doesn't feel ready for. The cultural pressure is to seize opportunity when it comes, no matter how it fits or feels. It encourages us to fear that, if we don't, the chance we've allowed to pass will never come again and that we'll regret missing it for the rest of our days. What a terrible lie to be taught to live by.

Life, the Grandmothers and my deep self show me repeatedly that opportunities that I don't feel ready for or that don't feel right to me are ones that I can allow to pass. Different, better-for-me opportunities will keep coming until the one that feels absolutely right arrives and I take it up. When we choose our moments out of an inner sense that the time is ripe (even if we feel crabby about it) we are being kindheartedly supportive to our growth. When we choose the moment because it's there and we've been taught to be afraid to let it pass, it's inevitably a rockier road for our tender selves.

If you don't feel ready yet for an opportunity that presents itself, consider letting it pass and trusting there will always be other more-right-for-you openings down the road.

Permissions and Things To Remember

1. There is no right way to be or right way to do anything. Be however and do whatever you feel like – as long as you don't hit or throw things at people or bother people who want to be left alone.

2. You don't have to do anything you don't want to do (even if "everyone else" is doing it). And, you can stop in the middle of anything you don't want to do anymore.

3. You don't have to share anything if you don't want to. And, it's absolutely okay not to want to.

4. The only grown-up you need to take care of or be-the-Mommy-to is your self.

5. Be as gentle and loving with your self as you possibly can. Always give your self the benefit of the doubt and avoid criticizing your self. If you can't avoid criticizing your self, at least avoid criticizing your self for criticizing your self.

6. If you don't see what you want/need, don't make-do, just **ask** for it.

7. If anyone is bothering you, tell them you want them to stop it.

8. If you feel sad, it's okay to cry; if you feel angry, it's okay to growl, yell or stamp your feet; if you feel scared, it's okay to slow down or to stop and rest.

9. Remember to breathe into your belly, it makes everything feel better.

10. If you feel tired, curl up and take a nap.

Part Two:
Calming Our Inner Critical Voices

Our inner-critics, although they now seem only to torment and batter us, originally came into being to protect our small and vulnerable selves. They came to prevent us from doing things and being ways that threatened to bring upon us more frightening and dangerous external criticism. This external criticism might well have also threatened us with withdrawal of the love and support that were essential for our survival.

Though this inner-policeperson usually speaks to us in the harsh and judgmental tones of the larger culture, it does this **still** with the intention of pre-empting the possibility of such criticism coming at us from the outside world.

When the critic is badgering us, it is important to stop and ask inward: "Who's scared?" and, "Honey, what are you afraid of?" and, "What can we do to make it safe for you to go ahead being all of you right now?"

At the very same time, it is important to help detoxify and calm our inner policepersons. We do this by encouraging them to begin to question the messages from the larger culture that continually push us to do or go more, bigger, better, further, faster, yesterday in order to feel worthwhile, valuable or loveable. And, if we are women, it helps to also question the cultural messages that tell us – at the very same time – **not** to feel too full of our selves, **not** to put our selves first (ever), **not** to feel empowered, **not** to be so emotional, **not** to be so concerned with process. We can gently encourage our inner policepersons to consider if these are really such healthy values to accept and to adhere to.

Pirouettes

Just One More Achievement, Accomplishment, Stretch or Pirouette to Perform

(A tale written in 1986, when I was 46, about the journey 15 years before.)

She was 31, a financially successful therapist in private practice in her home on analysts' row in New York City. She worked only with people she enjoyed, all of them referred to her by people who knew or worked with her. She was married to a gentle, feminist man with whom she shared life, housework and expenses as an equal partner. She worked in the Women's Movement, doing low-cost therapy, training peer counselors for indigent women, and helping found the first New York City Feminist Psychotherapy Referral Service. She even baked the exquisite pastries served at the Coffee Hours during which endless streams of New York therapists were interviewed for inclusion in the Referral Directory. She volunteered hours to match clients calling the service with appropriate therapists. She was interviewed for several television talk shows, public-broadcasting programs, and newspaper features both about feminist therapy and feminist marriage arrangements.

She designed and crocheted most of her own clothing (often while standing in line at banks and supermarkets), cooked and baked most things from scratch (as did her feminist husband), took time to develop warm connections with the shopkeepers she traded with in her neighborhood and even developed a small business (featured in *New York Magazine*) crocheting custom-made bikinis. She bicycled 18-24 miles around Central Park by herself three days a week and then again on the weekends with her partner. She was slender and shapely (though she never felt it). She did lotion massages, bubble baths, yoga and a little meditation every morning. She and her partner had come to considered decisions to have an open relationship and not to have children. In the course of non-monogamous relating, she became lovers with a woman friend who was also in a non-monogamous relationship. The partners of both women struggled consciously and feministly with accepting the sharing.

Despite all of her current achievements and constantly growing list of accomplishments (she also had received her Ph.D. at twenty-five, summa cum laude, while her dissertation had received honorable mention in a national competition) she was continually beset with a deep sense of not being or doing enough. She was never quite at ease with herself, always plagued with an inner voice (the Hatchet Lady she called her in therapy) that ceaselessly picked at and found fault with each thing she did, no matter how perfectly it seemed she had done it.

One morning she woke up with a severe backache that made it impossible for her to sit through the length of an ordinary therapy session. Undaunted, she worked for several weeks standing up or lying down. Her morning ablutions and preparations began to require that she wake three hours before her partner so that she could soak her aching back and weave herself together before facing her very perfect life. Then she started waking each day with the strong sense that she would die if she couldn't get away from the city's dirt and noise into a place where she would be surrounded by green growing things.

It took a week of searching rental ads to find a beach house in the woods that she rented for the winter season. She began doing all her work on three days and spending four days in the country-quiet, resting herself. Her partner took over most of the chores in the city and did the weekly two-hour drives to and from the beach. She did fewer of the perfectly done things that had filled her life. Yet, she got more and more exhausted. Her partner began having an identity crisis. He didn't trust therapists, so she began spending her four rest-days being-there for him. One week she decided to stay at the beach while he went back to the city for the workweek. She thought for long hours about moving to the beach and working there. Then, she understood that she would only do it all over again in this new place: creating the perfectness and suffocating from the relentless self-criticism in the midst of it.

Walking down by the ocean she realized that something was radically wrong in her life: that no matter how many pirouettes (as she called them in therapy) she continued to find to perform, she was never going to be able to quiet the critical voice that consistently made shit from her gold. She was filled with an overwhelming impulse just to stop: to stop all the doing and all the doing for, to hand in all her union cards and to give up holding up the superstructure of her life, the superstructure that was weighing so heavily on her aching back.

It took almost nine months to do just that: bit by bit, figuring out the way she needed to arrange things, selling off her possessions, letting go of her relationships, her work, her marriage, her ideas about who she was or would be and buying herself a van to live in while she went searching for the self she could feel was needing to emerge. Four months after her thirty-second birthday she left the City and headed west to California. The van and her freedom were funded by the financial legacy (as she called it in therapy) of her former life.

For the first three months she rarely spoke with anyone, except for long-distance calls to her husband, her lover and her sister. No one ever knew where she was. She had no phone and no address. She was erasing her past and becoming invisible. She lived from day to day, hour to hour. She woke only when she felt ready, ate what and when and as often as she was hungry, did whatever it was that came to her to do with her days and went to sleep when she felt tired (night or day). She moved from place to place along the coast of California and Oregon, spent her days hiking, bicycling and, once she discovered it, lying naked in the sun getting tanned. She had many adventures, alone and also with people. She felt giddy and pleased with herself for no good reason. She spent hours exploring the inside of herself, in between or during the hours she spent exploring the outside-of-herself places that were filled with green growing things.

And she discovered something remarkable. She was doing nothing out in the world and nothing for anyone else and she was feeling more okay about herself than she had ever felt in all her thirty-two years of being accomplished, caring and perfect. She began to feel like a revolutionary, never telling anyone she met anything about who and how she had once been, watching people move from drop-dead shock to intense curiosity when she responded to their "What do you do?" questions with a laughingly mischievous, "Nothing, absolutely nothing but work on my tan!" She felt excited (even when her inward explorations led her to painful and upsetting awarenesses about her undeveloped parts), alive, full of herself and more self-accepting than she had ever felt in her life – just being in the middle of herself, in the middle of nature, discovering the depth and richness of her own being. She continued doing mostly nothing for over three years, almost two of them while living in her van. Sometimes then and later she tried on other lives: baking in an organic bakery for some months, selling her crocheted bikinis and clothes, cleaning houses, being a doorperson cum bouncer at a women's bar, working as a health educator at a community clinic, doing a women's radio show. Occasionally she would almost forget what she had learned and make the mistake of doing or giving more rather than less when she was feeling uneasy with herself. Still, her back or shoulder aches would usually come to remind her to stop, to go inward at such times to find where she wasn't loving herself exactly as she was at the moment – unfinished, imperfect, and all.

Along the way (especially during the times when she found herself being seduced by circumstances into forgetting what she had learned, into going back to the old ways of doing), she came to a very power-filled knowing. She came to know with every cell of her being that she had lived in a world that stole what was her birthright: self-acceptance, unconditional self-love and inner peace; a world that then constantly dangled that prize package like the carrot-on-a-stick, forever just out of reach so that there was always just one more achievement, accomplishment, stretch or pirouette to perform in the world or for someone else's benefit before she could be set free.

What did at last set her free was giving up the whole ride, ending the journey of incessantly trying to prove to herself (and anyone else) that while she was as (or more) competent and successful as any man, she was equally as (or more) sensitive, caring and nurturing as any woman. She practiced saying no to everyone and everything until she could be sure that no would come as easily to her as yes. Daily she practiced just being in the middle of herself in the middle of life, not doing anything to be worthwhile, except growing her self, her awareness and her consciousness and sharing her truth with anyone who was interested.

Now, fifteen [in 2012, actually 40] years later, she is a financially successful therapist (who describes herself as a spiritual guardian) in private practice in her home. This time it is in the middle of the chaparral, orange and avocado groves of Ojai, CA. She still works only with people she enjoys, mostly referred to her by people who know or work with her (but often they arrive in her life by more varied and magical means). She is married to her Self, living in a deep and meaningful sharing with her various selves (among them those she calls the Ancient One, the Mommy-Inside and the Little One) and a very small number of both near and geographically distant women friends. She no longer works in any Movements, but she is always in growthful movement and always committed to helping women heal and whole themselves as a way to help heal the planet. She does not volunteer these days, but recently she was interviewed for the first time in many years.

She does not cook or bake much either. Instead, she makes artful arrangements of food for herself and for an occasional guest or two. She does not do much of anything on a regular basis except for an hour of Reiki upon waking, followed by yoga and meditation, at least on the two days a week [in 2012, two days every other week] that she does work. Other days, yoga comes and goes according to the flow of the day. She still does lotion massages every morning and is more likely to feel them as she gives them to herself. She floats in her hot tub or in her bathtub every day. She has at least one two-hour massage each week, often either the day after or the day before she does her two-day workweek.

On her five-day [in 2012, 12-day] weekends she putters a lot amid the plants, flowers and rocks near her house, still lies naked in the sun, walks a lot in the Ojai canyons, sings and tones with the mountain streams and trees, plays with colored pens, paints and sometimes fiber or clay and a variety of percussion instruments. She likes being with her close friends because they, like she, are committed to and fascinated with the luscious process of discovering themselves and their connection with the Universe. She loves to talk (and to listen, too) about what's happening in the moments they are together as well as to just be in those moments as they unfold. With her friends she practices saying the whole truth of what she feels, even when it seems embarrassing or awful. She loves the comfort and security of knowing her friends are also practicing to do just that. She finds that the more she practices telling the whole truth, even out in the real world, the safer she feels. She never does anything **for** anyone these days, but she is always delighted when sharing what she is doing to grow her self is helpful to anyone else. She rages and stomps when she is angry, cries when she is sad or upset, leaves when it does not feel good or safe to be wherever she is and, most important of all, she always listens to the little voice inside and she never scolds, shouts at or talks harshly to her self, no matter what.

Eating My Way Home

When I was eight (one year and who knows how many pounds after the birth of my sister), my fashionably slender, exasperated mother yanked me around the Chubbette Collection at Lane Bryant (known then as "the fat lady store") looking for skirts with expandable side zippers. She pushed me into the dressing room in the "Boys, Huskies" section of Friedman's Department Store with pairs of outsized fly-fronted slacks (long before it was even remotely thinkable for a girl to wear such things).

That same year, my favorite (and somewhat roly-poly himself) Uncle Charlie began greeting me daily with "Hey, Belly, where you going with that girl?" (Because, he told me, my belly came into the room before I did.) Uncle Charlie also began pointing out every large woman on the street, whispering that I would grow up to "look like **that!**" if I didn't start watching what I ate. I began noticing that my very beautiful mother and equally beautiful Aunt Toby rarely ate anything other than hard-boiled eggs and Melba toast. Not surprisingly, that year marked the beginning of my personal version of the American Everywoman's struggle of fear and self-loathing around food and body size.

By 1971, I was 23 years into the battle between the Food Fascist and the Ravenous Rebel inside of me. I was taking 75mg of Preludin (a then popular appetite suppressant and upper), two strong diuretics and four herbal laxatives daily. All were easily obtained with automatically renewing prescriptions from my unquestioning gynecologist. He, of course, completely understood my need to control my weight. Most days, a small glass of grapefruit juice, a poached egg and dry toasted English muffin with jam started a day in which I then subsisted on innumerable cups of strong black coffee and equally numerous cigarettes. These effectively erased whatever might have been left of my suppressed appetite.

On the rare days I ate more than that, I kept accurate and restrictive track of the caloric value of every morsel that passed between my lips. On the terrifying days when the Ravenous Rebel wrested control, I ate as much as I could stuff into my self of everything I wanted. As I ate, the Food Fascist verbally harangued and abused me even as the Ravenous Rebel made sure I got to eat what I longed for. I was, the Fascist told me, fat, out-of-control, disgusting, contemptible, hideous and (worst of all in those days) un-sexy. All this existed as the hidden underbelly of my life as a feminist psychologist in a successful private practice and a feminist marriage.

In May of 1971, while helping to birth the Peer-Counseling Training Program of the New York Feminist Psychology Coalition, I met an amazing woman. Carol Munter had spent the preceding year with a group of radical feminists she had gathered at the Alternative University. In a class she instigated and incited, they explored theoretically and practically the food/body-size oppression that was, even then, of unquestioned and epidemic proportions. It was for all involved an inspired experience of searching for sanity in their relation to food and to their bodies.

In those days, Carol was never without a large, fashionable shopping bag filled with food. She ate, un-embarrassedly, wherever and whenever she felt the need to. I was stunned: awed and excited by what I saw, felt and heard as she and I immediately connected around this very heretical, radicalizing behavior. An enduring and nourishing friendship began as I shared what I had learned about doing therapy and she shared what she had learned about feeding oneself sanely in a crazy world. I at once began the simple yet difficult practice she had developed for ending the crazy-making, constrictive compulsions of eating and starving that had so run my secret life for over 20 years.

In the early months of my practice, I spent many weeks lovingly feeding my self limitless amounts of all the forms of chocolate (cakes, cookies, candy bars, ice creams, sauces, thick shakes) that I craved. I ate chocolate before, during, after and mostly instead of breakfast, lunch and dinner. I gave up meals and mealtimes as external impositions. I discovered that it pleased me to eat little bits of things I wanted as I wanted them throughout the day. Food became a voluptuous way of pleasuring my whole being many times a day, always giving my self exactly what I wanted. As I moved through the various forms of chocolate (and successively all the other proscribed foods), my consistent behavior gradually assured the Ravenous Rebel that my commitment to no longer depriving my self was dependable.

The next layer of my practice involved discerning the difference between the hungers that were truly physical and those that were emotional hungers seeking comfort from food and self-feeding. As an anthropologist might, I watched whenever I felt moved toward food. I looked in and around my self to see if it was physical hunger or hunger of a different sort that led me toward a meeting with food. Without judgment, I noticed. With attention, I sought the foods I wanted. With love, I fed my self. With focus, I noticed when I felt enough-ness or an end to the hunger. Without pressure, I considered whether something other than the food would have satisfied me more directly. Without judgment, I explored whether I had the same loving permission to go toward that something as I now had to go toward food.

As I moved into these new dimensions of the practice, I discovered that I had hungers for many experiences other than food. I was hungry to speak more of my truths, hungry to say, "This isn't okay with me," or, "No, you may not speak to me in those ways." I was hungry for more rest, for more bubble baths with candles and soft music. I was famished for more quiet, empty space with just my self. I was yearning for less steel and concrete, more green, growing, unimproved-upon Nature. I was starved for a sense of timelessness. I was ravenous with the need to say, "No!"

The empowering process of learning both to feed my body lovingly and to find my natural rhythm in relation to food served to open a whole universe of possibility for me. I began to apply the practice to every other area of my life in which I was depriving my self or abusing my self with self-castigation, self-devaluing and self-loathing. In each such place, I noticed how I had been trained and acculturated to always look outside (and often upward) of my own being for information on how it was appropriate for me to be, think or feel. In each such place, I gave my self permission to listen inward to how I needed to be, think or feel, to what my needs and yearnings actually were. I gave my self permission to act from and on these knowings and yearnings, to act on them with the same dedication to careful, loving self-nourishment that I had developed around feeding my self with food.

I gave my self permission to set aside the diets of constraint, restriction and judgment by which I had been taught to keep my self tidily in-line and out-of-trouble. I practiced healthy responses to the voices outside of me that said: "You can't," "you mustn't," "don't you dare," or "It's not good for you to," or "it's controlling of you to..." I responded sometimes internally, sometimes vocally with some emotional version of, "Who says so, why are they saying that?" And, "What is it that they really want of me that leads them to try to stop me from being, doing, feeling what is, by my own reckoning, right for me now?"

The more I silenced the external voices, the more clearly I came face to face with the judgmental, stopping voice inside of me that I called the Hatchet Lady or Nazi Mother. She reacted loudly and nastily toward me every time I took significant steps in the new direction. She called me names, warned of dire consequences and made sarcastic remarks ridiculing my new ways. I struggled with the agonizing push-pull between this internalized critical voice and the inner knowing place that was now guiding my choices.

Gradually, I came to see this frightening harridan in me as a Wizard of Oz kind of image cranked up by a frightened little child. This mean, inner policewoman acted on behalf of that child. She did what she did to keep me from doing things that might bring unexpected and much more dangerous attacks from those outside of me. Slowly but surely, when this abusive voice rose up, I would stop and take time to search for the hidden frightened little part. I'd ask that Little One what she needed in order to feel safe enough to let me go forward. Her answers helped me to move more slowly and in ways that felt less dangerous to her. She was willing to venture forth in baby steps as long as she could trust me to stop and take a break the instant she felt fearful or overwhelmed. When I moved only as fast as the slowest part of me felt safe to go and she no longer had to get the Hatchet Lady to beat up on me in order to get my attention, the push-pull resolved into a gentler pace and the Hatchet Lady all but disappeared.

From the practice of feeding my body, I've learned that it's not okay to trust anyone else's ideas about what I need or don't need to do. I've learned that when I can make the space to listen inward to my knowing self, I will hear what I need to know in order to best nurture my being, my body, my heart and my soul. And, I've learned that if I do only what feels safe for the slowest part of me to do at this moment (even if or when it looks wrong or crazy from the outside), it will each time lead me to where I need next to go. It will do this even and particularly when I seem to have no conscious idea of where that next place is.

I have learned from the practice of lovingly feeding my body-being that it's important to always be as gentle and forgiving with my self as I can possibly be (especially forgiving my self for not being able yet to be even more gentle than I am being). I have learned not to force, push or rush my tender self to be anywhere I think I might like to be when I'm not yet ready to be there. I've learned most of all that my body and my being can truly be trusted. They have a natural rhythm and flow that is healing and healthy and safe for me. I've learned that whatever I do to control, discipline or externally impose pace or order on my process inevitably interferes with, distorts or subverts that magical flow. There is an organic, organismic order that always will emerge if given time and space enough.

Through this practice I have learned to faithfully trust in my body knowing and in my emotional responses. I have learned that when I give my self safe space in which to be raging, howling, crying, grieving, screaming, vegetating or sleeping when I need that, it never goes on forever. Only when I keep trying to control and transcend these emotions do they seem to become overwhelming and bottomless. I have learned that peace, serenity and true generosity of spirit are born out of a compassionate commitment to take loving good care of one's own being, first. I have learned not to trust any tradition, spiritual path or teaching that asks me to discipline, disconnect from, or get beyond my emotional and body feelings.

I celebrate this womanly, emotion-filled physical temple that is my body. I celebrate its often messy, complicated, juicy feelings and all its intense hungers. I celebrate the joyous process of learning how to nourish, nurture and care for it in an ever more sacred and honoring way, as a part of all creation. How I feed and care for my body and my emotional being is how I feed and care for my soul and how I feed and care for the circle of all beings and souls of which I am a part. I am always doing the best I can; if I could do better, I surely would. And when I can, I surely will.

2-1. Criticizing Your Self

When you find you're criticizing your self, stop...
Ask the critic-in-you what it's so afraid of...
Then do what you can to help this old and frightened
part feel safe enough to be comfortable with you being
just how you are being right now!

I was raised by a bright, beautiful and very wounded mother. Her pain, frustration and deep sense of inadequacy complicated our relationship from its earliest days. (See **Loving Acceptance**, page 159 for more about her.) She was extremely critical and competitive with me. She rarely praised or acknowledged any of my accomplishments. Instead she found much to criticize in anything I did. In fact, the more I did to seek her acknowledgement, the more virulent and dismissive was her criticism.

When You Find You're Criticizing Your Self, Stop... Ask The Critic-In-You What It's So Afraid Of...Then Do What You Can To Help This Old And Frightened Part Feel Safe Enough To Be Comfortable With You Being Just How You Are Being Right Now!

c5

I responded to this ceaseless disparagement with ever more agitated efforts to do better (See **Doing Better,** page 157 for more about this). Living with such poisonousness spawned in me a ferocious inner critical voice that became my constant companion for the first 40-some years of my life. This voice, that I called the Hatchet Lady, was the source of an unrelenting stream of belittling, ridiculing commentary and invective. The Hatchet Lady denigrated and found fault in all that I did or attempted. (See **Eating My Way Home**, page 131 for more about her.)

Whatever project or enterprise I worked at, the Hatchet Lady watched over my shoulder. She invariably had something nasty to say about what I wasn't doing right or acceptably enough for her unreachable standards. Any time I'd accomplish something that might seem of value, she would point out its triviality compared to what I hadn't yet done. Her most typical responses were "Big deal!" "So what!" and "So what's the big deal!"

One day (in my early-mid forties) I was at the Laundromat with my just washed, fairly new, originally 8 1/2 by 11 foot Flokati rug. (A very shaggy rug made from loosely woven sheep's wool.) I knew I was in trouble when, as I'd taken the rug from the washer, it'd felt very hot. I was baffled and upset because I thought I'd carefully set the dial to cold wash. Then, when I (after the fact) looked more closely, I noticed that the little raised marker on the dial was actually on its opposite side. The dial I'd set so carefully was in fact pointing to hot wash. I could feel the Hatchet Lady starting to rail at me. I suggested we wait till we got home to see how much damage had really been done.

When I laid the rug in its place, the shrinkage was evident and significant. The Hatchet Lady voice came on in full roar about my carelessness, my stupidity, and on and on. Suddenly, my still-new Mommy-Inside voice rose up. She spoke with love and authority to the furious Hatchet Lady. "There was no great harm done," she said. "We could use the rug just as well in its diminished size." If it felt too wrong this small, we were fortunate enough, at this moment in our life, to have the money to be able to replace it. We could use this one somewhere else in the house. "It wasn't such a terrible mistake," she said. "We **had** paid close attention, even though we had missed the little raised mark." "There was no reason," she said, for the Hatchet Lady "to be beating us up for this – it was an unfortunate, but **not** catastrophic, mistake." Surprisingly, the Hatchet Lady backed down, apparently mollified by the Mommy's words.

I was suddenly flooded with a towering rage. I screamed and stomped and roared around the house. And, in the middle of that raging, I cried and cried and cried. I felt outraged at how long the constant, mercilessness of the Hatchet Lady had been devastating me and running my life, at how long I'd spent quaking under the lash of her acid tongue. I could see, in just this moment, that all those criticisms – like these about the rug – were **way** beyond any reasonable response to the situations that had called them forth.

I raged and cried for all the pain and anguish I'd suffered for so much of my life. I curled up with my teddy bear and rocked my Little One selves. I felt filled with gratitude to the Mommy-Inside who'd taken such good care of us **and** who'd calmed the fury of the Hatchet Lady.

Until this experience, my response to the Hatchet Lady's attacks had been anxious agitation. I'd frantically scramble around trying to make things right. The Mommy-Inside voice showed me that I could respond differently. I could calm and reassure the critical voice. I could comfort her rather than be cowed and made frantic by her.

It was a moment of illumination. I saw beyond the larger-than-life, Wizard-of-Oz presence of the Hatchet Lady and her nastiness. Hidden beneath her fierceness was a terrified little being whose scared voice had never before reached me.

I saw that the Hatchet Lady had grown in me as an inner policing/ guardian person to protect the terrified Little One whose voice I couldn't (or wouldn't) hear. With her ferocity, the Hatchet Lady had been desperately trying to **protect** the frightened parts of me. Her searing criticisms were her way to keep me from being or doing what she feared would bring critical attacks from those **outside** of us. She was convinced that such outside attacks would be scarier, more damaging to the vulnerable parts of me. (That her criticisms were themselves devastating and demoralizing didn't seem to be taken into account in her reasoning process.)

This moment of realization was a mountain-moving turning time. From it began a practice that radically changed my life. Rather than continuing to be tyrannized by her meanness, I started embracing the Hatchet Lady.

Each time the she began belittling me, I told her that she didn't have to hit me over the head that way to get my attention. I told her that I understood that she was trying to let me know that some little part inside me was feeling scared. I told her it wasn't okay for her to talk meanly to me anymore.

I would call to the vulnerable Little One whose terrors were propelling the Hatchet Lady's condemnations. I talked gently and lovingly to that self. I invited her to let me know what was scaring or upsetting her. I promised I would keep working to hear her. I encouraged her to call directly to me. I promised I would respect her fears and do whatever I could to address them. I committed my self to working with her to choose paths that wouldn't be as frightening to her or, to find ways to help her feel less frightened with the paths that I had been choosing.

Sometimes, just my **hearing** that it was being scary for her was enough for her to risk moving forward with me into new ways of being. Most of the time, what she needed was for me to slow down and reassure her that I would stay in touch with her every step of the way. She had suffered for so long because I wouldn't allow my self to acknowledge her fears and her sense of overwhelm. She'd frequently felt pushed beyond what she could handle. She understood that I had, in the past, felt afraid of her fears. **This** had frightened her more than anything.

I have been becoming, over the years, a better and better Mommy for all the little and big scared parts of me. I'm much less frightened of being frightened. I'm much more willing to go only as fast as the slowest part of me feels safe to go.

And, I'm also becoming a better Mommy for what's left of the Hatchet Lady. She still occasionally pipes up, (though more and more rarely with each passing year). Most of the time it's a bleat of, "Well, you're only doing that because you're crazy/sick/screwed up/damaged/unable to do it the way normal people do!" While I still call behind her for the little one, I also now put my arms around her snarly old self and say, "Honey, so what if that's true? All the more reason to do it just this way!" She lets go of the snarliness every time. Sometimes, it even makes her giggle.

Next time you find your self talking meanly to your self, consider the possibility of listening deeper to hear who else inside of you might be trying to get your attention. If you can hear that scared self, consider the possibility of helping her feel more safe.

And, consider treating that scared part with great tenderness.

2-2. Being Too Much

You are never: too sensitive, too serious, too particular, too_____.
What you may be is: more sensitive, more serious, more particular,
more _____ than the people you're around feel comfortable with...
Consider not being with them at such times!

So many times in earlier seasons of my life I can remember instantly and painfully contracting physically and/or emotionally when someone with whom I was talking and sharing my feelings told me I was:

Too intense ("You make such a big deal out of everything, can't you just let it go?").

Taking everything too seriously ("Can't you ever lighten up?").

Being too compulsive about my space, my food, my plans ("You're so rigid! What's the big deal? Don't be so picky!").

Worst of all were those times I tried, for reasons of my own sanity, to check out my perceptions of peoples' vaguely hostile/angry/upset-with-me energy ("I'm not feeling anything like that, you're really being too weird! I can't believe you really think that!").

You Are Never:

Too Sensitive
Too Serious
Too Particular
Too _____

What You May Be Is:

More Sensitive
More Serious
More Particular
More _____

Than The People
You're Around Feel
Comfortable With...

Consider Not Being
With Them
At Such Times!

o7

I remember, too, many occasions when I've given my self a hard time for noticing what I'd noticed, feeling what I'd felt, saying what I'd said. I did this because my noticing, feeling or saying whatever it was clearly seemed to distress or threaten other people. Or, it seemed to give other people something with which to judge themselves. So many times in the past I've made my self smaller, dimmed my lights as it were, tried to be less or less likely to give offense.

It never really worked to help the other person feel any better about me or about the situation. And, usually, I would come away from the encounters filled with self-criticism: loathing my self for being who/how

I was, for betraying my own truth/needs/self by my trying not to create circumstances in which others might feel discomforted or diminished.

It's taken me many years and lots of inner work to come to understand that when someone tells me I'm being **too** anything, what they're in fact saying is that I'm **too** whatever it is for them to feel comfortable around. And, I've learned that it's **never** okay to betray or abandon my self just because someone else finds it hard to be around me as I am in my fullness (of joy, sorrow, anger, confusion, whatever).

These days, I might feel sad, disappointed or regretful that they find it hard to be around my energy. I might even feel irritated or frustrated that they choose to judge my behavior instead of being able to acknowledge their own difficulties coping with what my being all of my self stirs in them.

Most of the time now, I'm likely to respond by letting the person know that I understand that they're finding my way of being problematic for them in the moment. I'm usually willing to listen if they want to talk about what their discomfort might be about **in** them. If they're unwilling or unable to engage at that level, I'm more than willing to consider leaving the shared space. Whenever staying in the shared space with another asks that I pay the price of abandoning my wholeness, I will without fail choose to leave and go be with my self.

We've all had many times in our lives when someone's told us that we were being just **too** something-or-other. Our most immediate response tends to be to constrict, to feel badly about our selves and our behavior. We usually move quickly to consider how we might stop our selves from being that **too** whatever.

Instead of this knee-jerk response, we can encourage our selves to remember the truth about such comments. Namely, that they are in fact about the **other person's** unease or discomfort with our behavior rather than about **our** behavior. Their judgmental comments are intended (not necessarily consciously) to get us to constrict our selves so that they can regain their preferred comfort level. It **is not** our job to comply.

When we shave off parts of our selves trying to become the person that we think the other will better like or accept, we can't help but know that who they then like isn't the who we actually are. And, in the process, we are our selves rejecting who we truly are. This diminishes us.

As we practice letting our selves just be who we are – **all** of who we are – we grow to more fully accept our selves. **This** is the acceptance we need most of all. It is this acceptance that can heal us.

Consider hearing judgmental comments about your behavior as messages telling you something significant about the **judging person** rather than as conveying any truth about you. And, consider practicing letting your self just be exactly who and as you are.

2-3. Judging Difference

When you're feeling judgmental about some difference between your "way" and another's... Look for where you are not yet at peace with the rightness of your "way" for you! Give your self permission to be and do what's right for you!

I was exploring, with some women I know, about the different ways we had each chosen to cope with our outsider status when we were in our early days of high school:

One had dealt with being outsider by conceding and despairingly resigning herself to the feeling of being less than.

The other had figured out ways to compete with and prove that she was as good as or better than any of the in-girls.

My own resolution had been deciding that the belongers and belonging itself were dumb; that belonging was less-than and that being different, being outsider was the superior way to be.

Of course, the resolutions we chose in those early years significantly influenced the ways we've each dealt with our differentness and with judgment – our own or others'– throughout our three lives. (We all, inside of our selves at the very least, have continued to feel our differentness.)

When You're Feeling Judgmental About Some Difference Between Your "Way" And Another's... Look For Where You Are Not Yet At Peace With The Rightness Of Your "Way" For You! Give Your Self Your Permission To Be And Do What's Right For You!

o4

For most of my grown-up life, as I've tried to do what felt authentic and right-for-me, I've made choices that were over the edges of convention: Not birthing or raising children. Having an open marriage. Not going for post-doctoral training in psychotherapy before I started practicing. Dropping out of a high-rise, doorman, married, professional life-in-the-fast-lane. Living in a van on the road by my self for two years, doing nothing more than working on my tan. Choosing to expand and explore my conception of my own sexuality. Choosing to live voluptuously in a primary relationship with my Self. Choosing to reinvent how and what I do when I work as a therapist/coach. Choosing to live simply, to do as little as possible as I live in recovery-from-super achieving. Choosing to celebrate rest and moving only as fast as the slowest part of me feels safe to go.

Until my mid–forties (I'm now 72), while I neither noticed nor cared about how anyone else saw or judged my choices, I can see that I was always secretly involved in looking down my nose at the more conventional-seeming choices made by others around me.

My strongest judgments were focused (albeit secretly) around people's valuing partnered relationship, busyness and outward-directed lives as opposed to more solitary, unscheduled, inward/contemplative lives. And, to a lesser extent, I (still secretly) judged people for needing or choosing formal teachers and systems for the contemplative life rather than relying on their own inner guidance.

Over time, I began to question whether both my judging of other peoples' choices and my ideas of my own superiority were actually reflections of my being less than wholly comfortable with the acceptability – to **me** – of my own choices. As I explored this idea, I saw that my choices were acceptable to me only when I could see them as superior to or healthier than other possible choices. If I thought they might be coming from wounded or as yet unhealed places in me, they became problematic.

As I went further with the exploration, I discovered that it was impossible to figure out to what extent my choices were made from my limitations as opposed to being made from my wholeness. All I could uncover about them with any certainty was that they seemed to be the best choices I could make for my self at the times that I made them. They addressed and were in harmony with my own needs and capacities-available-in-the-moment.

Actually, that's what made them right-for-me. As I began to accept that this was so, I could compassionately and unconditionally embrace all of who I might be in any situation. I could see my choices simply as the most-right-for-me-in-this-moment. I could let go of both the trumped-up vision of my superiority and the secret judging of others that made them wrong in order to make my self right.

When we can accept that we each can only make the choices that are right for us in the moment, we can begin to let go of the idea that there are choices that are absolutely right for everyone – including our selves. As we become more generous and spacious with our selves, we can better allow that differences just **are** and give up the belief that differences are directional: good/bad, more than/less than, important/insignificant, etc.

Let your self notice whenever you are openly or secretly judging or feeling superior to anyone else about some difference in your ways. See if you can find more space for it to be okay just to be you where and how you are. And, do consider not judging your judging.

Consider being really loving with your self just exactly where and how you are.

2-4. Judging Someone Else

When you find your self judging someone,
look for what in your self you are not yet willing to accept...
Hold that part of you more gently!

It was early spring 1984, some nine months into my challenging year of moving back and forth as I continued the work of separating out of a very fraught seven-year relationship. (See **Others' Views**, page 259 for more about this.) I'd gone to the Santa Barbara airport to meet my step-sister-in-law who was arriving from the East Coast for some graduate seminars at the Fielding Institute.

Usually, when I'm out and about in the world, I move around inside my own sheltering psychic bubble at some energetic distance from the people-world around me. My bubble works quite well as insulation. (So well that my friend's teenage/early twenties children love to tell hysterical tales of their frantic antics trying unsuccessfully to get my attention when they drive by me in town.)

On this particular day, just as I walked through the door to the outside waiting-for-arriving-passengers area, the woman walking

When You Find

Your Self

Judging Someone,

Look For What

In Your Self

You Are Not Yet

Willing

To Accept...

Hold That Part

Of You

More Gently!

c2

next to me began to talk to me. Oddly enough, I heard her and actually responded to her conversational opening. Neither of us can remember how she started that interchange. Still, in the ten minutes before her mother and daughter and my sister-in-law arrived (on the same flight), we had discovered some remarkable parallels in our lives.

We were both Jewish psychologists who had had practices on the East Coast. We had both, ten years earlier, dropped out of our established personal and professional lives in order to come out West. We had both made those moves in order to do some deep inner exploration and healing that we'd felt was not possible in the middle of our former lives. We had both lived in Santa Barbara and were both now living in Ojai. The level of synchronicity astounded us. As our passengers arrived, we exchanged phone numbers with some vague idea of catching up with each other sometime in the future.

Within the month, however, I'd reconciled yet again with my almost-former partner. I left the ranch on which I'd been living rent-free while caretaking a menagerie of handicapped or ailing animals. Sharing a new rental we'd found in the East End of Ojai, the two of us began what shortly and clearly became an abortive attempt to construct a healthier partnership.

It was a devastating time in my life. I couldn't believe that I'd risked living together again after the enormous struggle I'd had trying to move out the first time, just ten months before. I was depressed and frozen, unable for the next few months to find my way to physically leave again.

During those awful months, the only peace I had (except for when I was working and focused on my clients' lives) came in the very early mornings. For the few short hours that I'd have to my self, before the full weight of my depression descended again, I'd do yoga, meditate and then walk a half-mile up the road to a forest trail. The trail led another mile up a chaparral covered canyon to a creek. Once at the creek, I'd melt into a boulder in the middle of the flowing water, awash in the natural sounds. For that small space of each day I'd feel held by Spirit, at one with the wonder of the natural world.

Living our separate lives – in and out of frustration and tension with each other – my estranged partner and I continued to share the rental house for just over four months. While doing errands in town during those months, numbers of shopkeepers and people I'd run into would ask me if I'd ever met Cynthia Rossman (not her real name). They'd each tell me, in almost the exact same words, how much I reminded them of her; how similar our energies were; how similar our ways of being in the world seemed to them. I recognized the name. It was that woman who'd engaged me at the airport. It all seemed odd and fascinating. Still, I was too completely immersed in my despair to think of trying to make contact and explore the possibility of a friendship with anyone new.

Then one morning, as I wandered up toward the trail, I picked up a scrap of paper lying in the brush alongside the road. (I often policed the roadside, picking up bits of trash to dispose of when I got back home.) I glanced at the scrap before stuffing it in my pocket. It was a very old Visa statement for several florist purchases made back East by one Cynthia Rossman. I burst out laughing. Spirit was certainly into nudging me, trying to get me to pay attention. I finally surrendered and picked up the phone once I got home.

It took several rounds of phone tag for us to get to talk with each other in real time that mid-July. As we tried to make a plan to get together, we discovered that she'd been living just across the road, up a few properties from where I was still living with my ex-partner. She was at that point in the process of packing up the last of her things in preparation for a move from Ojai back to Santa Barbara, with plans to visit her oldest friend in Santa Fe in between.

We decided that I'd come by right then, that we would visit while she packed. By now, I was quite curious about what exactly was up for me with this woman, wondering why Spirit seemed so determined to bring us together. I gathered some cheese, crackers and fruit, and went across the road. I was feeling some excitement about this meeting, about the possible adventure of discovering a new friend.

I was sucked right into a whirlwind. The woman actually seemed a bit of a lunatic. She talked and packed at warp speed. She kept pulling out and handing me photos of her "exquisite former house on the river," her fancy former sailboat, her former self in many upscale settings. She was intent on telling me stories that she obviously thought would help me understand that she had been "a somebody" before she chose to drop out of her former life.

I was a little dazed by it all. I couldn't have cared less about how much of a mover and shaker she had been before. In fact, for several years after my own dropping out, I'd consciously chosen to obscure my personal history. I'd been committed to meeting people simply as the person I was right then, diligent in not letting anyone know about all the pirouettes, accomplishments and degrees I'd used in my former life to create some sense of worthiness for my self.

I was just interested in who she was right now and who she seemed to be was one very insecure, frenetic woman trying to impress me by telling me things that she had no idea would have so little meaning to me. I was disappointed. I was dumbfounded as I tried to figure out what people could possibly have seen in this frantic, insecure woman that reminded them of my (as I saw it) very slowed down, calm self. (I didn't yet know that, out in the world, she was not this self I was seeing.) I couldn't understand what the point was of all of Spirit's nudging me in her direction.

Yet, after a while, she settled down and we talked more meaningfully. I could feel her warmth, her juiciness and the intensity of her genuine interest in getting to see/know me. The similarities people spoke of made more sense to me then. Still, she was off the next day for several weeks away and then on to Santa Barbara. I, on the other hand, had much to deal with in finding a new home and once again getting my self free of my enmeshment. So, that was that for then.

Five months later, after I'd finally extricated my self from the excruciating living-together situation with my former partner, found a beautiful new home and moved on to a further layer of healing my broken self, Cynthia turned back up in my life. I was at a fairly new friend's house for a small, intimate Christmas Eve gathering of five empowered and fascinating women who were (except for our hostess) all new to each other. The evening started with Lois telling us that we were missing one other woman that she had wanted to bring into this circle. The woman had an old friend visiting and the friend insisted on going to see Amadeus rather than coming to this dinner. The missing woman was none other than Cynthia Rossman, who had asked that we give her a call at some point in the course of the evening.

When we called, she told me that the old friend – her best friend since kindergarten, the friend that she had been going off to visit in Santa Fe that past Summer – was none other than the second of the only two close friends I'd had at college. It was peculiar, more than a little eerie. Once again, it felt like Spirit had a hand in it. So, we made a plan to get together after the New Year.

When she arrived at my cottage in mid-January, Cynthia dazzled me by reading, with awesome emotional accuracy, each of the many fiber masks (my Spirit-Mother Totem series) lining my walls. She read the masks to me in the same way that I had been able to translate into words the feelings evoked by the work of many of my own artist friends. It was yet another striking parallel between us.

That January 1985 meeting was the start of a powerful, complex, freewheeling, sometimes challenging, sometimes delightful, sometimes delightfully challenging, sometimes (mostly past now) crazy-making but always growth-provoking 28-year friendship. We came to the friendship each having done considerable personal work. We were both ferociously dedicated to our own healing. And though we each had our own wobbly places, we were both, for the most part, empowered and grounded in our selves.

At times, calling it a more-than-a-friendship has seemed an accurate description since it continually served each of us as a cauldron in which we were forced toward our fullest, most authentic and most transparent selves. Over the years it became clear to both of us that it's been for this work – and for the wisdom that comes with it – that Spirit has brought us into each other's lives.

Strangely enough, much of this growing and forcing has been a consequence both of how hotly we have judged each other and how unswerving we've each been about owning and learning from that judgmentalness in our selves and in the field of our sharing.

Though neither of us is particularly judgmental of others, we have each been furiously, aggressively, both secretly and outspokenly judgmental of each other, often in exaggerated and extreme ways. Typically, these judgments (mostly in the past now) came up in moments that were very particular for each of us.

When Cynthia felt insecure or self-doubting she would do what looked to me like putting up a front, sort of puffing herself up and acting in ways that I experienced as inauthentic or phony. I would get irritated with and critical of her when I felt this was going on. I would tell her how stupid her behavior seemed, how easy to see through and how insulting it felt to have her think that I could be taken in by these machinations. I hated them. Of course, she would take my judgmental behavior as proof of how unsafe it was for her to consider being her insecure self around me. We'd go round and round with this as I tried to explain it wasn't her insecurity I was judging, but rather her ways of trying to hide that insecurity.

We'd argue, argue, argue: I'd call her behavior insulting and stupid, she'd call mine mean and crazy. Gradually, with this particular repeating dance, we came to agree we'd each try looking more directly into our own stuff instead of continuing to judge and berate each other. We chose to each focus both on what was being triggered in our selves and what was happening between us, using these tangled moments as opportunities to do research into what the interactions might teach us about our selves and the dynamics in our relationship.

When we'd met, I was recovering from super-achieving, from using what I did or what I'd accomplished in the world as a measure of my self-worth or as a cover for my insecurities. I was working at being in the middle of my self-doubts openly, revealing my vulnerability rather than obscuring it. It was an edgy practice but one that seemed to promise me a sense of safety no other path had provided.

Cynthia's behavior served as a dark mirror for me. In it I saw the ways I had, for so much of my past, tried to hide my own insecurities from others and from my self, projecting instead an image of my self as a person who had it all together, who rarely if ever had a fraught or anxious moment. That effort had been exhausting and it had usually left me coping with constant fear that some perceptive someone might, at any moment, unmask me, leaving me quaking and terrified of ridicule.

My new path involved me unmasking my self, revealing any deficiency or insecurity I might be feeling. I chose to do this **as if** I believed it was perfectly honorable, respectable and okay with me that I felt insecure. The more I practiced living my shortcomings boldly and out-loud, the more they actually became honorable and respectable to me. As I treated them this new way, others seem to have little choice but to do the same.

In these still early days of this practice, I was doing what so many of us are inclined to do when we make a major shift. I was judging and devaluing the old ways (now being left behind) that I had used to make my self safe. But, I was doing this indirectly by judging and demeaning what I saw as those behaviors in Cynthia. In doing this aggressively and out-loud on her, I was becoming, for her fearful-and-hiding self, the very menace that I had always feared would unmask me.

I encouraged my self to honor and embrace the me that I had been when I had tried to make my insecure self feel safe in the same ways I believed Cynthia was using. As I could be more compassionate and accepting of that earlier me, the one that had grown me into this new place I was now learning and practicing, I could also be more spacious and generous with Cynthia's process. I stopped taking her behaviors personally, stopped feeling insulted by them and stopped seeing them as stupid. This was a great relief to both of us.

There have been, over the 28 years of our friendship, many more such tales of our judging and being judged by each other (albeit about other issues). In each episode, we used to have to go through many rounds before we would begin together to look for the inside stories behind our judgments. Lately, we are more likely, one or the other of us, to catch onto the very earliest moments such a research opportunity appears in the field between us. We argue less and explore more.

I've repeatedly judged in Cynthia ways she acts that (less than consciously) remind me of ways that I used to act; past ways that I haven't yet fully accepted as having been honorable parts of my evolution. She, on the other hand, (it seems to me) has been more likely to get judgmental of ways that I act that reflect back to her secret parts of herself that she hasn't yet embraced as honorable parts of who she is in her current evolution. But, then, this is only my story about it all.

In any case, the lesson around our judgings has been powerful and empowering. Whenever we are judging someone else's behavior it's highly likely (maybe even a sure thing) that we are, in this process, disowning a part of our selves. By heaping our negating judgment upon that behavior or aspect of the other person, we are almost always really saying, "I certainly don't act in that unacceptable/disgraceful/repellent way."

If we stop whenever we find our selves judging someone and look instead for what in our selves (past or present) we may be trying to separate from, every judging-moment becomes a doorway into recognizing and embracing more of all of who we are. Once owned, even our ugly, wart-ridden, foul-smelling parts become significant contributors to the fullness of our rich, fertile, juicy selves.

Consider using your open or secret judgments of others as opportunities to lovingly reclaim and embrace previously disowned parts of your self.

2-5. Doing Better

You really are doing the best you can in this moment.
If you could do better, you would do better. Trust that always!

I remember being both puzzled and pained by my report cards in public school. With rare exceptions (most of them in the works-well-with-others category) I received my school's equivalent of A's. Yet, every report period the comment section always included some words about how I could do better.

Each time, though feeling somewhat deflated, I returned to my schoolwork with intensified zeal. I kept hoping my teachers would some day acknowledge that **I was** doing my best. It never happened. Without fail, along with the A's, there would be the same old "could do better" note. And, each time, I would think that, despite how it felt inside of me, maybe I really hadn't done my best or done enough after all.

Years later, I got 99 and 97 on my New York State Regents exams in high school chemistry and advanced algebra. When my parents asked me "what happened to the other four points?" it didn't feel like the joke they meant it to be. Instead, it felt like another of the endless stream of messages that I could/should do better.

> You Really Are
> Doing The Best
> You Can
> In This Moment.
> If You Could
> Do Better,
> You Would
> Do Better.
> Trust That
> Always!
>
> o3

As I moved on through the first 30-some years of my life, I (no surprise here) took up the same chant. Having fully internalized the message, I was never able to look with pride or even simple acknowledgment at any of my accomplishments in either the external or internal realms of my life. Nothing I ever did seemed enough in itself. There was always more I felt that I shoulda-coulda-woulda done if I were really to be doing my best.

When I was 32, I abruptly ran out of any mores I could imagine doing. In an **"Aha!"** moment, I understood that all the mores in the world wouldn't be enough to prove that I was really doing my best or that I was enough just as I was. For the first time I saw that it was the standard of measure I'd learned that was at fault, not me. I had learned never to see anything I had **already done** as either my best or enough, simply because I had **already done** it.

I had been conditioned by the bizarre but mostly unquestioned cultural notion that praise (our own or anyone else's) gives us an inflated sense of our selves. The notion being that praise encourages us to rest complacently on our laurels while intimations that we could do better keep us motivated. This conditioning had left me unable to recognize that I **was always** doing the best I could. And, it left me unable to recognize that I was doing the best I could because that **was** and **is** my very nature.

None of us are (as that conditioning would lead us to believe) lazy slugs who would never do anything in our lives were it not for external prodding and fear of censure. Our actual natures move irrepressibly toward growth. The odd bends and twists that our growing may take have mostly to do with our beings' attempts to survive and thrive in the face of imposed obstacles: like the shapes of trees that twist and bend to reach toward the light in a crowded forest.

It is our basic nature to do the best we can with the capacities and consciousness we have available to us at each moment. As our capacities and consciousness evolve and grow, our best will grow better, too. Acknowledging and celebrating all the baby steps along the way helps to nourish this unfolding.

Remember to lovingly remind your self that you're always doing the best you can in this moment.

Consider being loving and tender with your in-this-moment self.

2-6. Loving Acceptance

The loving acceptance you so deeply hunger for...
Can never reach you until you've learned to give that gift
to your self. Practice holding your self as dear as you
would hold anyone else whom you truly cherished!

Like many of the women who came of age between the Depression and World War II, my mother spent much of her adult life feeling thwarted and embittered. Much had been made in high school of her considerable intellectual capabilities. Still, she'd been forced by her father to give up a college bound track for a business track in which she'd learn skills to help support her family during the Depression. She'd had a brief (and from her diary, seemingly exciting) career as a legal secretary. Yet, once she married, she was expected, according to the custom of the time, to quit and be solely supported by her husband.

The Loving Acceptance
You So Deeply Hunger
For...
Can Never Reach You
Until You've Learned
To Give That Gift
To Your Self.
Practice Holding
Your Self
As Dear As You
Would Hold Anyone
Else Whom You
Truly Cherished!

c8

During the war, she sent me to live with her parents when my father went into the Navy. She went back to work as a legal secretary and kept our apartment. For a heady year, she got to live alone and have a career that she enjoyed. She was part of a whole generation of women who had been strongly encouraged (in the spirit of patriotism and Rosie-the-Riveter) to move out beyond their traditional roles into the workforce to help the war effort. But, once the war ended she, like all of her peers, was expected to happily resume being a stay-at-home wife and mother.

She was miserably unhappy and frustrated. Over the years she became increasingly more depressed. She passed to me, albeit less than consciously, the mantle that had been taken from her. I was charged with the task of doing and becoming what she had been stopped from: making my way academically and into a professional career

From my earliest days at school I was a dedicated super-achiever. In primary grades, I usually brought home report cards filled with the equivalent of A's. In the later grades, when marks were in numbers, mine always ranged in the mid to hi 90's.

As I continued through the grade levels, I added numerous extracurricular activities. I wrote poems and stories for which I won small prizes. In high school, I was active in the productions of and also president of the Drama Society. I was president of the Speakers Bureau, Co-editor-in-chief of our school newspaper and a cheerleader for the Honor Society. I was part of an All-City Chorus and an All-City Actors Group, both of which involved traveling weekly to rehearse and to perform regularly on educational radio and TV stations. I graduated from high school with a New York State Regents Scholarship, as a Senior Celebrity – The Girl Who Did Most and as a Merit Scholarship semi-finalist.

I (wrongly, as it turned out) believed that by doing all this, I would make her happy. If she were happy, I thought, she would finally be pleased with and loving toward me. Despite the considerable accomplishments that I brought home to her, my mother was never any happier or more loving with me.

In fact, her responses, when she paid any attention at all, were cold and critical. I didn't then grasp that my achievements rather than fulfilling her vicariously (as I had hoped) were actually stirring jealousy and resentment in her because I was getting to do what she hadn't been allowed to. It was a terrible catch-22.

My own joy and excitement with what I was doing and bringing to her paled in the face of her dismissive responses. I would feel confused and despairing. Each time, I would head back out to do more or to do differently. I was forever searching for the key that would unlock her and win for me her love and acceptance.

Gradually, I internalized her scornful raised eyebrow look and icy voice. My inner critic, the Hatchet Lady, was born. The Hatchet Lady denigrated the things that I did or created even before my mother had the opportunity to do so. The Hatchet Lady ridiculed any delight in my self, any excitement with what I was doing. As far as she was concerned, whatever I did was never right or never enough.

The lavishing of love, attention, recognition from my dad, my aunts and uncles, my grandparents, my teachers – all this was as ashes to me. No amount of acknowledgment, no prizes, no honors carried any weight against this now internalized negative view of my self. Everything positive from the outside triggered the old Groucho Marx "why would I want to belong to any club that would have **me** as a member?" feeling.   By its valuing of me, the source was automatically devalued.

Nevertheless, I never stopped searching for the illusive, magical achievement that might finally render me acceptable and worthy of love both from my mother and from the Hatchet Lady inside of me. (**Pirouettes**, page 125 tells the story of this continued searching.)

When my mother died just three months after my 30th birthday, I felt no grief, no sense of loss. Instead, I felt a surge of relief and release. I felt set free from the weight of an impossible lifelong burden. She was no longer there to be unlocked. Now I had only the Hatchet Lady inside me with which to contend.

My mother's death opened the space for me to realize that no amount of more doing and no amount of further external acknowledgment could ever make me feel good about my self. That it was, in the end an inside job, one I had to do for my self. I finally understood that I had to find some different way to live with my self, some way to feed my aching hunger by my self.

Over the next couple of years, something within me kept nudging me along the path to leaving a whole way of life that now felt completely wrong for me. I had a persistent sense that if I didn't get to where it was green and still, to somewhere where I could be just with my self, I would literally die.

For years as either a friend or a therapist, I had encouraged others to give themselves permission to just be: to accept and love themselves however they were. Yet, entrenched in my doing-proving-achieving life, I could find no such permission for my self. When, two years after my mother's death, I left both the East Coast and that way of life, I started on the path toward embracing and loving all of me.

I stopped trying to be worthy, or trying to be any particular way at all and began to discover how I actually was. I came to be more and more in the middle of my own experiences: exploring and enjoying rather than always evaluating and monitoring. I began to care about my many-sided self with at least some of the tenderness I had, until then, brought only to my caring about others. I found a therapist who, for a while, could be for me what I had been for others: someone to help me to find permission to finally give that unconditional loving to my self.

Healing the wounds from (and in) the Hatchet Lady has taken many more years and an expanding commitment to embrace all my unfinished imperfectness. But, feeding the starveling inside of me began when I stopped looking outside of my self for her nourishment. (**The Little Ones Story**, page 9 chronicles this part of the journey.)

Until we can begin to treat our selves lovingly, any loving from the outside can't reach past our automatic invalidation of it. No one can love us into loving our selves. Their love can support the seed of our self-loving, like bringing coffee and donuts to the barricade. The starveling inside of us (on the other side of the barricade) needs **us** to feed her. She needs **us** to believe that she deserves our own loving care. She needs **us** to believe what's so: that she deserves that love just because she's alive and she breathes.

Often we begin this process by acting on faith, as if we believe these things are true. We act as-if because we've never had such truths modeled for us by those who parented or took care of us. It is a slow, often scary road. But, it is the way home.

Travel gently as you begin to give your self the love you've been hungering for.

2-7. The Power of Vulnerability

To be openly vulnerable is an act of power!

For a good many years of my life, particularly those during graduate school and my first years as a professional (clinical psychologist), I lived with an intermittent sense of fraudulence. This was so despite the fact that my work and my intellectual capacities were well received and respected, first by my faculty and academic peers then later, by my clients and colleagues.

Generally, I experienced my self as peer or as superior in capabilities to those in my student cohort. (See **Judging Difference**, page 145 for more about this.) While I could be intrigued by the occasional brilliance of some of my mentors, I was rarely impressed and never intimidated by them. Whenever my harsh inner critic (the Hatchet Lady) rose up to flay me with her invalidation and ridicule, she challenged how I used my capacities, not that they existed.

To Be Openly

Vulnerable

Is An Act Of

Power...

To Be Openly

Empowered

Is An Act Of

Vulnerability!

b2

Still, I was often beset by a disturbing sense that I was somehow an imposter, not really the person others (or I) thought me to be. I was plagued by a fear that some dangling loose end in the fabric of my being could be inadvertently snagged at any moment. I was certain that, were that thread snagged, my entire disguise would unravel revealing to all a much less impressive me.

It took several years of feeling baffled before the mystery of this long-standing sense of precariousness finally resolved for me. Some of the clues to its source came from what else had been going on for me while I was in graduate school.

During the years of my graduate and professional training, I had been learning more than just the subject matter of psychology. By far the more significant education I was getting was about the boys' (patriarchal white male) world. I was gaining an understanding of how the boys' game board operated around the issues of power, respect and status. I watched my professors and my clinical supervisors as they each projected (and supported each other's) images of self-assured, self-contained inviolability.

With my finely tuned emotional Geiger counter (honed in the process of surviving my childhood), I saw beneath these Emperor's New Clothes exteriors. I would pick up on the insecurities, feelings of inadequacy and uneasiness behind their projected images. I noticed that the more insecure a professor seemed to me, the more likely he was to be dismissive and humiliating to his students, the more likely he was to require (and be impressed by) slavish regurgitation of his words on the exams he gave. I also got to see that arrogant behavior was connected with underlying insecurity, the degree of outward arrogance being directly proportional to the degree of the person's inward insecurity.

Still, it was clear that the source of all valuing and respect in this community lay within these unchallenged projected images. Of the two women on the faculty at my school, one seemed quite unaware of the game board. As a consequence, and despite her obvious scholarship, she was viewed as inconsequential by faculty and students alike (my self regrettably included). The second woman seemed to know how to play the game the way the boys did. She was accorded respect in a measure fairly equal to what the boys accorded each other.

I grasped that projecting a similar image of my self was essential to garnering the respect of my professors, respect that would then assure my success in the program. I grew quite adept at this boys' game. My emotions and anxieties were for when I was at home or privately wrestling with the Hatchet Lady. At school I was the epitome of cool, self-assured unflappability.

With this image and with my high level performance in classes as well as on tests, I became a significant (sometimes daunting) figure both to other students and to most of the faculty. In my classes I would sometimes play with my professors' image of me by asking questions that, had they been asked by any other student, would have been treated as beneath consideration. I would marvel at the serious attention that my professors would give these inane questions when I was the one doing the asking. It was a way I could play with the boys' game and explore the edges of its distortions.

During those highly functional, successful school years, my personal emotional life was in constant turmoil. In private and in secret, I felt like a complete mess. Depressed and despairing to the point of seriously considering suicide, I finally took what (in that system) seemed an enormous risk. I confided in my female faculty mentor (the respected one) in order to get a referral to my first therapist. The dear and wonderful therapist that she recommended helped me to save my life and to learn to live more comfortably with my always-intense emotional life. Our work didn't, however, touch or relieve my recurring sense of fraudulence. That resolution came years later.

As, in my therapy practice, I worked with highly competent, functional-in-the-male-world women clients, I found that many of them also struggled with feeling out-of-control over what they also saw as the messiness of their secret emotional lives. And, many lived uneasily with a similar sense of fraudulence and fears of being unmasked or revealed as less than what they appeared to be. It was in the work with these women that the mystery behind the feelings of being counterfeit finally clarified.

In the boys' world (the dominant, patriarchal white male reality) vulnerability, empathy, emotions (other than anger – which only the boys are allowed to express without penalty) are read as signs of weakness, softness (as a negative quality), untrustworthiness or undependability. And, they are devalued in a specifically gendered way: "Don't be such a wimp/sissy/girl!" We women who cross into and are successful in that reality have often learned, as I had, to garner respect by acting like one of the boys. We learn to leave our vulnerable, feeling selves at home, or (in some cases) to leave them completely.

We learn to gain position and respect (power in their world) by disowning our very natures as emotional, relational creatures. The price is devastating. No matter how well we learn to suit-up, no matter how effective our external disguises, we do not fool our selves. We cannot avoid knowing that we do have a feeling life, that under the suit we are still our female, feeling selves.

Colluding with the system by denying the presence and value of a (our) feeling life, we may gain the boys' respect, have credibility, influence and power. Yet, in that collusion, we simultaneously give our selves the message that who we truly are is neither okay nor worthy of respect. ("If they knew how I really am, they wouldn't respect/value/ hear me at all!") This denial and suppression of our essential natures creates uneasiness and stress in us. We live feeling vaguely off-center, with an ongoing (if often less than conscious) fear that our true self can at any moment slip out and unmask us; or, that our careful disguise could, at anytime, be torn away – wittingly or unwittingly – by anyone around us. This precariousness arises from our less than conscious incorporation of the patriarchal white male cultural training to dismiss and disguise our vulnerable, feeling natures. This was my "Aha!"

With this "Aha!" came the awareness that our efforts to be powerful in the white male system actually dis-empower us on a being level. Feeling authentically empowered comes from respecting, affirming and living from our true self, not from denying and suppressing it.

With this "Aha!" came the decision to stop my own participation in the self-wounding, self-undermining attempt to obliterate my nature. My first step was consciously owning my vulnerability and beginning to explore it as an ally. I hung out with the possibility that my feelings: emotional states, moods, felt responses to all situations in my life might be sources of important information about those situations as well as about my self.

My acceptance of the wisdom in my vulnerability and my emotional responsiveness grew. As I felt stronger in my own valuing of these aspects of my self, I began the practice of claiming, naming and sharing them in my in-the-boys'-world interactions. As is the best plan with new practices, I took my first baby-step risks in circumstances where a neutral or possibly positive response might be expected.

Each time I took the risk of matter-of-factly speaking for my vulnerability/feelings, my own acceptance of these parts of me increased. It didn't seem to matter whether I was well heard or well received in the setting. All that mattered was that I spoke out simply and directly, as if I believed that what I said was honorable, meaningful and worth sharing. In these acts of sharing-with-conviction, I was empowering my self. And, typically, my conviction made what I was sharing quite compelling to those with whom I was sharing it.

One of my favorite tales of this kind of sharing comes from more recent history. At the time of writing this tale, I'd been working for about seven years with a mom-and-pop print shop. They had been doing the production of all the greeting cards and decks of affirmation cards that I've designed and been selling since 1991.

I arrived at the shop at 8:30 one morning after having stayed up all night working both at home and at a 24-hour Kinko's. I'd been doing and redoing layouts and paste-ups for a new set of twelve long postcards. When I came into their shop, soaring with excitement at the project's completion and at the edge of crumbling from exhaustion, John and Sarah (not their real names) were both there. With bubbling delight I handed over the six pages of layouts. John looked at them and, with great irritation, threw them onto the counter.

"These are impossible! You can't expect me to do three-sided bleeds!" he all but shouted at me. My eyes welled with tears at what was, to my exhausted, sensitive, full-of-self self, an unexpected energetic assault. I put my hand up, palm toward him and told him he had to stop talking at me that very minute. I took a few deep breaths. Then, through my tears, I told him that it was **not** okay with me for him to blow out his frustrations and anger on me, that it was misplaced, inappropriate and very upsetting to me.

I reminded him that I knew – from his frequent sharings with me – how much it upset him that many of his customers expected him to clean up the messes in their original work without respecting or being ready to pay for the time involved in his doing that. I reminded him that in the seven years of our collaboration – of my learning how to do my preparations so that he could more easily do his job – I had never asked or expected him to do my part of the work and had always paid him for every bit of his time.

Then, as he tried to respond, I picked up my layouts and told him I didn't have the room right then to listen to him about anything other than the information about what exactly was problematic about the work I'd brought. He gave me a calm, concrete explanation of the problem, apologized profusely and then I left.

During the ten-minute drive home, a very simple remedy presented itself to me. After a nap, I made that change in the layouts and went back to the print shop. John took the pages, nodded his head and began to write up the order.

"John," I said, "wait!" He looked up at me, clearly a bit uncomfortable.

"What?" he said. "Well," I said, "if, when you're teaching me how to work with you, you're going to give me a hard time when I've done something badly, you're going to have to learn how to acknowledge me when I've done something well! You could try saying: "Robyn! What a brilliant solution you found! This is great! It makes my job so much easier! Thank you!" I said.

John turned scarlet with embarrassment. Sarah said, "That's so right. He's always quick to criticize, but he rarely gives compliments."

John apologized again and actually found words of his own with which to acknowledge the clever and simple solution I had devised for the 3-bleeds problem.

Through the years of our collaboration (until he retired), I still occasionally had to remind John to remember it was me he was talking to and how he could better communicate with me. Yet, on the whole, he did get it that very day. John and I joked about this dialogue repeatedly as time went on. And, his wife Sarah often teased about how that interchange had impacted his behavior in general.

I've gathered many similar tales since I've begun bringing the whole of my vulnerable and empowered feeling self into every situation in my life out in the so-called real world. Often it feels like I'm doing one-woman guerrilla theater. I know that the combination of my forthrightness, my conviction that feelings matter and that vulnerability openly acknowledged is powerful, can often be disconcerting. It's usually so unexpected and off the ordinary continuum that it winds up being quite disarming. I am heard. It does make a difference, for the moment at least, in business-as-usual.

When people occasionally respond to me with raised eyebrows, disdainful faces or attitudes or other suppressive behaviors, I usually address it directly. Often, I'll ask, " Is there something –" or, "What is it – about how I'm being (or what I'm saying) that's making you uncomfortable?" Of course, this is still more guerrilla theater, since one is ordinarily expected to respond to such censorious hints by stopping the misbehavior or shutting up.

Perhaps the most empowering thing I've discovered about respectfully owning my vulnerability is that when I choose, matter-of-factly, to acknowledge whatever I've been encouraged to be afraid of having revealed about me, I am finally and truly safe. Whenever I have my own permission to be my whole self, I am living from the center of what is so for me. This is an act of power, an act in which I authorize my self to be all of who I am, out-loud as it were.

Consider exploring and claiming the fullness of your vulnerable, feeling self.

[Because the simple message of this card – To be openly vulnerable is an act of power… To be openly empowered is an act of vulnerability – turns out to have such a complex underpinning, this tale reflects only on the first half. The next tale goes on to explore being openly empowered as an act of vulnerability.]

2-8. The Vulnerability of Power

To be openly empowered is an act of vulnerability!

During my first year in private practice (1967, my second year out of graduate school) one of my former mentors called to refer one of his male patients to me for diagnostic testing. The mentor was a well-known, highly regarded elder psychiatrist who had taught our psychotherapy practicum. He had also become, outside the confines of that seminar, an odd sort of friend and emotional-overseer to me during one summer when my first therapist (a close friend of his) was out of the country on vacation.

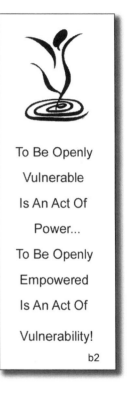

To Be Openly

Vulnerable

Is An Act Of

Power...

To Be Openly

Empowered

Is An Act Of

Vulnerability!

b2

Dr. X offered the referral as a grand gesture of faith in me at the start of my career. He said he "was trusting" me to do the testing and write the report. But, he stipulated, I must, "in light of your inexperience," consult on the results with Dr Y, the woman who had trained my class in advanced diagnostic testing techniques.

Dr. Y, an elder of some considerable reputation in **her** field, had consistently astonished my class with her capacity to uncover the bones of the people we had examined. She never failed to weave our piles of test results into living breathing beings revealed in their complex, nuanced vulnerability. In her seminars I had often felt mystified, clod-like in my bumbling attempts to follow her trance-like flights into the unconscious symbolic language of our clients. I felt uneasy about returning to consult with this woman with whom I had never felt quite comfortable.

Still, once I had set up the testing time with the patient, I called Dr. Y to arrange the consultation. She was surprisingly warm and cordial with me, so I relaxed and prepared for our meeting. We had a marvelous time working together on the materials and preliminary conceptions that I had brought. I felt none of my earlier cloddishness. Delighted with my reflections on the test results, she enthusiastically applauded the richness and depth of my understanding of this patient's psyche as we laughed and played with the materials.

I returned several days later, bringing a draft of my report for her review. In this second hour together, I sought her counsel on how to charge for my work. I was paying her for two hours of consultation time. I'd spent almost two hours testing the person, another two hours or so ruminating and pondering the results and yet another two hours working up the two-page report. She told me that it was appropriate for me to bill the client for my pondering time, my composing time and my time consulting with her as well as for the consulting fee I was paying to her. While the final figure of $250 ($160 for my eight hours, $90 for her two) seemed fair, I felt a bit uncomfortable with it.

In addressing my discomfort, Dr. Y reminded me of something that she thought I already knew. Apparently, Dr. X had first called her to do the testing for him. When she'd told him that she was no longer doing testing, he'd asked for a referral to someone "who'd do the kind and quality of work you would." Dr. Y had immediately recommended me to him as her "finest protégé." Dr. X had also asked her if she would consult with me on the case. She'd told him that, though she thought that it would be unnecessary, she'd be happy to work with me again if that was what he wanted.

I sat there stunned: Amazed by the news that she had so respected my capacities that she would consider me her finest protégé and refer him to me as someone who could do the kind of job she could do. Astonished that I'd never had any sense that she had noted or valued what had felt like my clumsy efforts in our seminar.

I felt even more stunned by the realization that this man – whom I had considered a benevolent friend/mentor – had, by the way he presented the referral and his request that I consult with Dr. Y on it, misrepresented the truth, neglecting to disclose both the fact and the content of his conversation with Dr. Y. Such disclosure would have involved him in acknowledging her respect for my expertise, her glowing recommendation of me as a stand-in for her and her acceptance of me as a full colleague. Instead, he'd presented his referral as a boon he, as grand pooh-bah, was generously bestowing upon me – the very green, inexperienced, not totally qualified novice who would need an expert's consultation to assure the quality of the report produced.

I went home to type the final draft of the report (essentially unchanged by the consultation with Dr. Y) feeling perplexed by this new view of Dr. X. The next day, I hand-delivered the report to him at his office before I began afternoon hours seeing my own clients. I wasn't sure what I wanted to do with the new perspective I had on the episode, so I said nothing. As agreed, I mailed the bill for my services directly to his patient, a corporate CEO living in an affluent suburb north of New York City.

A week later, at 7:00 A.M. one morning, Dr. X's call woke me from a sound sleep. (A habitual early riser, he never considered that other people might not be awake when he was.) Sputtering in a fulminating rage, he was shouting so loudly that I had to hold the phone well away from my ear. Standing there in my nightshirt as he ranted like a man possessed, I slowly got the gist of what had so infuriated him. The more I understood of what he was saying the more appalled I became.

His patient had, the evening before, told him about my bill for $250. Apparently the patient's wife had simultaneously been psychologically tested by "a very well experienced" male psychologist in the affluent suburb in which the couple lived. **That** psychologist had charged $250 for **his** evaluation of the patient's wife. **That** psychologist's report had been typed "without any strikeovers or erasures on an IBM Selectric typewriter" (a rather classy electric typewriter fairly new in those days). Dr X was enraged that I had the audacity – with my "inexperience, short skirts, long hair and poor typewriting"– to think that I had a right to charge $250 for **my** work.

Dr. X raved on about how he'd had to struggle, suffer and pay his dues. How he'd had to live on a pittance for many years while making his way up through the ranks as a medical intern and resident before he could begin to be paid reasonably for his time. He was furious with me for having the temerity, at this early point in my career, to ask to be paid the same rate as the much more senior male psychologist.

I listened with shocked disbelief. This man had been my proud mentor: an outspoken supporter, frequently articulating his appreciation of my skills and development as a clinician. Now, after lying by omission about the circumstances surrounding the referral and consultation with Dr. Y., he was acting like a raving lunatic, saying things that were unconscionable and deranged.

Though the intense energy of his raging left me physically trembling, the absurdity of its content left me clear-headed enough to respond immediately with a cold anger of my own. When he'd finished blasting at me, I calmly pointed out that what I wore, how long my hair was, how proficiently the report was typed and how long I'd been in the field were totally irrelevant to the quality of the insights offered in my report. I told him that I believed, and Dr. Y concurred, that the quality of these insights was excellent and highly pertinent to the questions he presented to be addressed in the testing.

"That the harsh protocol of medical training required financial sacrifices from you," I told him, "has absolutely no bearing on my decision to charge a reasonable fee for my time. I'm my own sole source of support; I can't afford to give away my professional time. Besides, why would I **even** consider doing such a thing?"

I told him how despicable I thought it was of him to treat me as if he were doing me some great favor by offering me the referral. I told him how appalled I was by his deliberate misrepresentation. I informed him that Dr. Y had told me that when he had asked, she had recommended me as her choice of the best person to stand in for her.

I informed him that $90 dollars of the $250 fee was to pay for the consultation time with Dr. Y, time that he had stipulated. I told him that I now knew she thought that that consultation was unnecessary. I informed him that the fee I set for my time had been arrived at in the consultation with Dr. Y who thought it was a reasonable fee for the number of my hours involved.

He responded saying that if I were "going to act in this way, to charge these rates," he'd surely "never again refer anyone to" me. My response was immediate: "If you're going to act and talk to me in this completely unacceptable way, you can keep your referrals." Then I hung up. We never spoke again.

The whole situation had been a minefield. A psychiatrist in the position of having to request psychological diagnostic expertise to help him to understand the psyche of a patient was, in those years, rarely happy about needing such assistance. That it was a female, considerably junior psychologist who'd actually been a recent student of the psychiatrist made the situation even more fraught for him. That the patient involved was an outwardly imposing, traditional, powerful male whose psychological profile revealed an inner life of extreme fearfulness, insecurity and emotional stunting along with a desperate yearning to be taken care of by a mothering figure – well, that put it all over the top.

I chewed for a while on what had happened between my mentor and me. Obviously, he was unable to tolerate my fledging into my own fullness and competence. His message was straightforward: were I to choose to step into my own authority rather than to defer to his, he would no longer be willing to mentor my professional evolution and would completely withdraw his support of me.

Earlier that year, when I had sent out formal announcements of the opening of my private practice, both my other primary mentors had reacted in parallel and equally shocking ways. One of these mentors was the professor who had been the chair of my dissertation committee, my research mentor through all four years of graduate school, the person for whom I had run a research lab before he invited me to enroll into the graduate program he chaired and a man who generally introduced me as his professional protégé in a variety of research settings. This mentor mailed back my formal announcement with a handwritten note penciled on it: "Et tu Brute!"

I never saw a way to respond to this, to his feeling betrayed by my choice to practice as a clinician rather than as the research/experimental psychologist he would have had me be. We never spoke again.

The second of these other mentors was the woman professor who had helped me to find my first therapist. She had been a significant influence in my decision to expand my academic concentration from experimental psychology into clinical psychology. She had hired me as her teaching assistant for the laboratory sections of the Rorschach course even before I had officially changed my major. She was ardently vocal about my creativity and intuition as a clinician, always lobbying for me to make a commitment to honoring those skills.

She, extremely distressed, called me the day after she received my announcement. She told me she couldn't believe that I would presume to be ready to set out on my own at this stage of my development. She told me that I had "no business" starting a private practice until I had, as she herself had had, several years of postgraduate training under my belt, that there was still so much for me to learn. I agreed that there was still an enormous amount to learn. And, I reminded her of our many discussions of how much of the learning came from just doing the work and having some quality supervision/consultation available. I explained that postgraduate school felt like boot camp hazing in which I had no interest. "Well," she exclaimed, horrified, "there's absolutely no way I'd ever refer anyone to you if you didn't enroll in a program!" That ended our relationship. We never spoke again.

In these experiences with my three official mentors, I learned a stark, painful lesson about how vulnerable we can become when we act confidently from our own inner authority inside a system where such empowerment is viewed as a threat to the existing power structure.

In the patriarchal white male paradigm, power is measured by the degree of one's authority over others. One is seen as powerful in the exact measure that one can command and direct the behavior of others hierarchically beneath them, under their jurisdiction. In most settings, this power (power-over) is viewed as a limited commodity in a closed system. The more power one person claims the less there is available for all others in the system. One's power, thus construed, is guarded jealously.

When someone lower in the pecking order attempts to take up their own authority, those in power experience this as a threat to their position. Typically they respond suppressively to such attempts. Invalidation – undermining the credibility of the person they see as a challenger – is frequently the form that suppression takes. Invalidating others becomes the way of revalidating one's challenged self. This "I have it, you can't get it!" "You're less therefore I'm more" stance is a power operation. Power operations are the acts and stances by which insecure people, unable to authorize and empower themselves, move repeatedly toward diminishing others to enhance their own illusion that they are more powerful.

In the Sacred Feminine paradigm, power is construed as self-empowerment, emerging from and expanding with our growing capacity to authorize our selves, to give our selves permission to own and to manifest all of who we are as beings. When we have our own permission to be and to be becoming all of who we are, we recognize power as an unlimited quantity. We have room for those around us to claim all of their own authority as well. Their self-authorizing behaviors do not in any way limit our own. We are in an open system where, in fact, one's empowering her self can encourage and engender the conditions under which others feel freer to similarly empower themselves, claiming their own authority.

When we are empowered, we have no need for power operations: everyone's truth and everyone's being matters. We can and do rejoice in others' fullness. My experience with Dr. Y's delight in and encouragement of my fullness and competence was a perfect example of the Sacred Feminine paradigm in motion. The world-at-large, regrettably, does not yet generally reflect this paradigm.

When we authorize our selves to act from our own fullness in a world where power is still primarily perceived as power-over and limited in availability, our behavior may call forth unpleasant responses from those around us. Perceived as having something others may not feel themselves to have, we may become vulnerable to their resentment, envy, and/or attempts to "cut-us-down-to-size." On the other end of the continuum, we may be subject to their idolization, adulation and the uneasy objectification that comes with such idealization.

In the midst of such challenge, we learn to continue to practice acting from our deepest selves; we practice being openly vulnerable and openly empowered. We keep learning about how to hold our selves more safely at these edges. We commit to not dimming our lights. And, as we continue, we are lighting the way for each other. For those at the edge of birthing themselves into their own fullness, our continuing gives hope and kindles belief in the possibility of a world in which we are each and all empowered and safe.

A footnote to this tale: It was actually many years before I finally recognized that I had been abandoned by all of my significant mentors at the moment I fledged into my own independent practice as a psychologist. Sadly, the repeated, similarly unrecognized abandonments by my mother throughout my childhood and adolescence had prepared me to take these events in stride. I experienced them as unpleasant but not really unexpected responses to my choosing to listen to my own heart. Like so many of us, I had figured out, early on and by necessity, how to go on by my self when no one outside me was there to support me.

My first psychotherapy practice actually grew easily from word of mouth through friends and then though the people who'd become my clients. I've always been grateful that I chose not to pay the price required to stay connected with those mentors. Still, as I've come to recognize the repeated abandonment to which that young, ebullient me was subject, I have grieved deeply for the losses she never quite felt on a conscious level. And, as I've been writing this piece, so many years later, I've found my self experiencing an even deeper layer of sorrow than I'd yet felt for that dear, courageous young woman that I was.

Consider holding your empowered self gently and with great care.

2-9. Procrastinating

If you think you might be "procrastinating..." Try listening inward for the feelings of the part of you who isn't so sure that whatever you aren't yet doing would really be all right for you to do at all!

In the midst of a month that was feeling overfull and was challenging my capacity to stay in balance, a woman who'd worked with me intermittently over the preceding 18 years called me for a consultation. She wanted to process her struggle with the decision to go off the chemotherapy treatments for her lung cancer now that those treatments had begun to feel like they were killing her. Renewing her dedication to work with visualization tapes was an integral part of her feeling safe in making this decision.

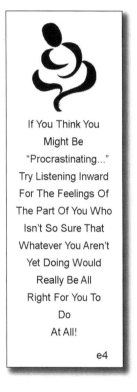

If You Think You Might Be "Procrastinating..." Try Listening Inward For The Feelings Of The Part Of You Who Isn't So Sure That Whatever You Aren't Yet Doing Would Really Be All Right For You To Do At All!

e4

Using the tapes that I'd made for her four and a half years before no longer felt appropriate. The level of health being visualized in those earlier tapes seemed beyond anything she could now reasonably expect herself to achieve. We agreed that I would make two new tapes for her, ones that would progress toward improving health in much smaller steps. I promised that I would get them done as quickly as I could. She planned to revive the many prayer circles that had supported her healing work during earlier crises and to begin her visualization practice without the new supporting tapes.

On my way home from our meeting at her house, I stopped to buy the high quality 30-minute tapes that I'd need. I was certain that I'd be able to get to the task within the next few days and deliver the tapes within the week. Yet, days passed with the project repeatedly slipping to the bottom of the heap of the January paperwork and chores before me. I felt uncomfortable about not getting to it. I felt some urgency about getting the tapes to this dear woman. Yet, I'd feel paralyzed every time I considered beginning what was likely to be at least a 2- or 3-hour project.

By the end of a week, I had progressed only as far as listening to the old set of tapes (to remind my self of how we had designed the relaxation and preparation process). I felt stymied by the prospect of recreating and redesigning the visualizations. At that point, I called Sarah and Jane (not their real names) to check in on how Sarah was coming along. I reported apologetically that, to my consternation, I hadn't yet been able to create the tapes. They were much less perturbed about the delay than I had been.

For the first few days of not-doing-the-tapes, I'd felt uncomfortable with my self. Unlike earlier times in my life, the inner critic's voice wasn't noticeably activated. I wasn't either berating or beating up on my self for procrastinating on this urgent project. Rather, I was simply experiencing an uneasy perplexity about why I seemed to be so frozen in the face of it.

Briefly one morning I had an old style "what's wrong with me, why on earth can't I **just** do this!" thought. All my years of working with calming my inner critic (the Hatchet Lady voice) helped me to recognize immediately that I did not have to go any further down this self-flagellating road. Instead, the self-critical thought simply served as a flashing neon sign letting me know that the part of me that was having trouble with what wasn't happening was in need of my attention.

I sat down quietly and talked with this upset-with-my-self part about what we've learned over the past many years of our healing journey: that what looks like procrastination to our own (and others') outside-eyes is usually a sign of one of two inside-eyes truths. Either we're asking our selves to do a thing that's not right for us to be doing **at all** (the wrong thing). Or, we're asking our selves to do a thing that's not right for us to be doing **now** (the wrong time).

When it feels as if something is sitting on me, as if I am frozen or paralyzed or procrastinating, I reminded her, it's likely that some less than conscious, deeper knowing place in me is, in fact, taking very good care of me. And, no matter how uncomfortable it feels to be in this place, I reassured her, I will, at some point, come to consciously understand what isn't clear at this moment about the rightness (for me) of this not-doing.

I also reminded my upset self that whenever I agree to create anything, all I can really do is commit me to making my self empty, to becoming available to and waiting for Spirit to move through me. I cannot force the flow of Spirit and I cannot create without the grace of this flow. This loving conversation with my upset self calmed me. I was able to let go of expectations, to relax into patience and into calmly waiting for the next step to reveal itself.

Three days later Jane called to tell me Sarah was in the emergency room in severe respiratory crisis. The doctors advised calling in Hospice, believing that Sarah wasn't likely to survive more than a month or so.

When I got to the hospital that evening, Sarah was under heavy morphine drip sedation and no longer conscious. While other close friends kept vigil with the sleeping Sarah, I drove Jane home to gather some things to make it more comfortable for her to stay the night at the hospital with Sarah. Jane had a strong sense that things would move very quickly now, that she needed to get right back to the hospital.

At seven the next morning, Jane called to say that she'd just awakened from a two hour nap to discover that Sarah "had passed."

Two days later, the night before Sarah's memorial, Jane called to ask me if I would speak at the service. I turned the computer on even before we hung up.   Words of celebration for Sarah's life easily poured from my heart and cascaded onto the screen. This was the right thing at the right time.

Consider the possibility that what you usually call procrastination is really the sign of a deeper, wiser part of your self taking good care of you. And, consider being really loving and gentle with that part of your self.

2-10. Growth is a Process

Growth is a process, not an achievement. When you feel discouraged, take time to lovingly acknowledge how far you've already come... There is always further yet to go!

I remember, at 23, sitting with my first therapist – a warm, compassionate, fiercely maternal man (who helped me to save my life). I had come to him awash in soul-crushing despair, suicidal and desperate to find a way to fix my broken self. He seemed so wonderfully calm, so beyond the kinds of problems and conflicts that plagued me. His whole being radiated peace and serenity.

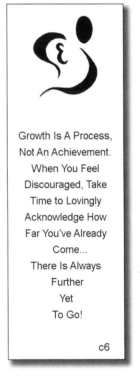

Growth Is A Process,
Not An Achievement.
When You Feel
Discouraged, Take
Time to Lovingly
Acknowledge How
Far You've Already
Come...
There Is Always
Further
Yet
To Go!

c6

That impression of someone living-in-Nirvana, beyond struggle, became my benchmark, the image of the place I wanted to reach. Though the gap between that place and how I was living in my own life felt huge and nearly unbridgeable, I enthusiastically signed on for the project.

As with anything I undertook in those days, I hurled my self into the work, hell-bent to be the best-ever patient: to be cured in record time. If he addressed my hurry, I mostly did not hear it. Whenever the barest hint of a question about it might reach me, I dismissed it as being patronizing. Already a dedicated super-achiever, I was perpetually racing ahead of my self, often able to make enormous strides at incredible speeds. All the while unaware of the cost to my being of this break-neck pace. (See **Going 75 mph**, page 321 for more about that.)

When I graduated from our working together a year and a half later, I felt substantially fixed. No longer suicidal or immersed in despair, I had learned some empowering skills with which to navigate my typically intense emotional life. I continued to believe Nirvana was attainable. But, by then, I'd realized that some time and living might be necessary in order to arrive at that serene place from which life would become a matter of coasting. Twenty years, five therapists, considerable spiritual searching and several cycles of great despair later, I finally got that Nirvana, as I'd imagined it, didn't exist.

During those twenty years (until, at 43, I began the work I started with my last therapist) I would be filled with self-loathing, disappointment and an abject sense of failure each time I, once again feeling broken, cycled through yet another season of despair. During these feeling-broken times, I was convinced that the strong sense of self and wholeness I'd felt in the preceding periods had simply been delusional. If I'd truly been as whole as I'd believed my self to be during those periods, how could I possibly wind up so undone again?

In that last therapy (that ended some 26 years past), I first discovered and then began reclaiming and re-parenting, the wounded Little One(s) inside of me. (See **The Little Ones Story**, page 9 for more about that.) It's work that I continue to do even now. My own immersion in this process and my witnessing the healing journeys of the hundreds of women with whom I've worked during my more than 48 years as a therapist, has given me a very different vision of the ways in which we grow throughout our lives. This one is more generous, more realistic and more forgiving than my old vision of reaching Nirvana and then coasting.

All of these journeys repeatedly teach me that growth is an ever on-going process, **not** an achievement. The way of our healing is not a linear but rather a spiral path. Over and over again we pass through the same fixed points, but at a new level each time we spiral around. These fixed points, the coordinates through which our spiral of growth unfolds, are the issues we have come to work with in this lifetime. At each new threshold in the spiral – each time we are moving to the next layer in our process – we are likely to encounter another, more subtle version of these issues that we had indeed resolved at each earlier level in that spiral.

A narrow, shortsighted view of these moments leads us to criticize and disparage our selves for being-in-the-same-old-garbage again. The same shortsightedness makes us believe that the progress we thought we'd made till this moment was illusory.

The truth is that when it seems that we are passing through the same old place again, it is a new self that is passing through a new iteration of that old place on the way to a still newer emerging self. So, each time we notice that we are confronting some form of the old dragons again, we can – instead of doubting our selves – feel assured that we are indeed in the midst of moving forward, through a threshold.

Like so many of us, I grew up having the psychic/emotional responsibility for mothering/parenting my own mother. With this emotional initiation, one of my fixed points/coordinates is the repeating terror and challenge around choosing to respond to my own needs before responding to the intuited or spoken needs of any other who touches my heart. At each new threshold in my spiral of growing, Spirit pushes me into making some new, more fine-tuned form of this choice. As I make the choice I inevitably feel, in some little part of me, a familiar (though lessening) terror of murderous, dangerous retaliation from the person to whose needs I am not responding.

I hold this frightened part of me close. I lovingly remind her of how many times we have passed this test without something terrible happening to us. I promise her that I will continue, without fail, to protect her. I assure her that I will always stand between her and whatever anger the other person might have about how we are choosing. I let her know it will be safe for us to hear the other person's feelings, that those feelings cannot/will not destroy us. In time she feels safe again.

Another of my fixed points: in my emotional history, a recurring wave of unaccounted for despair, of feeling broken and lost is usually a clue that I'm about to open into a whole new place/part of my self. This lost, despairing feeling is the anticipatory grieving (in some little part of me) for the imminent ending either of a chapter/season of my living or of a way of being in my self.

The little part of me needs my reassurance that she will not be abandoned by me as I move into the new spaces of my life and my self. She needs my loving comfort in her fearfulness and grief. I hold her close. I remind her of how many times we have gone through this kind of threshold before. I remind her of how very far we've already come without me ever leaving her behind or alone. After some while, she seems done with feeling both the fear and the grief. We move into the new season of our life-long adventure holding hands.

When you feel discouraged about your progress, consider reminding your self of the more generous view of the growing process offered here. Remember, too, to be loving and comforting to your inner little one.

And, consider lovingly holding your own little one's hand as you grow.

2-11. Applaud Your Self

Applaud all the tiny baby steps along the way in your journey...
Acknowledge the wonder of your persistence in the difficult times...
Marvel at the miracle of your courage and trust-in-the-process...
Delight in your self at every possible opportunity...
Watch how much you flourish with enjoyment as the motivation!

It's fascinating to watch young babies as they discover themselves. Their whole bodies radiate joy, vibrating with delight in the moments when they discover their fingers or feet, shake a rattle, splash in water or set a mobile in motion.

Applaud All The Tiny Baby Steps Along The Way In Your Journey...

Acknowledge The Wonder Of Your Persistence In The Difficult Times...

Marvel At The Miracle Of Your Courage And Trust-In-The-Process...

Delight In Your Self At Every Possible Opportunity...

Watch How Much You Flourish With Enjoyment As The Motivation!

b5

Young children, too, if they haven't yet been damaged, are similarly delighted with themselves. They brim with excitement – thrilled with themselves over what they say, or do, or make, or their made-up songs or dances. Their glee in just being suggests that this unself-conscious enjoyment-of-self is our natural state, our true birthright.

Yet, early and often, our experiences teach us to cut off from feeling so simply full-with-our selves. We are frightened or shamed out of the unself-consciousness. We become uneasy about our selves. We start doubting, becoming critical about what we are doing, how we are doing it, how we look and how we are. Much of this damage is done to us in the guise of socializing us to fit into the world more safely.

For those of us who grew up in certain minority cultures (e.g., African-American or Jewish), praising, openly acknowledging or simply feeling and acting full-of-oneself was seen (often quite validly) as an endangering invitation to punishment or malevolence from the larger collective (or the evil eye).

Those of us over thirty grew up in an era when conventional wisdom held that praise was likely to go to a person's head, encouraging both conceit (swell-headedness) and a tendency for one to rest on one's laurels. We learned that feeling excited with oneself and/or openly showing that excitement was socially unacceptable, evidence of "getting too big for your britches!" We were often warned, "pride goes before a fall."

Many of us had wounded mothers and/or fathers whose own critical competitiveness took these cultural biases even further. Unwilling and, perhaps, unable to acknowledge or to celebrate anything about who or how we were or what we had accomplished in the world, they instead responded with criticism and dismissiveness.

It's no surprise, then, that many of us have persistent toxic inner voices that undermine and disparage much of what we do and how we are. These inner critics serve to keep us in our place. We feel constricted: cautious and self-deprecating in the moments that we might otherwise have felt expansive – joyously full-of-our selves and delightedly self-affirming.

My own emotionally crippled mother died when I was just 30. But, the legacy of her mean-spiritedness toward me continued to live on in just such an internalized, disdainful voice, a voice I've called the Hatchet Lady. (See **Criticizing Your Self**, page 137, **Loving Acceptance**, page 159 and **Doing Better**, page 157 for more about this and her.)

It wasn't until my mid-forties that I began to free my self from the Hatchet Lady's constant tyranny. My ongoing struggles with her, nevertheless, had had a significant impact on how I worked with clients from the earliest days of my grad school psychotherapy practicum. My own bitter experiences had taught me about what we who've suffered in these ways might need to help us to heal our selves. I spent my first twenty years as a practicing psychologist helping people find the permission to be more loving, accepting and acknowledging of themselves than I had yet been able to be with my self. Though I encouraged clients, friends and even grumpy or mean service people to give themselves this permission, I never felt allowed to give it to my self. For many years it was a case of teaching best that which I most needed to learn.

I witnessed the ways my clients told themselves negating and demoralizing stories about who and how they were. It was all quite familiar to me from my own parallel inner process. I learned to invite my clients to look for ways to tell stories that would give them the benefit of the doubt. I supported them finding the stories they might tell about those same experiences or struggles if they were consoling a beloved friend who was upset and hurting over those very experiences or struggles. As they continued with this reframing practice, they gradually developed the capacity to bring that same compassion to themselves. Though many of them grew to look more kindly and unconditionally lovingly at themselves, I continued to berate, find fault with and be undermining of my self.

I helped my clients to acknowledge the tiny baby steps along the way of their healing process. They learned to celebrate these small bits of progress that they had before dismissed as insignificant. Yet, I continued to belittle what I saw as my own negligible progress.

I encouraged my clients to see, acknowledge and even marvel at their persistence, their willingness to hang in there with themselves. I fostered their ability to develop an appreciation of the miracle of their courage as they struggled. They learned to have this appreciation of themselves even in the middle of the most challenging passages in their lives. Nevertheless, the standards I held for my self left me still critical of my own ways of being.

Toward the end of this most disheartening period of the Hatchet Lady's reign, a friend told me about a creative arts therapist with whom she had started working. She described a session in which she had, scribbling intently, covered sheets and sheets of paper with angry red and black crayon and pastel. Then, while shouting ragefully, she'd torn sheet after colored sheet into jagged confetti. Afterward, she and the therapist processed the experience and came to the end of their session. Then, my friend got to leave the therapist's studio **without** cleaning up **any** of the mess she'd made.

Some inner part of me started shouting **Yes! Yes!** I didn't understand why this felt so right to me, but I **knew** that I needed to call that therapist and try working with her. I called the very next day and saw her before that week ended. It was **such** a right and life-changing choice. This wise woman was able to be for me what I had been for my clients. She found ways to encourage me to give my self permission to be me, just as I might be at any moment. In her studio, she offered the safety and unconditional acceptance I had never before been given. (Or, perhaps, never been given in ways that I could trust and be ready to let in.)

In some fantasy work – while dreaming to music – I discovered the tiny, exuberant and vibrant little being that I had been before the early damaging experiences had begun. I felt her breaking free into my consciousness and I adored her. I couldn't imagine being anything but fiercely protective of this precious creature who seemed to know just what she needed, just what was right for her. I could hear her speaking in my heart. I wanted nothing more than to listen to and to take really good care of her. (For the story of this process, see **The Little Ones Story**, page 9.)

Taking this Little One home with me, I began, at last, the process I had been teaching my clients about for years. I started becoming a fiercely protective, compassionate, unconditionally loving Mommy to **all** the parts of my self. I could no longer allow the Hatchet Lady to be mean to these vulnerable parts of me. I even began to work with that inner critic, to talk with her, to find out what she needed from me so that she might stop being awful toward me.

As I practiced mothering my self in this new way, I continued meeting with that therapist over a period of almost three years. The Little One and I called our intermittent meetings with her our play therapy. It was wonderful to have someone who had magical toys and who was delighted to have us come and play in her space. It was also mind-boggling to have permission (for what seemed the first time in our life) to make messes that we didn't have to clean up our selves.

It's been a long, slow, layer-by-layer process to come to this place where, these days, I can almost always delight in my self all the ways that I am (even when I'm in the most crabby, whiny, pissy places). In the more than 29 years since I first met the Little One inside of me, I've been living the practice that, before then, I could only teach to others.

It never ceases to amaze me how much more richly we all grow and flourish when we work on being kinder, gentler and more loving with our selves; when we practice being more accepting and – in the safe spaces we create for our selves – more permitting of **all** the ways that we are. We **all** deserve this sort of treatment from our selves, as much of the time as we **possibly** can give it. And, we deserve it **most especially** when we think that we probably don't deserve it at all.

Consider treating your self with exquisite tenderness and acceptance.

2-12. Speak Kindly to Your Self

Remember to speak softly, kindly and lovingly to your self!

On a summer weekend when I was around 9 or 10 years old, my family went to visit some close relatives in their country cottage out at the end of Long Island. We all tramped out to the beach one day, everyone's arms filled with all sorts of picnic and sit-on-the-sand stuff. For whatever reason, I chose to walk along the edge of a tarred road up a little rise from the path that everyone else was on. As we all chattered away, I was looking over my left shoulder toward my cousins rather than watching the road ahead of me.

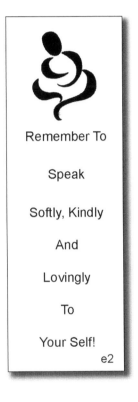

Remember To

Speak

Softly, Kindly

And

Lovingly

To

Your Self!

e2

Suddenly I was in excruciating pain. I had walked, head on, into the corner of a rusty stop sign. My hands flew up to cover my right eye and cheek as I howled with pain and terror, dropping whatever I'd been carrying. My mother came up the incline, roughly pulled my hands from my face and began screaming at me. "Stop making such a racket! It's only a little cut on your cheek! From the way you're carrying on, you'd think you'd taken your eye out!" When I couldn't stop my convulsive sobbing she began shaking me by my shoulders as she continued to scream at me to "Just stop it! Stop it this instant or I'll really give you something to cry about!" And, "If you'd look where you were going, things like this wouldn't happen to you!"

I understand, from friends who are mothers, that such behavior is not necessarily that extraordinary or bizarre. Getting angry with her child can be in the emotional mix of the agitated upset a mother feels when, for example, her child has run out into the street and nearly been hit by a car. Still, this was just another moment in a, by then, infinite stream of experiences I'd had of my mother raging at me when I came to her hurt, sick, terrified or needy.

The grown-up in me understands that my neediness, terror and pain frightened and overwhelmed her. The grown-up in me understands that she was so ill equipped emotionally that rage/anger was, generally, her only available response when she felt threatened by my upsets/injuries. The grown-up in me understands that she was in fact doing the best she could, given her own damaged, stunted emotional capacities.

Still, the child that I was in those years was repeatedly devastated and tyrannized by the screamed recriminations, the threats and mean responses that came when she went to her mommy seeking solace. When I'd come hurt or sick, her responses invariably led me to feel it was my own fault, my own stupidity or carelessness that was responsible for my predicament. Or, her reactions made it clear that she thought I was "making a big deal out of nothing." Or, that I was malingering. In all cases, the message was that I deserved no sympathy.

The legacy of these interactions was an awful one. I would feel terrified whenever I'd hurt my self. Then, I would be petrified by my own terror because I had no safe place to go for support or comfort. I learned that I had to find ways to handle all of it by my self. As a young child, though, I had no real resources to do that. I developed an internal version of my angry, belittling mother's voice that yelled at me even when I was all by my self with my pain. It was all I knew to do.

For much of my life I met every accident or illness that befell me with the same meanness that I'd experienced from my mother. Every trip or fall or bump-into-something (and over the years there were many) would have me calling my self stupid, careless, klutzy. I'd feel full of guilt every time I'd get sick with a cold or flu, unsure whether I was malingering, not really as sick as I felt, worried that my illness might be a manipulation on my part.

With anyone else in similarly distressing plights, I would be tender and sympathetic, solicitous and compassionate. Only with my self was I so negating and so harsh.

This mean, unforgiving way of speaking to my self extended beyond the times of physical trauma. Any of my emotional upsets, any mistakes I made, any slips or forgetfulness, any social mishaps, etc. – all these called forth in me reactions that were equally critical and unsympathetic. My response to my self was typically the very opposite of what I needed and craved. It was the opposite, as well, of what I freely offered to any and everyone else.

When someone treated me compassionately or solicitously in these moments that I saw as lapses, I'd feel guilty, fearful that I had somehow manipulated them into this undeserved caring toward me. Or, on the other hand, I might feel irritated by what I saw as their being patronizing. Needless to say, these reactions of mine confused everyone who might act caringly toward me.

When at 43, in the depths of despair, I first uncovered and began to connect with the Little One inside me, this awful pattern began to change. The precious, delightful little creature inside of me stirred a love, compassion and caring for her/my self that I had never before imagined being able to feel.

Suddenly, it was unthinkable to allow anyone, **including me,** to be mean or harsh with my self. For the first time in my life I found permission to speak as lovingly and kindly to my own hurt, upset, imperfect self as I'd always spoken to others. (See **The Little Ones Story**, page 9 for more about this.) The more lovingly I treated my self, the more kindly and sweetly I spoke to my self, the more I began to blossom and grow. The transformation that began with that phenomenal shift has led me to the who that I now am.

Along the way to here, I've come to understand that no one ever deserves to be spoken to cruelly, to be undermined by words, to be denied a sympathetic hearing. And, I've come to trust (despite what our culture would have us believe) that more real change grows from tender nurture than from drill-sergeant-like blastings of criticism or ridicule.

Along the way to here, I've learned that speaking with love even to the parts of me that have mean, nasty, self-serving thoughts and feelings helps me to grow. When I am kind with these usually abandoned, angry and unhappy selves, they feel safe enough to reveal their woundings to me. Then, I am able to help them find healthy ways to release their pain and to begin to heal.

Along the way to here, I've learned to talk generously to my self even when I'm somewhere or doing something that I don't like for me to be being or doing. Only when I caringly allow my self to be where I am while I'm there, can I ever move beyond that there to somewhere else.

Along the way to here, I've learned the language of tenderness toward my self. When I fall, trip, stumble, fumble, spill or break something, inadvertently (or sometimes advertently) or do something that hurts or upsets someone else – I hold my self and say, "Poor Honey!" And, "I'm so sorry you're hurting/upset/unhappy that you did that!" And "It's okay, Honey, we can make it right/fix it/tell the truth!" And, "I'm right here with you Sweetie, we'll be okay!" And sometimes I rock and rock and cry and cry. And, I feel really, really sorry for my sad little self and let her feel really, really sorry for her self until she's done with feeling that way.

It's not easy to change a lifetime of mistreating our selves in the ways we've been mistreated by others. Still, beginning consciously to choose to speak kindly to our selves in all the moments of our lives is a practice that can and does begin to turn the tide. In the middle of starting such a practice, it's especially important to speak caringly to our selves when we notice that we've slipped into speaking cruelly to our selves!

Consider talking tenderly and gently to your self as much of the time as you possibly can.

Part Three:
Keeping Safe through the Difficult Times

When we're in the middle of intense and challenging times, it becomes even more urgent than usual for us to have compassion for our selves: for us to be tender and loving toward our frazzled, stressed or feeling-stuck selves.

It is especially important to remember that we each have our own rhythm and style with which we process crises and impasses. It isn't okay to use anyone else's way as a standard against which to measure our progress.

It's important to remember that what look like detours, avoidance, and running away may simply be ways we are taking exactly the time that we need in order to get to the next place.

When change is accelerating and everything is moving very quickly, it helps to try living in the very thinnest slice of now that we can define.

It helps, as well, to remember that pulling the covers over our head and feeling sorry for our selves can be very relieving and helpful respite. It's one sure way of taking a rest before we go back into the fray.

The Madwoman

*(Written in the earliest days of the 40+year journey
that has led me to the spaces where I now live and write.)*

There is a madwoman who, naked and alone, lies on the beach whenever the sun shines. Greased with oils and floured with a fine spray of sand, her full body glows golden brown. Breathing with the breaking waves, tuned to the hum of that earth place, she is soaring on the winds: sensing, exploring, gathering strange and tantalizing networks of information. If you listen with the proper ear you can hear she is talking to herself inside the opalescent haze.

The madwoman and I have lived together for 35 years. For 32 of those years I have played the part of her keeper. Thanklessly and dutifully I have tried to contain her, to restrain her from visiting her madness on the world. On the whole, I fear, I haven't done quite as well as I've meant. Like a mischievous child she is wont to pop up, sticking out her tongue, making obscene faces and weird noises just when I'm sure I've finally gotten her tightly in hand. Inopportune to say the least.

Still, sometimes I've been able to feel both fascinated and tickled by the ingenious ways she finds to make her presence felt no matter what I do to hide her. Perhaps that in some way accounts for the more recent developments in our life together. The balance has changed between us. I've grown less afraid for her and less afraid of her. I've grown weary of the cat and mouse games we've played, tired of draining my energy to build a proper fortress to contain her – especially since none I've built were ever in the least way adequate. Sooner or later, I was left there, sweating, holding tight the cell door only to discover she was already outside, cavorting some place or other. She is quite an artist of escape and escapade.

She has now become my protector. But, while I as keeper tried to hold her in, she seems to be a guide for getting me out of our drama and into strange and wonderful new worlds of experience. Always before it's been excruciating to accept the student position. I needed to structure the teachers' teaching in my own manner before incorporating it. Still, the madwoman's method is Socratic and infinitely patient. She leads me gently to the edge of discovery and waits without expectation until I dare to open my eyes.

A strange and marvelous sense of adoration for the madwoman fills me – I for whom loving has been such a challenge. In the past, I've feared the vulnerability of loving, the loss of the power I needed to keep her contained. Now I'm romantic, tantalized, fascinated – totally absorbed in this crazy lady.

Songs of The Madwoman

I

I hear the songs of the madwoman
The moon-mother-goddess power
Within me
Within all women.
The holocaust has started
She is rising
Howling
Shrieking with joy!
And I am
Allowing
Knowing
Being with
Her power
The power
That comes with letting go.
I am becoming
The madwoman–mother–child I was born to be
I am becoming a wild woman-child in the world.
And Great Mother guides me through
The threshold
To the wisdom of madness

II

The madwoman has wrested the controls
We are careening
A mad roller coaster ride
Hair and scarf tangles
Riding gales of shrieking laughter.
See me here
Plastered to the ceiling
By the forces of my own gravity.
Features distorted in terror

Held back
By the straining to be free.
I fish
My intellect a net
To gather in the turbulence –
A holy war
My endless crusade
Counting fingers and toes
I make my self real
Reeling in the force of her
Blasting me
Fragments of oblivion
Terrified
Plasticine and Thorazine my weapons

Her head is always just beyond
The reach of my mace.

I am being run away with,
Is this panic my fear
Of delight.

3-1. Safe for Feelings

The thing to do with feelings is to make it safe to feel all of them!

Walking through the arcade area at the San Francisco Airport some years ago on my way to the restrooms, I was listening to a loudly screaming little person. So was everyone else I passed, most of them indignantly shaking their heads. Almost all wore expressions of outrage that such emotional excess/noise was being allowed by some presumably incompetent parent.

The Thing To Do

With Feelings

Is To Make It

Safe

To Feel All

Of Them!

o2

As I rounded the corner to the restrooms, after walking almost half the length of that part of the terminal hearing the powerful little lungs sending out rage, I came to the source her self. A little being in overalls, probably about two years old, lay roaring and kicking on the carpet near the wall behind an escalator. Three or four feet away, amid bags and suitcases, holding the little person's jacket, stood a serene looking woman in her mid-late thirties. Leaning nonchalantly on the chest high wall, she watched the screaming little one, her expression tender.

As I passed near them, the racket stopped – as abruptly as if a switch had been flipped. The little one lifted her head, looked up at the mom who asked, in a gentle voice, "Are you finished now, honey?" The little one's face broke into a huge grin as she shyly but energetically nodded her head. All the while, a steady stream of glaring head-shakers passed by unnoticed by either of the two.

I was captivated: awed by what I had witnessed, amazed at the love and comfort both with self and intense emotion that seemed involved in mothering that way. How different that child's world was (and would be) from what I and almost everyone in my world had known. I found my self wishing we'd all been given such open, accepting space for being our selves; for feeling our feelings as they were happening inside of us; for knowing that expressing our strongest emotions could be safe and acceptable; for discovering that feelings, felt, do resolve.

Leaving the restroom stall, I passed the mother diapering her child on the fold-down baby station. The two of them were laughing and being silly together. I stopped to share with the woman how moved I was by her calm patience as she stood letting her child's temper tantrum run itself out; how astonishing it had been to watch her do that while so many people walked by "Harrumphing" with the judgment of our culture. The woman smiled, shrugged her shoulders and said, "What else is there to do?"

Over the years, this experience has become my favorite teaching story about feelings: about how they really are, about how we might be with them, about what we might do with them if we are to heal our selves into wholeness. It's a story that sets in relief the false messages our culture has given us about emotions and how our beings have been damaged/stunted by those messages.

Feelings are a natural part of being human, of living in a body. They come in response to our inner and outer experiences of the present moment, in response to memories of past experiences evoked by the present moment or in response to our anticipation of moments yet to come.

We don't need to know **why** we're feeling what we're feeling in order to have the emotion. (We don't **even** have to know **what** we're feeling in order to feel it.) There's no way a feeling can itself be wrong or bad (although we may feel badly). A feeling just is.

And, it's **always** a lie when anyone (including your own critical self) tells you "You can't possibly be feeling (fill-in-the-blank) about that!" or "You have no reason to be feeling that way," or "You shouldn't feel so (fill-in-the-blank)."

Feelings of any sort don't go on forever. When we can give our selves safe, protected space and our own permission to be in the middle of whatever we're feeling, it does run its course. Often, this takes longer than we (and others around us) may think it should.

As we practice engaging with each emotion, with its energy in our consciousness and in our body, as we find ways to release its intensity (by crying, yelling, stomping, banging, rocking, drawing, writing, etc.) and ways to comfort our selves in the midst of the storm, each particular experience of grief, sadness, rage, terror does come to an end. Sometimes it comes to an end because **we're** exhausted. Other times, it comes to an end because we've exhausted that emotion for the moment, having felt our way through it.

Each time we can break the cultural taboos against taking our emotions seriously by choosing to respect our right to have them or by allowing our selves to feel them for as long as we feel them, we are reclaiming more of our natural wholeness.

Remember to be kind and compassionate with your self as you practice making space to feel your feelings.

3-2. Covers Over Our Heads

*Sometimes the best thing to do is to give your self permission
to pull the covers over your head and to feel sorry for
your self – just until you're good and ready to stop!
(And, you really will be ready to stop sometime!)*

In the spring of my 42nd year I began the years-long journey of extricating my self from an intense, symbiotic seven-year relationship. What had started as a love that took me to never explored edges of my being had become a painful enmeshment in which I'd gradually lost the threads of connection with my inner self.

We were both experiencing the deadening undertow of what we had become together. For a long while despair and frustration paralyzed both of us. We spun round and round in repeated, ultimately useless attempts to fix our selves, each other and the relationship. Consultations with a therapist only deepened the morass.

That June, in desperation and terror I packed my clothes and papers into the van in which I had once lived and tried to leave. I unpacked back into our house later that same day, too panicked to go ahead and take the step of leaving. Two more days of anguish (and the mounting terror of staying) finally allowed me to repack the van and drive away in the blistering heat of an Ojai summer day.

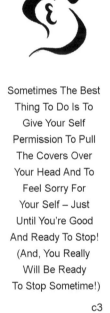

Sometimes The Best
Thing To Do Is To
Give Your Self
Permission To Pull
The Covers Over
Your Head And To
Feel Sorry For
Your Self – Just
Until You're Good
And Ready To Stop!
(And, You Really
Will Be Ready
To Stop Sometime!)

c3

At first I lived in the van parked in my friends' driveway with access to their air-conditioned garage-office and guest bathroom. Then, I found a partly furnished guest apartment on a ranch where I could live rent-free in exchange for feeding a large menagerie of physically challenged animals and birds.

Except when I was seeing clients or feeding the animals I was unable to stop crying. Breathing was a struggle: I'd stand in doorways and force my self to exhale so that inhaling would become a possibility.

I would occasionally, for a moment or two, recover a small scrap of my once familiar balance. Then, a phone call with my ex would catapult me back into the anguish and terror. It was as if we'd been conjoined twins and the outcome of our separation surgery was in doubt. Did we each have enough of an internal life support system to survive? That I had done the actual leaving mattered not at all; I felt abandoned and bereft, completely betrayed by the loving.

Never before had my capacity to function been so undermined. Never before had I been so unable to find or feel my own strength and wholeness. Never as an adult had I felt so devastated, so helpless in my anguish.

It took all the energy I had to drag my self through the day. Typically a night owl, I'd crawl into bed at 8:30 or 9:00 P.M. I packed lots of pillows all around me and literally pulled the covers over my head. I rocked and wept and thought I'd never get through the pain and suffering. I howled and keened and slept and dreamed.

And, I felt unremittingly sorry for my self. It didn't occur to me to think that this wasn't okay or that it was weak or self-indulgent, useless or unproductive. I seemed to have no choice in the matter of how I felt just then. Thinking positively was beyond me, even though it had, before this, been my usual way of coping with challenging times. I was entirely out of cope, bereft of hope.

I surrendered into the feeling sorry for my self. It felt comforting and nourishing. It felt real and appropriate. It felt compassionate and caring to the broken, wounded parts of me. It went on for a very long time. After a while, it became more of an intermittent experience. In between covers-over-the-head times there were occasional hopeful moments, brief flashes of feeling that survival and resurrection might be possible. Gradually, there were more and more of these hopeful moments and, after that, longer and longer hopeful periods between shorter and shorter sieges of feeling sorry for my self. At some point I noticed I no longer had anything about which I needed to feel sorry for my self. (In that growing season, at least.)

Giving way to feeling sorry for my self had always before seemed a dangerous entry into a downward spiral from which there would be no return. Everything I was ever taught inspired this fear of "giving in" to feeling bad. In the past, I'd had the strength and energy to fight the pull to collapse into feeling bad. I'd get busy, do constructive things or get into doing for others (how many articles about depression counsel just this!).

In this extremely trying time, when my suffering was too severe for me to use my old ways, I experienced a powerful and liberating truth. Feeling bad, feeling sorry for my self, is not dangerous, not the start of a spiral into hopelessness. When I can surrender into the middle of it while being tender and compassionate with my aching, wounded self, it is a process: a path to my deepest self, a doorway to healing.

We live in a culture in which feeling bad, sad, despairing, grieving or depressed leads us to feel like a pariah, a carrier of some awful contagion. We are everywhere and every way encouraged to get over it: take an anti-depressant; think positively; focus on envisioning better feelings; don't be a drag on our friends/family/colleagues by showing our sad faces. Submitting to this inexorable pressure leads us to close off from the rich, empowering discoveries that come from compassionately embracing our darker moments. It also keeps us from discovering the truth that the only real way out of hard feelings is **through them**!

Consider taking some time for pulling the covers over your head, curling up with a teddy bear and feeling sorry for your self the next time you're having a hard time.

(Lesley Hazelton's *The Right to Feel Bad*, SARK's *Transformation Soup* and Elizabeth Lesser's *Broken Open* offer words – if you want them – to help support you as you risk being with the darker moments and risk feeling sorry for your self.)

3-3. Safe Space to Scream

When you give your self permission to find and use a safe place to scream, rant, rave and stomp when you're angry, you'll find a way to communicate your feelings in the situation that stirred them!

The woman who raised me was filled with anger and bitterness that she frequently and unpredictably poured out on me. The flashes of her rage, in their heat or their iciness, devastated me. I would, each time, feel flayed: reduced to a cold, hard, walnut-sized knot suspended in a dark, freezing emptiness inside my skin.

For many of my earliest years I had a frequently recurring nightmare of standing, terrified, on a huge white parchment-like surface that was tearing and curling up over my little self while my mother's icy rage-filled voice relentlessly reverberated around and within me.

As I grew into my teens and her meanness toward me became more extreme, rage at her started to grow inside me. My agonizing experiences of having her anger directed at me made it impossible for me to consider doing that to anyone one else, including her. I couldn't yell back. Instead, I would flee to my room, close my door, stuff my pillow over my mouth and keep screaming "I hate you!" and "Leave me alone!"

When You Give Your Self Permission To Find And Use A Safe Place To Scream, Rant, Rave And Stomp When You're Angry, You'll Find A Way To Communicate Your Feelings In The Situation That Stirred Them!

s3

Even this imploded exploding terrified me. So, fairly quickly, I learned to cut it off inside of me by "understanding" that my mother was a disturbed and damaged person, incapable of behaving more humanely. I promised my self I would never get that angry about anything or spill anger onto anyone. I would rather have died than become an angry, mean person like her. I felt so virtuous as, through the first 30 years of my life, I never got angry.

Instead, I ignored or made excuses for others' mistreatment of me. I was understanding and forgiving. I rose above the messy unpleasantness of conflict. I obeyed both my own personal commitment to my self and the overriding imperative of the larger culture: "good/nice girls don't get angry." Not surprisingly, I suffered periods of depression and self-loathing. (When we cut off from parts of our authentic selves, that loss of connection often manifests in our consciousness in just these ways.)

In my mid-thirties, as I began on a path of conscious spirituality, the culture's "nice girls don't get angry" message was overlaid by the "enlightened beings don't get angry" message of New Age philosophies. Beguiled by the light, I mostly evaded the darkness of anger. The familiar darkness of despair and depression was generally more comfortable, more acceptable to me.

Despite this three-layered suppression of anger, something would periodically seethe inside my belly bringing hateful thoughts and litanies into my head. I called this my craziness and struggled to abort or nullify it. Instead of feeling this anger, I would leave the situations and people that were stirring the unacceptable feelings in me.

In my early forties, I met and began a deep friendship with a woman wise in the ways of anger. Her ease and comfort with her own and others' angry feelings caught my attention. She didn't blow up at people when she was angry. She didn't walk away from conflict. She expressed her anger without meanness, without saying damaging things to the person with whom she was angry. I had never before experienced that as a possibility; it fascinated me.

She refused to believe that I never got angry about anything. **That** angered me – at least at first. Then, her disbelief became a doorway. Through her mentoring, I learned that anger is a normal part of everyone's emotional repertoire, neither good nor bad in and of itself. I opened to the startling possibility that anger could be felt and expressed without devastating me or the person with whom I might be angry.

The key here was recognizing that anger is both an energy and a content and that these two components are separable. We can work with the energetic portion by doing something physical to release it. We can do this releasing in ways that are **safe:** by our selves rather than on other people.

We can scream, rant, rave, or curse (in our cars in the slow lane, if it's not private enough elsewhere in our worlds). We can do that stomping around the house or we can do it while having a heel kicking, fist-pounding tantrum on our beds. We can (kneeling beside them) beat on cushions or our mattress with our hands clasped into a single fist, beat at door jams with a beanbag pillow or slam balls against a backboard with a tennis racket. We can beat on drums or gongs (this and screaming in my car worked best for me). We can make safe places to break things we gather just for this purpose (plates from Goodwill/garage sales or glass bottles we're going to recycle) or pound on scrap wood with hammers. (Beating a repeatedly malfunctioning calculator to smithereens with a hammer was exhilarating!) We can throw rocks at boulders or into water. We can tear or shred paper or fabric we've set aside to use just for this. Whatever we choose to do, we need to be careful that it not physically hurt us in the doing. Otherwise, we're giving our selves permission for the releasing while (with the hurt) punishing our selves for doing it.

If you consider exploring your angers, experimenting with how it feels to release some of that energy in any of these ways, it's good to think about whether it might feel better/safer to buddy with a friend, alternating being witness for each other. If actually doing some releasing activity feels too scary, just playing with visualizing the doing helps move us along. Remember to go slowly and to breathe while you do any of it. Start with just a few seconds of it and, as you get more comfortable, gradually add more time. Having palpitations, feeling anxious, sobbing or laughing hysterically are all likely possible accompaniments. Stop, take breaks, go on to other things and come back another time. Don't push. Baby (or even nano-) steps are the rule for starting on this journey. (This kind of energy releasing can also be done as a daily practice like teeth-brushing as a way to unpack years of unexpressed anger/rage.)

When we've blown the energy out for the moment, or done as much of this as we feel ready to do just now, the content of our anger typically becomes clearer to us. We can see just what triggered it. Knowing this, we can explore what it is we need to do differently in the situation where it was stirred. Or, see what it is we need to communicate to the people with whom our anger was stirred. We can do this straightforwardly and calmly without fear that the unaddressed energy of our anger will spill out.

Remember, when we women express the content of our anger, we often cry or fill with tears. It is important to know (and let the people you're confronting know) that the tears **do not** take away from the anger we are communicating.

Consider taking time to be with and release the energy of your anger in ways that feel safe.

3-4. Owning Our Fears

When you can openly name and own your right to your own fears – without apology… You give your self permission to be just where you are… And, you honor your capacity to "be there" for your fearful parts. This always deepens your sense of your own strength and empoweredness!

One beautiful early fall weekend some years ago, my friend Cynthia and I set out on what was, for each of us, our first backpack trip without a more experienced guide along. She'd been on her first backpacking trip earlier that summer with her son as guide. I had been on three trips with different women Vision Quest guides some years before.

We'd had fun shopping for (and then deciding to return some of) the equipment we needed to fill in for what our guides had contributed to our earlier trips. We'd read an article that taught us how to jerry-rig our own bear-proof containers using lengths of PVC pipe and PVC end plugs. We'd negotiated about food, organized and packed everything we could imagine needing for any emergency. We weighed and divided our equipment, supplies and food into two piles of roughly 35 pounds each. We had our topographic maps, compasses and whistles – all the right stuff. We were both excited, eager and only a little bit edgy about the stretching we were each about to do.

When You Can Openly Name And Own Your Right To Your Own Fears – Without Apology… You Give Your Self Permission To Be Just Where You Are… And, You Honor Your Capacity To "Be There" For Your Fearful Parts. This Always Deepens Your Sense Of Your Own Strength And Empoweredness!

o8

Our first day of driving, arriving and setting up our initial camp (in the vicinity of the car), went easily and well. We spent the night at 6000 feet practicing with all our gear and getting acclimatized to the altitude.

Next morning, we began to pack our way up to the camp at 8000 feet where we expected to spend three days. The weather was glorious, the skies filled with dramatic clouds, the sun bright and the air a little nippy. It was exhilarating to be on our way. For the first twenty minutes, that is.

At that point, it became obvious that the trail was going to be a relentlessly steep and narrow one. The boulders of the mountain loomed on one side; a sheer precipice fell away at the other. A precipice without even the smallest bit of chaparral to mask its edge: a huge test for me.

Just the tiniest veil of low shrubs gives me a sense of groundedness when I'm walking near a cliff edge. When there's nothing at all between the drop and me, I walk with low-level terror as my companion. With a heavy pack and the steepness of the grade adding to the struggle of keeping my self balanced and grounded, the usual level of my terror escalated. It was hard to revel in the magnificence and beauty all around me. It took almost all of my energy to keep walking and to keep my eyes away from the edge.

And, I kept walking-two-ways-at-once. My anticipatory dread of the steep-downhill-return-trip-with-pack to come kept adding to the terror I was experiencing on the uphill climb. Coping with the weight of my fear on top of the weight of my pack was exhausting. I kept talking gently to my petrified self. I promised her we could stop and turn around any time we felt we couldn't handle it anymore.

Despite the terror, I wanted to get to camp in the alpine meadow ahead. So, I practiced going very, very slowly with many, many breaks – each for however long my frightened self needed in order to be ready to move again. I kept gently reminding my self not to be walking two ways at once. I kept giving Cynthia updates on how I was doing. And, I kept making sure I still had her agreement that she'd turn back with me at any point.

We did **a lot** of stopping and resting. At some point we were stopping almost 15 minutes for every 10 minutes of walking. Though Cynthia wasn't frightened by the edge, she was more than happy to be stopping to rest as often as my fearful self and I wanted. Her pack, like mine, seemed to be getting heavier and heavier as we climbed. And, as my most regular hiking buddy, she already knew and was sympathetic to how scary physical edge-walking was for me.

Then, the worst happened. We met an eight-mule pack train with four horsemen coming downhill and had to move off the trail to let them pass. That meant standing on the very edge of the precipice. The grumpy, brusque leader of the train was impatient with me as I very slowly tried to find some secure footing on the small, rocky outcropping at the edge of the drop. I was almost frozen when he told me I'd have to take off my pack because it/I was too close to the trail and likely to spook one of the more skittish mules into shying. Cynthia, standing further out at the edge, helped me out of the pack. Then, I collapsed to the ground in a petrified puddle as the mules and horsemen passed by.

It took a while to put my self together enough to crawl back onto the trail, slow the adrenaline and get Cynthia's help putting my pack back on. Amazingly, when I checked, the inner consensus was still to continue on. So we did.

When we crested the mountain and arrived at the meadow surrounded by pine forest and ringed with yet higher mountains, it felt well worth the struggle.   It was awesome and completely our own private domain. The campsite was near a creek, had a huge downed tree trunk that would do perfectly as a counter on which to set up our kitchen and another smaller trunk that would work as a backrest for sitting. Upturned roots provided hooks for all sorts of miscellany.

A small, deserted nearby weather observation cabin with a tiny sheltered entry proved immediately useful. Just as we stood there, gaping at the beauty, the clouds broke open in a downpour with thunder and lightning.   Both of us and our as yet unopened packs fit neatly under the entry for the half-hour of dramatic storming.

The storm left as suddenly as it had arrived and we began the business of setting up camp, filtering water, and preparing our evening meal. We managed to get a small fire going for a little while.

Once we gave up on the damp fire and crawled into our sleeping bags in the tent, we discovered that our sleeping bags were not fulfilling their promise: our feet were freezing. Making foot pocket linings out of our Mylar emergency blankets warmed our toes but set us off into hysterical cackling as they crackled raucously at any slight movement. Our cackling led to each of us having to wriggle out of bag and tent to pee. Of course, that led to more uproarious cackling and crackling. In the midst of all this we heard cowbells. It wasn't an auditory hallucination. We peeked out and saw a herd of cattle grazing in the meadow. More cackling, it was hysterical. My earlier fear and panic seemed distant. (I still celebrated my Little One for having been able to make it up to the meadow despite how scary it had been for her.)

When we were finally warm enough and quieted enough to say goodnight, I was surprised not to be fast asleep in my typical five minutes. Instead, I found my self overwhelmed with a resurgence of fears. I worried that it might rain again over the days we planned to stay up here, making the already terrifyingly steep, narrow, edgy downhill trail muddy and slippery. The cowbells and the lowing of the cattle kept coming closer as I lay there getting more and more anxious about the trail. Then, I started to be afraid that the cattle might wander into our camp and trample us as we slept. I felt claustrophobic and vulnerable in our tiny little tent.

The Mommy part of me was there watching as I moved from anxiety and terror into what was rapidly becoming a full blown panic attack. That part kept holding me, rocking me. She kept talking gently and lovingly to me, acknowledging how really overwhelmed I was feeling, how scary this all was being for me. She reminded me that I was not alone, that she was with me and would stay with me.

The panicking part felt a desperate need to be down from the mountain, back near the car, back to where it was safe. She wanted to leave that very moment even though she knew it was not possible or safe to go then. She could hardly breathe. She was afraid to wake or to share her panic with Cynthia; afraid that the intensity of her panic, so rare and unusual in her, would frighten Cynthia. If her panic frightened Cynthia, she would feel even more overwhelmed.

The Mommy reminded her that Cynthia was not like her biological mother, that Cynthia probably wouldn't get terrified by the Little One's terrors. And, the Mommy let her know she didn't have to tell Cynthia now, in the middle of it, if that was too scary. The Mommy promised the petrified one again and again that she would stay with her no matter how frightened the Little One was. She crooned and soothed and promised her that we could tell Cynthia in the morning that we had to go back down the mountain. That we would, together with Cynthia, figure out a way to do that safely. That we could even ask Cynthia to make two trips and take our pack down for us if we couldn't do it our self.

The Mommy kept reminding us to breathe out so that we would be able to breathe in. She reminded us to breathe slowly, deep into our belly. She reminded us that she loved us so much, that it was okay to feel scared whether or not there **really** was anything scary happening, that she would never leave us alone with our fears or be angry at us for having them – no matter what. Gradually my body relaxed from its clenching. The panicked, exhausted Little One began to calm and finally drifted into sleep.

When I woke in the morning, the cattle were very close but had miraculously kept outside some invisible perimeter. It was another glorious day. I wasn't feeling terrified, but I still felt sure I needed to get off the mountain early on in the day. Over breakfast I shared the saga of my night with an astonished Cynthia. She was absolutely willing to break camp and head down as soon as I needed to leave. And equally willing to help deal with my pack if I needed her to do that.

We took a short breathtaking hike further up the mountain (with only our fanny packs on) before heading downhill with all our gear. Of course, the downhill trip turned out to be a piece of cake: the trail was dry and hard, didn't feel nearly as steep going down as it had seemed it might as we made our way up and, this time, we didn't meet up with any mule-trains.

Setting up camp in the valley at 6000 feet, I felt sort of blue that I had needed for us to come down. I felt a little sheepish about having been so panicked at the prospect of a downhill trip that was, in fact, not particularly difficult. But, the Mommy reminded me, it didn't matter that it had turned out to be so much easier than I'd thought; it didn't matter that there was nothing to be afraid of after all.

What mattered was that we had listened to the fears we were having, honored them, taken them seriously, and taken good care of our self in the middle of them. It mattered that we had asked our friend to be as respectful as we were of our fears and that she had been. It mattered that neither we nor Cynthia had tried to belittle or to talk us out of our fears. We had made it safe to be afraid, no matter what was so on the outside.

It is **such** a huge and empowering step to openly own our right to our fears, to name them, to honor them without apology or excuse or shame. It is how we can begin to stop abandoning our frightened selves. It is how we can say, "No! That's not the truth" to anyone (including parts of our selves) who would think less of us for being fearful, for having fears. It's not fear that we need to be afraid of (with all due respect to Franklin Delano Roosevelt) it's our fear of fear. When we commit to listening to our fearful self and to helping her find safety, she begins to trust our care-giving enough to risk walking her edges. This always helps her grow stronger.

All the me's of me learned so much, grew so much and did so much healing of early woundings in the middle of this scary experience. It was exciting to be able, at last, to be taking such good care of my frightened self. And, an added bonus of the journey is that I have learned not to walk two ways at once when going up steep trails.

Consider being gently respectful and loving with the fearful parts of your self.

3-5. Comforting Our Selves

When the wounded parts of you feel sad, frightened, unhappy, lonely or yearning... It's almost always your own attention and comforting they are needing. Practice taking time and space just to listen to those parts with the same gentle, loving patience with which you'd listen to the distresses of any beloved friend!

Like so many women, I was raised by a woman whose own emotional limitations and damage left her unable to cope adequately with mothering me. Like so many of us who were poorly or damagingly mothered by such women, I grew up dedicated to trying to mother my mother into wholeness. Even without words or language I and others in this cohort grasped early on that our mothers felt overwhelmed, traumatized or enraged by our needs, pains and fears. Like so many of us, I became precociously adept at protecting my mother from my normal childhood dependencies in order to be safer in her presence. To do this required cutting off from conscious awareness of my own needs.

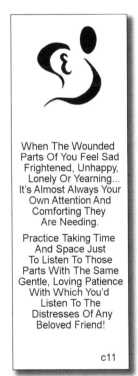

When The Wounded Parts Of You Feel Sad Frightened, Unhappy, Lonely Or Yearning... It's Almost Always Your Own Attention And Comforting They Are Needing.

Practice Taking Time And Space Just To Listen To Those Parts With The Same Gentle, Loving Patience With Which You'd Listen To The Distresses Of Any Beloved Friend!

c11

In this process I, like other women in this cohort, became fiercely independent well before that was developmentally appropriate. (Or socially prescribed.) We became highly empathic: sensitive to and committed to nurturing our supposed nurturer's unnamed neediness. From the shape of our own unacknowledged starvation we understood what these hungry women might need. As remarkably good babies, girls and women we've spent and spend much of our lives being tuned to the unspoken neediness not only in them but, as well, in anyone else who might cross our path. Often we are particularly tuned and responsive to the needs of those who are in roles (supposedly) of providing for us: teachers, mentors, boyfriends, husbands, mates, etc.

We've developed the capacity to anticipate and subtly attend to comforting and nurturing others without their ever having to own either the fact of their neediness or of our tending to it. In our secret hearts, we keep believing that our loving will heal the other into wholeness. A wholeness that we (often less than consciously) imagine will allow them then to nurture and love us back in this same way. The sad truth is that this never happens and they never do.

We become chronic, knee jerk nurturers. Everywhere we go, we are recognized as intuitive, caring and generous "Mommies." In our disconnected and self-serving world, this endears us to a great many people. The people whom we nurture typically see us as sources of limitless caring, complete unto our selves, unlikely to need anything from folks such as they are. They do not intuit back. They rarely give much of anything to us save the gift of their receiving from us and, occasionally, the gift of their gratitude. This rarely deters us from our ministrations.

Over the years, I've realized that this relentless, driven giving away of what we've never gotten is a secret process by which we try vicariously to nourish our own less than conscious hungers. By secretly identifying with the recipient of our bounty, some little starving parts of us can have the illusion of being lavishly fed. We remain unaware of our own suppressed neediness by focusing on the neediness in others.

In the end, it's a poor bargain. The hungers we attend to in the other are most often based in their early deprivations. These ancient unmet yearnings are locked behind the shield of time; inaccessible to ministrations from anyone outside of the person in whom they live. Satisfying these needs can only be an inside job.

But, from early in our lives it was not safe for us to recognize that we had needs of our own that required tending. So, we often stay trapped in this unsatisfying vicious circling. When feelings of sadness, fear, loneliness, yearning push up toward consciousness, we throw our selves into finding someone else to whom we might tend.

What we are drawn to do for others neither fills us up nor fixes what's broken in them. When it doesn't, they sometimes get angry with us. They believe that our nurturing isn't making them feel better because either we're not doing enough or we're not doing it right. We, on the other side of it, throw our selves more avidly into the tending – until or unless we begin to feel resentful about what appears to be the insatiability of their hunger. The little starveling in us believes that **we** would use such nurturing to much better advantage – were it being given us by someone as loving as we are being. We get resentful that it is always still the other person's turn, that they never get whole enough to give anything to us.

When I dropped out of my complex and successful life in New York City taking to the road westward in my house-on-my-back womb of a van just after my 32nd birthday, I inadvertently broke out of this vicious circling for the first time. (See **Pirouettes**, page 125 for more about that transition.) With only my self to be with and take care of and little else to distract me, I gradually became conscious of the hungers that had been disowned and locked away, stored in my body. As I began to listen to my body, a new emotional landscape emerged into my consciousness.

In this new terrain, unfamiliar longings surfaced: a profound hunger for the mothering I'd never received and till then did not consciously miss; an aching for the comfort of caring, accepting touch that till then had not been a particular yearning; a longing for someone outside of me to love me into loving my self in ways I seemed so incapable of doing by my self: this, too, a possibility that till then had never entered my mind.

I wrote in my journal and spent endless hours with these newly conscious and uncomfortable yearnings, learning how to live in the middle of them. In those first days, I believed that only the unconditional love, care and touch of someone outside my self could ever bring me true healing. At the same time, I couldn't begin to imagine how I would ever find such a person much less how I'd be able to trust such a person were I to find one.

So, I practiced living with these now conscious longings without having much hope of ever having them met. I muddled along making room to immerse my self in feeling the feelings when they rose up. In other moments I continued exploring the rest of the newnesses that were emerging in my on-the-road journeying life. Now that I was aware of and being with my neediness, I was no longer inclined to get involved with people in the old let-me-take-care-of-your-wounds way.

Those early days of experiencing what had been buried below the level of my consciousness came almost ten years before I first connected with the Little One(s) inside. Here and there through those ten years and even afterward, I would occasionally meet someone who appeared to offer me some of that for which I was longing. Inevitably, I would quickly discover how impossible it was for me to trust that what was being offered was real or safe or okay or even healthy to let it in.

For example, someone might offer to hold me while I sobbed. Once in their arms, I'd feel as though I had to hurry up and feel better: so that they would feel that they were being effective; so that they wouldn't feel overwhelmed by my neediness; so that they wouldn't be done with giving to me before I was ready to be on my own with my feelings again. And, I'd worry whether they'd offered only because they assumed I'd say no. If I took them up on this offer I was supposed to reject, would there be a price to pay? Would they be furious with me? Would they humiliate and ridicule me later for needing to be held? What would I have to do to redeem my self in their eyes? How often would I be reminded of "all they did for me?" What would I have to do to make us even again? How would they use this against me? How might they use this to manipulate me? How withholding would they become once I'd allowed my self to lean on them? Or, I might wonder what it was they really wanted from me while they appeared to be giving to me? What were they needing or getting out of this giving? All these questions would come up in an eye blink, more a cascade of fears than actual thoughts.

Every fear and worry I would have was what I had learned to have around my mother's so-called nurturing behaviors. Nothing from anyone else felt any safer. The prospect of adding all this worried obsessing to my already upset self made it much easier to refuse all offers. Being with my upset by my self, just bumbling through, was the only safe, if not fully satisfying alternative.

When I began the process of connecting with and re-mothering the Little One(s) inside, everything about this changed. (**The Little Ones Story**, page 9 and **Coming Home**, page 287 tell that story in more depth.) As soon as I'd met the Little One, I was filled with ferociously protective, unconditional love for her. Suddenly, I had permission to give to my little inner self all the tender nurture that I'd only been allowed to give to everyone else. Day by day I practiced, growing more able to be a safe, loving harbor for my starving Little One. I became the dependable Mommy for whom she had been yearning. Being with my own upset became fully satisfying.

Over the years since I began mommying my self, I am sometimes able to allow my dearest friends to be there to support the Mommy in me as she cares for the Little One. I've learned that it is never safe to let anyone but the inner Mommy relate directly to the Little One. And, in truth, nothing anyone else has to give can reach across the time warp to where the Little One inside lives except by going through the Mommy.

We as women have so much cultural training (on top of whatever familial nurturing history we have) that pushes us to give nurture to everyone but our selves and to look for nurture from anyone but our selves. Practicing and developing our capacity to nurture our selves whenever we need nurturing is vital to our process of becoming more whole. Nurture from others can add on to and amplify what we do for our selves. But to take the very best care of our selves, self-nurturing is the essential baseline from which we must start.

As I watch my own unfolding, and as I write this tale, I'm aware that I am still not comfortable with others' ministrations when I am going through tense or difficult times. Though I no longer go through the obsessive worrying about such help, I typically find it's either not relevant or even distracting for the Mommy. At this moment, I'm not sure that I care about that becoming any different for me. Still, I suspect that as I continue in this process of aging, changes in this may come organically from necessity. It feels like that will be okay with me, too.

Consider bringing your own loving patience and attention to your own hungry or wounded parts.

3-6. Mistakes Are Opportunities

Mistakes are always opportunities for learning and growth.
Be kind and gentle with your self when it seems you've made a
mistake... You'll need to take responsibility for any harm or damage
you've caused and, you'll need to "set things to right."
But, growing can happen only if you don't beat your self up!

For the first 43 years of my life, I lived in dread of making mistakes. The shame and self-loathing that came with any slip-up were overpowering, to be avoided at all costs. The fear of mistakes drove me to extremes of perfectionism. It drove me, as well, to drop out of anything I couldn't do reasonably well right from the get go.

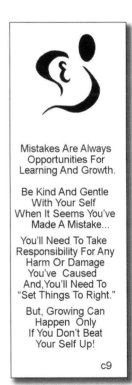

Mistakes Are Always
Opportunities For
Learning And Growth.

Be Kind And Gentle
With Your Self
When It Seems You've
Made A Mistake...

You'll Need To Take
Responsibility For Any
Harm Or Damage
You've Caused
And, You'll Need To
"Set Things To Right."

But, Growing Can
Happen Only
If You Don't Beat
Your Self Up!

c9

While our everyday world generally has little tolerance for blunders, the intensity of my struggles were more a consequence of the damaging mothering to which I'd been subject until I was 30, when my mother died. From my youngest days, I'd been humiliated by her angry impatience with anything I couldn't or didn't do right. Her corrections were freighted with the message that I should have been able to figure it (whatever it might have been) out on my own. She let me know that having to correct my mistakes was an infuriating imposition on her time and energies. Always anticipating her cold ridicule of my ineptness, I would be filled with nauseating anxiety whenever I faced doing something new.

Needing help of any sort, in any circumstances, fell into the same category as making a mistake. My mother's help came with irritated harshness and the implication that my incompetence was both beneath contempt and burdensome in the extreme.

The fear of getting anything wrong wove its way through all of my school years. I felt shamed when I made errors in class or on tests. Convinced that I should have known better, I'd verbally pummel my self and constantly push toward some unachievable standard of perfection.

(Several years ago, my dad told me about an open school night meeting my parents had had with my teacher when I was in third grade. It was the year I'd memorized the whole of Longfellow's epic poem, Hiawatha, as a special credit project. The teacher suggested to my parents that they ease up on their pressure on me to achieve. She felt that I was on overdrive too much of the time. In great surprise, they informed her that they were not pressuring me at all; that I must be driving my self.)

When I began seeing clients during my graduate psychotherapy practicum, I was given one hour a week of supervision for each four hours of client contact. The supervision process is intended to help student-therapists learn how to do therapy. Nevertheless, I would face each weekly session with gut wrenching anxiety. I'd feel devastated by any teaching that attempted to correct my awkward efforts at doing treatment. Anything that was viewed as a gaffe filled me with shame and a sense of worthlessness. Despite performance evaluations that were reasonably positive, I felt certain that my supervisors found my efforts contemptible. It didn't help that one, a world-renown (male) author of a classic in the field, actually **did** approach most of us with a large measure of disdain. Or, that the other **was** a cold and emotionally distant woman.

As I moved on into my professional practice with private clients, I was a pitiless critic of my own work. Even without supervisors to point out my mistakes, I kept count of my failures of insight and my off the mark interpretations. No matter how well I did otherwise, my focus was usually on the lapses for which I excoriated my self.

The shame I felt at any misstep in my everyday interpersonal relationships was similarly extreme. Inadvertently hurting someone's feelings undid me. My apologies and attempts at recompense were as limitless as my guilt and self-berating. I'd feel worthless. Everything I'd ever done right would pale before whatever apparent wrong I'd just committed.

There was no area of my life free of the scathing self-deprecation hurled at me by what I came to call the Hatchet Lady voice inside me.

The self-berating was as vitriolic for the smallest missteps as it was for larger gaffes. **Any** mistake led to her disparaging everything I might have held dear about my self, shredding whatever sense of self-worth I might have built from other accomplishments. (See **Criticizing Your Self**, page 137 and **Eating My Way Home**, page 131 for more about this devastating process.) No amount of therapy or self-work seemed to change this horrible pattern; a life free from its recycling torment seemed unimaginable.

Then, at 43, I discovered the Little One inside of me and everything shifted. As my heart opened to this vibrant, vulnerable creature, I was instantly committed to cherishing her. I couldn't imagine allowing **anyone** (even the Hatchet Lady) to treat her tender being with impatience or harshness. Something fiercely protective awakened in me: an inner-Mommy absolutely devoted to this precious Little One that I was coming to know. (See **The Little Ones Story**, page 9 for more about this experience.)

It was inconceivable to me that anyone could **ever** have been impatient with her, expected her to be able to do more than she was capable of or expected her not to make mistakes. She was so defenseless and delicate. She needed tenderness and loving support to grow and thrive. She stirred both in me, immediately, unquestioningly.

And, I knew, in every cell of me, that this Little One and I were both truly okay, lovable **just exactly** as we were. I understood that this had always been so: from infancy through all of my life up to that moment. I had been trying, for years, to accept this truth about my self. Even though I'd been, all along, helping my clients to know and accept this truth about their selves, it had never taken root in me as an in-the-belly/heart knowing about my own self. The Hatchet Lady had typically trampled the idea with her ridicule before it could implant itself. Not so this time.

Embracing the reality that we were lovable just exactly as we were brought with it the realization that we (the Little One and I) had **never** deserved the terrible, crushing emotional abuse to which we had been subject. We finally understood in our belly and bones that my mother's mistreatment of me had been about what was so **in her** and not at all about what was so **about me**. I **knew** – finally and beyond any doubt – that the absence of love from my mother was about **her** inability to love/love me. It was never about **any** not-rightness or unlovableness in **me**.

There had never been any way I could have been that would have opened her loveless heart.

Before this realization, I had, with the lacerating voice of my inner Hatchet Lady, perpetuated my mother's mistreatment of me. Maligning my self as my mother had, I'd affirmed that her criticism, her condemnation of my mistakes and her lack of love for me were entirely my fault. If I believed that there was something wrong with me, I could keep alive the hope that if I could figure out how to be the right kind of kid, I might finally get the loving I so craved from her.

At last, I accepted that there was no hope. I began the process of dismantling the self-destructive ways I had been using to keep that hope alive (even as she was long dead!). The Mommy-Inside, strengthened and fed by the Grandmothers and by Spirit/the Great Mother, gradually became the boundless, ever-present source of the love for which I had been so hungry. An ever more substantial inner reality, she was displacing the ragged dream-of-the-impossible: an outside good mother who would never be.

From the beginning of her emergence, the Mommy-Inside lovingly assured me that mistakes are things that happen in everyone's life, frequently. "No one can do everything right all of the time," she said. She's helped me to see a lot about so-called mistakes. They do not make us bad or wrong. They are nothing about which to feel shamed or guilt-ridden. They can provide us with chances to learn more about what we're involved in, what we're trying to do. They give us the opportunity to stretch and grow. If we're afraid of mistakes, we rob our selves of the adventure of exploring our furthest edges. Fixing a mistake sometimes opens us to new possibilities by awakening our inventiveness and creativity. Sometimes, what looks like a mistake turns out to be a doorway-in-disguise that leads to something unexpectedly magical and nourishing.

In the beginning of this new season in my healing process, when I'd make a mistake, the Hatchet Lady would still start to rev up her meanness engine. But, the Mommy-Inside would be right there, telling her she didn't have to do that, that there was no reason for her to be mean to us. She would remind the Hatchet Lady that we were lovable even though we might have done or said something wrong. She would remind the Hatchet Lady that nothing terrible would happen to us because of the mistake. She would help the Hatchet Lady and the rest of me to not feel so scared.

The Mommy-Inside would hold us all safely as we did what needed to be done to make things right. We would take responsibility for what we'd done or not done, apologize, figure out how to fix or replace anything we'd messed up or broken or, even, invent some way to make the mistake into something new and exciting for our self.

Over the years since those earliest days of this shift, the Hatchet Lady has finally hung up her fangs. Every once in a while she gets to grumbling a little. I'm always kind to her, reminding her gently of what all the me's of me have come to know and trust. I remind her that she doesn't have to feel scared or be mean to me anymore because we are safe and lovable no matter what we've done.

When I make mistakes these days, even really big ones involving clients or hurting someone's feelings, I still feel **very** sorry to have done that. I'm able to listen caringly to whatever the person has to say to me about the pain/upset my words, actions (or inaction) have set in motion. I can listen even when they might be very furious with me. I'm able to acknowledge and take responsibility for what I said/did/didn't do. I'm able to express my sincere regret that my words/actions/inaction have created the space for their pain and grief. And, I'm willing to look – with the other person or just with my self – at what there is that I might do to make amends and/or how I might avoid making the same mistake the next time.

What I no longer do is feel like a terrible, worthless person or feel shamed or feel that everything good about me is invalidated by the misstep. And, I don't any longer berate or verbally abuse my self for simply being a fallible human being.

When we can acknowledge that we might have done something terrible, without falling into feeling that this makes us a terrible person, we're much more available to the person we've injured. We can make room to hear their upset and anger. We can be listening attentively instead of trying to defend or justify our selves as they're trying to express themselves to us. And, we don't create a situation in which the one we have injured feels that sharing their upset will be devastating to our self-esteem. This allows healing to happen.

Remember to be especially tender and compassionate with your fallible, mistake-making, simply human self.

3-7. Angry Feelings

Angry, nasty, mean-spirited feelings come when
something "not good for you" is going on...
Listen inward for what that something is!

At 27, I was dating a dear, unique man. He was the only man I'd ever met who seemed wholeheartedly to enjoy my independent, intense, intellectually acute and articulately outspoken, oddball self. The other men I'd been with before then had been, if not entirely unavailable, then either threatened by or competitive with the who that I was. He was different. We could and did talk about everything. Including my struggle – at the time we started seeing each other – with trying to extricate my self from a tangled relationship with a very possessive woman that I was also seeing.

Two years into our relationship, we'd been through seven iterations of my moving in with him or having him move in with me and then my moving out or having him move out. For reasons that seem unfathomable to me now, we decided to see if making the commitment of marrying each other would move me beyond this ambivalence about having a live-in relationship. We married as an experiment rather than as a forever thing.

Angry, Nasty
Mean-Spirited
Feelings Come
When Something
"Not Good For You"
Is Going On...
Listen Inward
For What
That Something
Is!

s1

We made our own tiny, elegant wedding in my apartment (into which he moved yet **again**). Just our parents, siblings and the Rabbi were present. My partner and I had jointly prepared a small, beautiful and delicious feast for the celebration.

So began five years of what quickly became an open (non-monogamous) marriage. Sharing the emotional details of our intimate and/or sexual experiences with other people became a deepening part of our intimacy and connection with each other. For a time it felt like a creative (if inherently contradictory) resolution to what was, apparently for **both** of us, the sometimes claustrophobic experience of living together.

Our wedding, in late 1967, came during the rise of the second wave of feminism. We both were actively involved in and dedicated to the movement. And, we were committed to developing ours as an egalitarian, feminist marriage – an oxymoron perhaps?

We shared housework, marketing, cooking and baking (which we both did from scratch). We each did our own laundry and ironing and button sewing. We kept our monies separate and divided household and capital expenses according to the proportion of the total joint income that we each provided. (We started at a 65 him/35 me split, moved through a 50/50 split and wound up at a 35 him/65 me split when he left his job in research psychology to enter training as a Rational-Emotive Psychotherapist.) On (and somewhat beneath) the surface, we were functioning as equal partners. There was never any assumption that either of us would be called upon to give up anything that mattered to us "for the sake of the relationship." We even were interviewed for a *New York Post* series on feminist marriages.

One summer, midway through our years of being married, he was asked (at the job he was planning to leave that coming fall) to spend the month of August doing research work. This would have involved living for the month in the mosquito-ridden boondocks of New York State. There he would solicit visitors to the County Fair as potential control subjects for an ongoing research project in his department. We took a brief trip to check out the area and to see what kinds of resorts or vacation rentals might be available – August was usually the month we would take our joint summer vacation.

The area was depressed and depressing, the available rentals gloomy and uninviting. None of it was any match to the charming French-Canadian hotel/resort to which we had planned to return before this new wrinkle had appeared. At Mont Tremblant we would again have had our small motel-apartment on a lovely mountain property at the edge of a glorious lake. There'd be luscious country French meals in a tasteful hotel dining room with simple but caring service. There'd be several canoes, sail and paddle boats to take out on the lake, an adjoining executive 9-hole golf course (where I could chase a ball around the magnificent countryside) and a genteel, discreet, mostly

European clientele with whom we could choose to engage or not. We had a sweet connection with the warm multi-generational family that owned and managed the resort. We'd again have been bringing our cat, our bicycles, our books, a scrabble set, my crocheting and L's collection of things for his mathematical/theoretical explorations.

At Mont Tremblant we'd be exquisitely pampered for a month of complete relaxation with no responsibilities other than our personal laundry. For me it was a no-brainer. He was welcome to figure out how to manage **his** August in the middle of mosquito-ridden-nowhere in New York. I was heading back to the solace, beauty and chore-free deliciousness of Saint-Jovite, Quebec. I thought the whole idea of his doing this project was ludicrous, particularly since he was planning to leave his crazy-making boss and stressful (literally headache producing) job by October anyway. But, it wasn't my place to interfere in his process. I simply had no intention of interfering with my taking good care of my self in order to support this choice **he** apparently needed to make.

In the end, my not being willing to ruin my summer by going with him made the choice a no-brainer for him as well. He quit his job two months early and came to Saint-Jovite and Mont Tremblant with me. We had some wonderful adventures: Getting caught on the huge lake in a tiny sailboat during a thunderstorm we watched approaching over the well-named "Trembling Mountain." Dodging lightning as we worked to beach the boat at someone's magnificent summerhouse. Getting our selves and my bulky crochet project (a long skirt) totally soaked on the way. Capsizing a canoe during my first, very nervous canoe ride. Going as guests of the bartender cum golf pro to play a round of golf (i.e., me chasing a ball all over the back of beyond but playing the best round I'd ever played) on the nearby majestic world championship golf course at which he taught. We played countless games of cutthroat after-dinner Ping-Pong, went on hilly bike rides, laughed our way through silly and ridiculous attempts to teach me tennis and enjoyed lots of luscious lazing about drifting, dreaming and reading. (Something I loved even that long ago.)

And, then, there was a life-changing day of realizations. After a morning doing I-can't-remember-what together, I'd stretched out and voluptuously fallen into a fascinating book (*Knots* by R.D. Laing). After wandering back and forth for a bit, L decided he wanted to take a bike ride to town – five miles of scenic, steep hilly road. He announced his plan and I wished him a good ride. Apparently, that wasn't the response he'd hoped for. He grumped and rattled around our room for a while, distracting me from my book with the racket he was making. Then, he began a concerted attempt to whine and wheedle me into going with him because, as he said, he **really** wanted both to be with me **and** to take a bike ride. Absent my usual good-humor, I did at last respond to his imploring looks and words. I put my book down, gathered my gear and headed out with him.

Halfway up the first big hill, not very far from the hotel, I realized I'd left something I needed back at our room. (I can't now remember what it was, just that it seemed essential at the time.) I sped up to within hailing distance of him and told him I needed for us to go back so I could get whatever it was. He waved and said I should go on back, that he didn't want to turn around. That he would just continue on ahead and I could meet him whenever it was I would finally get to the town.

I turned around and rode back to the hotel fuming. I wanted to strangle him. I was furious. How childish, how typically male and self-absorbed he was, how unable to tolerate the absence of my attention to him when he wanted that attention. Pestering me out of my own lush space with my self because he supposedly couldn't bear to go without my company. Then, once he had my full attention, deciding to go off on his own while I went back to get whatever it was I'd left behind. I couldn't believe what I'd let my self get seduced into. I raged my way back to the room, knowing there was no way I'd go back to meet him in town.

It was impossible to calm down. I was in turmoil. I stormed around the room muttering to my self like a madwoman. Finally, I ran a bath with scented oil and bubbles to soothe my agitated soul. I needed to make space for me to listen inward to understand what was underneath the uproar I was feeling.

A flood of memories came of many other experiences that had marginally irritated me at earlier times. Previously separate things suddenly came thudding together in my brain and my feelings. I was sick of him, my self-described feminist partner; sick of my own complicity in the veiled dance we'd been into for so long without seeing it.

When L came back from his ride, he hadn't a clue about what he was walking into. He was totally baffled by my anger, perplexed about why I hadn't ever gotten to town. From my perch, still in the bathtub, I gave him my calm pronouncement. I was done, I announced, with taking up the slack in our partnership. Done having my flexibility be the critical element in making it possible for us to spend time together. I reminded him of how he was invariably such a pill about going along with me if I insisted on us doing something I might want to do. I acknowledged that I had learned that it was easier for me to do those things alone rather than have my friends, my family or me put up with how ill humored and pouty he'd be when he grudgingly agreed to come along. I pointed out that what time we spent together usually involved doing what **he** wanted to do. This, because we both understood that I could and would inevitably be more flexible, more good-humored, more present wherever or with whomever it might be, even when it was far from my first choice.

I was, I informed him, no longer going to be flexible in those ways. I was, I said, no longer willing to go along with doing things that were of no interest to me in order to make it possible for us to be spending time together. He turned quite pale standing in the doorway to the bathroom. Stunned, he asked, "Do you realize what you're saying? If you do what you're saying, we might never spend any time together!"

I couldn't believe my ears. I exploded. "Do **you** realize what **you're** saying?" I asked. Obviously, he had already known precisely what I was just coming to see: that in our so-called egalitarian marriage, things were not all that equal. He **and** I had **both** been in the habit of placing his needs/comfort in social situations first because, of course, he wasn't as flexible as I was.

A lot changed in our partnership after that. We became much more conscious of the subtle ways our gendered acculturation insidiously undermined our intentions to operate as equals in our sharing. A lot of our emotional and practical arrangements came up for re-examining. And, we did begin more often to go separately to do what we each preferred.

That day I learned a lot that has continued to be important to living healthily. I had allowed my self to feel all the angry, mean and nasty feelings that were welling up in me. I went with them; let them go to their max rather than talking my self down from or talking my self out of them. As I trusted and followed those feelings, they led me to an understanding and awareness of exactly what was going on that wasn't good for me. Once I knew that, I was able to make some choices that would deal with changing what was not okay for me.

These days, when I find my self having angry, mean-spirited and nasty thoughts or feelings about someone or in some situation, I know that they are a righteous signal that there's something not-good-for-me going on. I stop and go inward to hear what that something might be. Usually, though sometimes it takes longer than others, I do get the message of my anger. Then, I listen to what I need to do to remove the not-goodness from my space. Sometimes that involves speaking out about what's affecting me. Sometimes it means removing my self from the situation or person. When I address and do something about the source of the feelings, the feelings simply dissolve. Just as I'm reluctant to medicate away a physical pain before I grasp what/where it's coming from, so, too, I don't ever want to transcend my anger without listening to the message it's trying to give me. Both physical pain and emotional anger are signals for us to pay closer attention, to take better care of our selves. I believe it's essential for us, without fail, to honor, respect and attend to these powerful signals.

Consider listening to your angry, mean-spirited or nasty thoughts and feelings as messages from deep within about what's going on that's not okay for you.

3-8. Surrendering

What you resist, persists... Accepting and surrendering into "what-is" doesn't mean you have to love it... You can feel sad, cranky or angry about it and still surrender into it at the very same time!

I spent seven years through the end of my forties living an inward, hermit-like existence. Committed to healing both my life and the profound re-wounding from a recently ended relationship, I was living in the slow lane.

I'd spend two long days each week seeing clients. The next five I'd be mostly solitary, immersed in whatever was nurturing and healing for me at the time. I'd work a couple of hours each week with a creative arts therapist, essentially doing play therapy for grown-ups. I'd arrange for two hours of massage and/or other bodywork (Rolfing, energy work, Polarity work) every week.

Then, by my self, I'd play and explore using the tools I'd been gathering in the play therapy. I'd do authentic (spontaneous) movement, create child-like art and rhythm-band percussion music, journal with colored pens using my non-dominant hand, spend hours cuddling my teddy bear and listening to the Little Ones inside me. I'd go hiking or walking in the mountains and canyons of Ojai singing to my inner Little Ones the lullaby-chants that came to me from the Great Mother as I wandered.

What You Resist, Persists... Accepting And Surrendering Into "What-Is" Doesn't Mean You Have To Love It... You Can Feel Sad, Cranky Or Angry About It And Still Surrender Into It At The Very Same Time!

s5

Early on in that period, I became absorbed in an extensive project: relocating a huge volume of rocks, boulders and construction debris that had, till then, littered the neglected back and side yards around my rented cottage. As, over the months and years, I levered and rolled the boulders, moved or sometimes hurled the rocks, I created several beautiful rock-walled outdoor havens – sacred spaces for my self all around my house. Moving these mountains of debris, one rock at a time, was nourishing and comforting. It provided an education in slowness, patience and the process of transformation.

I occasionally spent small amounts of time with one of two or three friends. But, most of my people time was spent at four-times-a-year, five-day retreats, sitting in a lodge-circle with a small group of women in northern California. We had come together to explore and experiment with how women hold and share power. All of us were working as healing mentors while simultaneously engaged in our own inner work. Sitting with this circle, I got to practice being the fuller version of me that was emerging during my alone time.

Shortly after I turned 50, a very different chapter in my life opened. Little by little, I was being nudged back out into the world. It began with an invitation to speak at a Women's Council on Aging into Power organized by some of the women in that lodge-circle. As the time of the conference approached, I moved into a period of heightened creativity and synthesis.

First came the birth of the deck of Rememberings and Celebrations Cards. Then I resurrected all the cards, treasures and amulets I had, every winter solstice over past years, created for friends and clients. I reprinted and produced these in quantities that could be made available to people beyond my own usual circle. All of it went with me to the conference as give-away for the women who came to participate in that Council.

Over the next two years, I developed a small mail-order catalog/ business to sell my creations. Every step along the way felt magical and perfectly timed. I never decided or figured anything out. Amazing possibilities and coincidences kept presenting themselves to me. An overflow of money came from my work as a therapist to fund all the stages of this budding enterprise.

Quite serendipitously, at an opportune moment, someone turned me on to a list of feminist women's bookstores around the country. Spirit/the Grandmothers nudged me once again, this time into doing a mailing, sending out 200 decks with letters inviting these stores to consider selling my work. (Several chose to do that.) An old friend in Key West, Florida created a Robyn Corner in her one-of-a-kind boutique and began selling lots of decks of cards. Another old friend who ran Overcoming Overeating workshops across the country began selling decks at OO conferences, seminars and centers. Those who bought the decks in these places frequently sent requests for the catalog of my other works.

It was a time filled with periods of intense activity, creativity and production. And, as more invitations and opportunities arrived for me to speak about my work, my life and what I was learning, there were seasons when I was constantly nudged out of my solitary refuge.

The out-in-the-world times were followed by long periods of my till-then-more-usual deep resting: reading and daydreaming in the hammock, in front of the wood stove or while wandering in the mountains and canyons. Despite the additions and changes that came in these times, it still felt as though I were living my familiar, slowed down life – if only more intermittently now.

Then, I was swept into an even higher gear out-in-the-world cycle. Everything I was doing continued to feel directed and pushed by the energies and guidance that came from Spirit/the Grandmothers. But now, I no longer felt I had any veto power in the proceedings.

This newer cycle began with the birth of designs using my images and words for imprinting T-shirts. Shortly after, I followed the promptings of Spirit/the Grandmothers arranging to have the T-shirts produced and then moving out into the world with them as an itinerate peddler.

On my non-work days I was buying or building portable components for displays, gathering inventory and filing applications to be a vendor at an ever-increasing number of Women's Festivals, Spirituality Festivals, Pride Festivals, and women's or professional conferences of one sort or another. Then, I started being on the road at least once a month in California and the Southwest.

At the various festivals and conferences, the Grandmothers' energies cajoled me into giving talks and workshops. When I'd do a talk or an experiential workshop, I'd feel inspired and guided. I did little preparation for the presentations. My job was simply to calm, center and clear my self; to get my mind out of the way so that I could come into the space available to speak whatever of my experiences and learning was appropriate to be spoken about with that particular audience.

Even though the talks and workshops were generally exciting opportunities to edge-walk/dance with Spirit, none of this was anything I wanted or would have chosen to do with my otherwise open, empty time. Often I'd be terminally cranky about all the planning, packing, schlepping, loading, setting up, tearing down, reloading, driving, unloading, and unpacking. I felt over the edge much of the time – as though I were spinning out of control, careening at impossible speeds into unknown territory.

I would have tantrums and rail at Spirit: "Whose life is this?" "I hate this!" "I want my real life back!" "Please, please just let me rest and stay at home!" I'd try to go on strike: I'd dig my heels in, refuse to travel anymore. I'd try to shut out the pressure, the relentless nudging. But, there was no way out of the flow that kept pushing and herding me out into massive amounts of people contact. At some point, it finally became clear to me that this **was** what my real life was for now. I gave up the useless resisting. I gave in. I surrendered.

Surrendering into the middle of the new shape of my existence did not **ever** include loving it or even liking it. Surrendering meant accepting that this was what my life was to be about for a time (or maybe, forever more). Surrendering meant letting go of struggling and railing against what was so about my life in these moments. Surrendering meant looking, instead, for what lessons there might be for me in the midst of all this unavoidable unpleasantness. Surrendering **did not** mean that I was required to give up my gripes about what I was having to surrender into. In fact, surrendering was much easier when I could allow my self to continue hating the situation.

During the next three years I moved in and out of extreme crabbiness, in and out of hating the course of things. At the same time, I no longer resisted the flow in any way. The flow continued – unremittingly outward. While I hated it, I watched, I listened and I learned. My vision of my journey expanded. The me that had emerged in solitude moved out to explore her self in a wide variety of unfamiliar settings.

I had many opportunities to witness the impact of my work on passers-by who stopped and with eyes closed, randomly picked a Rememberings and Celebrations card from a basket outside my booths. I'd be as stunned as they were by the synchronistic appropriateness of the cards they picked. People who came into the booths to buy my cards and shirts and amulets were stirred – by the words and images in my work – to share intimate healing stories from their own journeys.

I got to watch how separate I felt from my work, how little it felt mine in any self-aggrandizing, ego way. I could accept credit for the tremendous work I'd been doing to get out of the way so that Spirit could use my life, my experience, my emotional fluency as a vehicle. I could feel amazed by what had come through me. I could be fairly comfortable receiving acknowledgment and gratitude for the healing impact of this naked sharing of my own process.

And, through those busy out-in-the-world years about which I so often griped, I began what has been a phenomenal, catalytic collaboration. My friend B – whose nudging and coaching over the years brought me (kicking and screaming) into the world of websites and computer literacy – introduced me to the magical possibilities of collaboration as we created shared sacred spaces for showing our wares at festivals.

It distresses me that so many spiritual traditions imply that equanimity always comes with (or from) surrender. Or, conversely, that still having considerations or gripes implies that one hasn't really been surrendering. It distresses me, as well, that our larger culture continues to view surrender negatively, as a passive, disempowered caving in.

I see surrender as an active, empowered and empowering choice to accept and allow what is so, to be so. It involves committing our selves to fully embracing what is. Yet, it does not require, **ever**, that we suppress or give up our considerations, irritation, sadness or crabbiness about whatever it is that we're embracing. Allowing our selves to grump about it is often what allows us more easily to surrender.

Giving up the struggle of resisting the inevitable (rather than giving up our feelings about it) is what enables us to use our energies to harvest the gifts hiding in the middle of what feels so awful.

Consider lovingly honoring your willingness to surrender your resistance without surrendering your feelings.

3-9. Feeling Unsafe

When you're feeling uneasy, unsafe, untrusting or just vaguely "not okay" in any situation... It doesn't really matter where that feeling is coming from: inside or outside, past or present, accurate or distorted perceptions... Or even if your response is "appropriate..." What matters is that you do whatever you need to do to find safety for your self in the moment. Removing your self from the situation is always an acceptable option!

The vulnerable little parts of me have almost always been able rapidly to sense when the circumstances in which I found my self were unsafe, unhealthy or simply not-okay for me. Yet, for much of my life, I rarely paid attention to their rumblings. If they ever actually got through to me, my conscious mind would dismiss or invalidate these apprehensions. So, until my mid-forties, these parts suffered through a good many unpleasant and undermining situations out in the world with people.

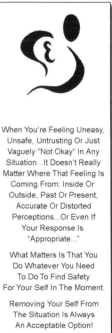

When You're Feeling Uneasy, Unsafe, Untrusting Or Just Vaguely "Not Okay" In Any Situation...It Doesn't Really Matter Where That Feeling Is Coming From: Inside Or Outside, Past Or Present, Accurate Or Distorted Perceptions...Or Even If Your Response Is "Appropriate..."

What Matters Is That You Do Whatever You Need To Do To Find Safety For Your Self In The Moment.

Removing Your Self From The Situation Is Always An Acceptable Option!

c10

Having been mothered by a woman who had no tolerance for my fears, I had learned to respond to my self the same way: I was critical and impatient with any anxieties I noticed in me. Although the phrases had not yet become popular, my self-talk was the equivalent of "get over it" and "get a life."

Through the years, as I became more psychologically sophisticated, I found a whole new vocabulary to use as I continued to find ways to invalidate any misgivings about my safety that might be stirred in me by interpersonal situations. I'd view these feelings as arising from either my distortions of what was going on or my past experiences being incorrectly overlaid on current circumstances or my projecting my inner reality onto the actual situation.

At 32, shortly before I was scheduled to leave my life in New York to begin my cross-country journey into the unknown, I went to a one-day experiential workshop introducing us to Charlotte Selver's Sensory Awareness techniques. What happened there was a perfect example of my typical way of dealing with my inner warnings.

The workshop came just ten days after I'd had my first-ever surgery: the removal of a small fatty tumor from the front of my right shoulder. That day-hospitalization procedure had involved general anesthesia and a small number of stitches. These had been removed just the day before this workshop that I'd been eager to experience.

As the group of ten of us gathered, the facilitator had us go round the circle introducing our selves and our intentions for the day. As I listened to these people describing themselves, I experienced intense visceral queasiness and nausea. None of these people with whom I was to spend the day felt kindred. Most were male. The male facilitator, who had come highly recommended, seemed overly impressed with himself in a puffed up kind of way. Almost without exception, the self-descriptions offered by the participants had, for me, the ring of posturing, as though they were engaging in a sensitivity competition. This was an odd sort of dance that many men seemed inclined to play out in those early days of the second wave of feminism. In ordinary social situations, I found this more-sensitive-than-thou posturing irritating. In this workshop where the agenda was for intimate connecting with our selves and each other, it stirred considerable unease. I felt I was in an unsafe environment. I felt very untrusting of the whole set-up. Nothing about it felt okay.

For seven hours and through the many exercises we were doing, I constantly argued with my self about these apprehensions I was trying not to have. I told my self that I was being excessively critical of the male participants and facilitator because of my strongly feminist orientation and my then-general cynicism about men's motivations. I told my self that I was projecting all of these feelings onto the situation because it was really hard for me to allow my self to be taught something I didn't already know by someone I didn't know, especially a puffed up male authority. I told my self that I was feeling uneasy only because I was feeling fragile, still healing from the cut in both my physical and energetic body. I told my self that all the strong body/emotional messages were the consequence of my distortions and inner realities that had little to do with what was **really** going on in the workshop.

Repeatedly invalidating my gut feelings, I kept pushing my self to "get over it" and just be there with the work proposed. The intense struggle inside my psyche made it nearly impossible to find room to attend to the sensory awareness of such things as the weight of a stone in my upturned palm as I walked in circle with the group.

In only one exercise was I able to be in the middle of what was going on inside of me and, simultaneously, connected with what was going on outside of me in the work of the day. We'd paired off, one of each pair sitting with our back against a wall. Our partner began to move toward us from a starting position against the opposite wall of the room. The task was to discover "at what distance between your self and your partner you feel safe." Only when I had my partner move two rooms away, to the opposite side of the house, did it feel safe to me. In the sharing afterward, I finally was able to talk some about the extreme uneasiness I'd felt all day and about the intensity of my inner battles around being there at all.

If I were to feel even a small measure of such disquiet in a similar situation at this stage of my life, I'd have unobtrusively gathered my things, slipped out, gone home and written the facilitator a brief note indicating I'd left because it had felt unsafe for me to be there. (In fact, I recently did just that at a movement workshop that I'd hoped would offer me new tools for some body releasing I'd been working on.) But, back more than 39 years ago, I had not yet learned how to take such good care of all of my selves.

Only when, in my mid-forties, I first met my inner Little Ones did I begin the practice of becoming a consistently protective, unconditionally loving Mommy to all of my intuitive and sensitive selves. (See **The Little Ones Story**, page 9 for more about this.) It's this practice that's helped me to be with my vague (or strong) uneasy, untrusting, not-okay feelings in a more caring way. I know now that it does not matter **where** these feelings come from. I know now that as a good Mommy I must **always** take them seriously. That means hearing them, acknowledging them with respect and responding to them with concern and tenderness. Only when my fearful selves feel protected can we then sit together and explore the sources of the anxious, uneasy feelings. Only then can we safely and together, look to find new ways to cope with these fears or new choices to make.

In our feel-the-fear-and-do-it-anyway/get-over-it culture we, constantly and from very early on in our lives, are being socialized to disregard our inner voices, to attend only to so-called objective reality (whatever **that** is). To openly acknowledge and appreciate that we can act **only** from what feels so for us in the moment – no matter what an outside eye might see as the supposed truth-of-the-matter, this is a revolutionary stance. It is a radical act of self-care to honor our inner voices above all others. And, it is equally radical to act to protect our selves from what might, to others, seem to be imaginary fears.

When you feel uneasy, unsafe or not-okay in any situation, consider taking your apprehensions seriously (no matter where they may be coming from) and honoring them by practicing such radical self-care.

3-10. Being Exactly Where You Are

If it's not okay to be where you are while you're there,
you can never truly be anywhere at all...
You don't have to love or even like what's so for you now...
But, to grow, to heal and to flourish, you do need your own
permission to be just exactly where, who and how you are
in this moment and for as long as it's so!

For much of my 42nd and 43rd years I was mired in agonizing struggle. Seriously depressed, I was trying to extricate my self from the challenging relationship in which I'd been enmeshed for seven years. (See **Others' Views**, page 259 for more about this time in my journey.)

If It's Not Okay To Be
Where You Are
While You're There,
You Can Never Truly
Be Anywhere At All...

You Don't Have To Love
Or Even Like What's
So For You Now...

But, To Grow, To Heal
And To Flourish,
You Do Need
Your Own Permission
To Be Just Exactly
Where, Who And How
You Are In This Moment
And For As Long
As It's So!

e12

My partner and I had moved back to California just days after my 42nd birthday. This after a difficult two-year sojourn in South Bend, Indiana where we'd moved to support my partner's terminally ill sister and the sister's young adult children. Even before we'd made that move to Indiana, I'd known that I needed to leave the relationship. Yet, the complicated inner turmoil I felt around breaking away and the press of her family crisis both combined to keep me from doing what I needed to do. While we were in Indiana, I'd been able to push the issue out of my mind.

When we came home to California, we had a trying re-entry. We'd planned to live in my bed-sitter van in a friend's driveway, hoping this arrangement would allow us some time to decompress after the cross-country move, the driving through blizzards en route and the stress we'd lived with for two years in Indiana. We'd anticipated having a few quiet weeks at our friend's before beginning the search for more permanent living arrangements. That wasn't to be. Our two road-weary cats, unusually heavy rains, unexpected leaks in the van, soaking mud all around us and our friend's life having pretty much fallen apart just before we'd arrived, made this plan untenable.

We tried a week-to-week arrangement at a motel with a hot plate and our ice chest. In the continuing monsoon rains, this was another depressingly gloomy situation. Having neither a real nest nor any comfortable separate space added to the stress of our dislocation. Attempts to deal with the taxing physical circumstances exaggerated the already problematic differences in our values, coping skills and interpersonal styles – the differences that had been at the core of our ongoing struggles with each other.

I wanted desperately to throw in the towel, to end the desolation I felt in our painful integration. I'd repeatedly come to the edge of giving voice to this truth and then be overwhelmed with fear. Gut-wrenching terror would constrict my breathing, blur my thinking, leave me panicky and in confusion. From standing at the brink of speaking, I'd bolt backward into the mire of the intolerable situation.

I felt intense hatred for my self around this failure of courage. As we moved forward together into finding a place to rent, buying stuff to replace what we'd left behind in Indiana and beginning to make a new home for our selves, I felt humiliated by my self-betrayal.

For months, as we did this and as I worked to build yet another psychotherapy practice, I sank further and further into despair and self-blame. The Hatchet Lady, my vicious inner critic, kept up her tormenting litany of my failings. I was depressed, feeling hopeless and being plagued by sleepless nights filled with obsessive self-condemnation.

My partner and I would move between tense, cold silences and long hours of trying to process what was happening between us. I couldn't speak the truth of what I was feeling, so my need to leave was never given voice. I hated how I would dissemble during those hours of our attempting to problem-solve issues that were, for me, truly beside the point. I hated my self for feeling so crazed. And, most of all, I detested my self for violating my commitment to always speak my truth.

The self-loathing around being unable to find a way to extricate my self from living this lie-of-a-life further undermined my already devastated self. I could barely get out of bed each day. I wanted to die: it seemed the only way I'd ever get free of this suffocating enmeshment.

Being ready to die opened a tiny crack of possibility for me. I finally found the strength to risk leaving physically, even without being able to speak about my reasons. The emotional entanglement continued and escalated as I left. There were several short, repeating cycles of moving back and moving away again. Still, being in my own separate energy field even some of the time was calming. In my desperation, I was able to let in some loving support that a local couple (new friends) generously and unconditionally offered. They were okay with me being as confused, obsessed with and self-destructively addicted to the relationship as I might be.

Their ability to stay with me without judgment, their acceptance of my process, their willingness to let me be wherever I needed to be until I was done being there, their belief that I would indeed somehow, someday be done being there and their capacity to stay out of trying to fix me – all this gave me a template for new ways to be with my self. Gradually, I began talking differently to my self and being more generous with what felt like my craziness – the despair, the inability to speak my truth, the inability to let go of this destructive involvement. I began holding all of it without the scathing self-condemnation, reminding my self that I was doing the best I could in the moment. I started giving my self permission to be exactly where I was – even if I hated being there – because I grasped that I'd have to be where I was for however long I needed to be there.

Despite how convoluted it all looked to my inner critic, I felt certain that I was involved in a healing process. Everything inside of me felt so different when I gave my self the same room I'd been helping my clients to give to themselves for years: room to let me be without judging me for where or how I might or might not be. Now I, too, could be allowed, honorably, to be clumsily bumbling along until I found my way. My friends' unconditional acceptance had given me the seed from which I created a loving, accepting internal voice. This new-inside-of-me voice evolved into what I called the good-Mommy-Inside-me.

Baby step by baby step, I grew better at accepting my process. I could hate how tangled I was feeling without hating my self for feeling so tangled. Instead, I felt sorry for my poor struggling self. As I grew more accepting of and compassionate toward this beleaguered self, I became more present in my experience, able simply to witness all of my turmoil.

More present in the experience and as witness to it, I had glimpses of insight into what my struggle was about; glimpses that the judging and criticizing had prevented me from seeing. I saw into the complex primal attachment that was keeping me tied to this relationship.

When we had first begun our sharing, my partner and I had appeared to be two significantly empowered go-to figures in our community. Yet, I had been magnetically drawn to the damaged little selves I saw beneath the surface of my partner's public big-person persona. Unasked, I nevertheless instantly dedicated my self to nurturing those unacknowledged wounded parts of her. Though I'd never had permission to own or to nurture the similarly broken little selves hidden within me, in this relationship (and unbeknownst to me) my wounded parts identified with my partner's. Then, as I nurtured and mothered her, my own unacknowledged hungers were, through the identification, being able to have an illusory (and secret) sense of being fed by me.

Leaving the relationship would have meant cutting off the vicarious nourishment that till then was the only sustenance these parts of me were getting in the world. The starvelings in me were petrified that they would die if I left the relationship, if I stopped nurturing my partner. Every time I took another step toward emotionally separating from the relationship, I would feel I was teetering on the brink of annihilation, both of my self and of my partner. It was this terror that would, each time, pull me back into the enmeshment.

Giving my self permission to pay attention to the hungry parts of me provided a doorway for deep healing to happen. As my inner starvelings became more visible to me I – without judgment – began to own how impaired I was beneath the layers of strength from which I'd lived. I began to feel as loving toward and devoted to my own needy self as I'd till then only been able to feel toward my partner's neediness.

As I turned my capacity for unconditionally loving and nurturing toward what was broken in me, I could directly feed my own till-then-denied hungers. This change in focus was the start of the arduous but successful process of individuating my self out of the entanglement with my partner.

Giving our selves permission to be exactly how and where we are while we're there allows us to be fully present in/to our most challenging experiences. The more present we are in/to these, the sooner we get what it is we need to learn in and from them and the sooner we come to the other side of them. This is true even when where we are is someplace we hate. And, it's especially true when we seem to be staying in that hated, uncomfortable place for an excruciatingly long time.

Consider giving your self permission to be just exactly where you are while you're there – even when you truly wish you didn't have to be there at all.

3-11. Feeling Sad

When you feel sad, depressed or in grief...
Be tender and gentle with your self.
Take the time and space to fold inward,
to be with the aching and the tears until they're done...
Trying to "cheer up" before you're ready to surface
deepens the wounding you already feel!

I spent most of my 42nd year and a good part of my 43rd year awash in inconsolable grieving. The anguish was part of the process of ending an intense, symbiotic seven-year relationship in which I had all but lost my self. (See **Others' Views**, page 259, **Being Exactly Where You Are**, page 249 and **Covers Over Our Heads**, page 207 for more about the relationship, the leave-taking and the grieving process.)

When You Feel Sad, Depressed Or In Grief...

Be Tender And Gentle With Your Self. Take The Time And Space To Fold Inward, To Be With The Aching And The Tears Until They're Done...

Trying To "Cheer Up" Before You're Ready To Surface Deepens The Wounding You Already Feel!

e10

Despair and waves of depression were a steady undertow that drained me. Amazingly, I was able to pull my self together to work with clients part of two or three days a week. I also found some solace in daily feeding, tending and mucking out the stalls of a menagerie of disabled animals I care-took in exchange for a rent-free living situation.

But, most of the time, I would be sobbing or near to tears. Breathing was often difficult. Food, for the most part, was nauseating to contemplate. Sleep and the lush nest of pillows on my bed beckoned constantly. Walks in the mountains and to the streams around Ojai offered some comfort when I could gather the energy to go hiking.

Being with friends and talking with family proved challenging. Most of the people in my life were relieved that I was finally removing my self from the destructive enmeshment in which I had been caught with my now ex-partner. It was hard for these people who loved me to hear the depth of my pain and grief over the ending that, for them, was cause for relief if not celebration.

It was hard for my friends and family to tolerate the upheavals that came with my efforts to stay connected, at least in a friendship, with my ex. Especially when each contact with her re-opened the wounds I was working to heal. The people who cared about my wellbeing would try to distract me from my suffering. They'd attempt to jolly me into other parts of my being or remind me what a miracle I was creating in my life by setting my self free. They wanted to get me to focus on what lay ahead instead of what I felt I was losing.

Since there was no way to be with my friends and in the middle of my pain at the same time, I mostly chose to spend my time where I needed to be: immersed in my anguish and by my self. One dear couple was the exception. As individuals and as a couple, they offered companionship, open ears, silent presence. They were willing, caringly, to bear witness to my up and down, in and out struggle.

They had no prescription for how I should be doing this mourning or this separating. They shared their home and their hearts without needing me to do my process in any way other than how I was doing it. They were able to be with my suffering, even when my own actions intensified my anguish. They didn't try to advise or fix me. They could let me be in the pit and still have some loving company, if and as that might be of comfort to me. They didn't expect the comfort to get me out of my funk. They didn't expect that their presence would make me feel better. Yet, and perhaps because they didn't expect or need it to, it often did.

They took me out to dinners, lunches and coffee with them, when and if I could stomach being around food. They didn't expect me to eat unless I could. They didn't cajole or push me into eating what I'd ordered when I found that I couldn't. My weeping at the table didn't distress them. They invited me out with them for movies or in for videos if I might want some temporary diversion or a break from the emotional intensity. And, they accepted when I'd need to leave abruptly, often just moments after I'd arrived.

They were a remarkable gift during one of the most difficult passages of my life. Their simple presence mirrored and supported what I was learning. Spirit was teaching me to have the courage to feel all of my chaotic, turbulent feelings without cutting them off or dimming them down. This couple's undemanding presence, their willingness to bear witness without intruding upon or diverting my process was perfect support. It helped to nourish my growing understanding that surrender into the fullness of the dark feelings was the only doorway to my healing. It was a blessing to be able to have some company when I needed it without having to pay the price of lightening up or cheering up when I still needed to be in the blackness.

The culture we live in is seriously dark-phobic. Feelings of sadness, despair, hopelessness and grief engender considerable discomfort, both in us and in the people around us. When we're sunk in these feelings, we feel less-than. We feel that it's not okay to feel badly. We feel that it's somehow shameful, an imposition if we are unable to put on a cheery face for those around us. Yet finding the courage to risk diving into these intense emotions – taking the time to plumb the depths of the darkness – offers us the only real possibility of moving through them/it into healing and greater wholeness. To be with our selves in those places is to honor our wounding, to be tender with our broken hearts, to allow our selves all the time we need to experience and release our pain.

We might, in these times, yearn to reach out for the simple warmth of human caring, believing the presence of a loving friend could offer comfort as we go on with our thrashing in the pit. Unless we're particularly fortunate in the people we have around us, it can be difficult to find anyone able to simply be with us without trying to cheer us up or to fix us. It can be difficult to find others willing to accept that it can be comforting to have their presence even as their presence doesn't appreciably cheer us up.

In these moments, we make a challenging choice. It's important to refuse to pay the price of prematurely lightening up, of trading off being with our difficult emotions in order to keep from discomforting others. To pay that price or make that trade off is to further wound our already suffering selves.

In these moments, we learn instead to practice reminding our selves that depression, grief, despair and feeling blue are natural and expectable parts of being alive and growing. We remind our selves that this is so even when others are put off by these feelings. We practice reminding our selves that these feelings are as much signs of life as the more generally acceptable feelings of joy, excitement and exuberance. We practice reminding our selves that all emotions have a trajectory:

they reach a peak of intensity, hang out there for a time and then slowly lessen and decay.

As we courageously yield into our dark emotions when they arise, we gradually increase our skill in riding them. We grow more adept at feeling all the way through them. In this process we uncover the wisdom and truths that our darkness has to reveal to us. We learn that, when we don't prematurely pull our selves together, we can actually observe our selves organically coming together on the other side of the turbulence.

Consider treating your self with gentleness and compassion in the dark feelings times.

3-12. Others' Views

*When others are interpreting, analyzing, advising or directing you –
they are really only communicating what they believe would be
appropriate for themselves were they in your situation. Remember this
if you choose to hear their views...Remember, too, that in the deep
knowing place inside of you, you are the world's best and only
authority on you! Practice listening inwardly instead of outwardly!*

Some months past my 35th birthday, after three years of being my own significant other, I entered a relationship that changed my life. It was compelling from the start, stirring longings that I hadn't experienced since my painful, childhood relationship with my mother. My heart opened in ways it never had in any other adult relationship and I loved with an intensity I'd never before experienced.

When Others Are Interpreting, Analyzing, Advising Or Directing You – They Are Really Only Communicating What They Believe Would Be Appropriate For Themselves Were They In Your Situation.

Remember This If You Choose To Hear Their Views... Remember, Too, That In The Deep Knowing Place Inside Of You, You Are The World's Best And Only Authority On You!

Practice Listening Inwardly Instead of Outwardly!

e11

I was drawn to the woundedness I saw in my partner. It resonated with my own. Each of us had been the rock, the nurturer – the one upon whom everyone else could depend. Those who looked to either of us for understanding/support repeatedly and unconsciously collaborated with us in keeping our own vulnerabilities invisible. So, we each were quite alone with our inner struggles and suffering.

At first, our coming together involved a conscious commitment to risk becoming visible (at least to each other) in these damaged places. We'd thought we might, at last and safely, explore being both our strong **and** our vulnerable selves with one another. Yet, less than conscious agendas and reluctances in both of us quickly led into more tangled emotional territory.

My partner, though sometimes sympathetic and tender was, more often, coldly distant and sarcastic. I readily got caught up in gyrations of conciliation, preoccupied with finding ways to re-create closeness and warmth in the midst of the freeze. I was persistent in my attempts to nurture, express love, placate, propitiate, cajole. More often than not, my attempts to bridge the gap between us only widened it. Still, occasionally warmth re-emerged seemingly in response to my exertions. These random rewards encouraged my escalating efforts and kept me obsessed with trying.

I was confused, filled with self-doubt, hurting. During the few years just before this, I'd begun to feel that I pretty well knew both my self and what I wanted. Now, for the first time in my adult life, I seemed completely lost to my self: utterly stripped. I could watch it happening. I would twist and re-invent my self in my efforts to avoid her glacial, critical distancing. I felt devastated by all of it, depressed most of the time. I loved and hated my partner in equal measure. Yet, I repeatedly dismissed my hating and my internal rageful ranting as my craziness, a perverse resistance to partnering.

Despite the intensity of the anguish and turbulence, I felt bound to the process: the struggle to make this relationship blossom. I felt sure that I could love my partner into a wholeness that would include her becoming able to love me in ways I longed for. I kept meeting her coldness with tenderness and understanding. I felt certain that my willingness to do this would eventually help my partner to heal the wounds that led her to be so mean and cut off from me.

My close friends were horrified as they watched me coming undone. They suffered anguish of their own on my behalf. They reflected. They interpreted. They implored. They offered all kinds of support to help me sever the connection. One couple even arranged for me to seemingly accidentally meet someone they thought might be attractive to me. Unable to fathom my participation in my own unraveling, they demonized and blamed my partner for all that was happening.

In the midst of my turmoil, I was continually bombarded by others' views, interpretations and advice. Friends, even a therapist I consulted during the worst of it, kept pushing me to leave the relationship. All agreed I shouldn't put up with what they saw as my partner's emotionally destructive treatment of me. All agreed I would be better once I'd left.

With all of this input overlaid on my agitation, I had to work hard to stay with my own inner knowing that it was important for me to continue being right where I was; that something important for me was going on here. It was work to keep honoring my conviction that this suffering was teaching me, growing me and taking me somewhere I needed to go. My coming undone felt like a significant (if still incomprehensible) part of my healing journey – not the doing of a demonic partner.

I asked my friends to stay out of it. I implored them to handle their own upset about my situation without expecting me to make changes in how I was handling my life. I asked them to trust with me that, despite appearances, healing was happening in me. Very few were able to give me that trust. With most, I had to disconnect entirely.

It took a long time for me to work my way through this challenging life experience. I was cracked open, scoured to the bone. Finally, after seven years, I began to accept that no amount of my caring or nurturing would ever heal my partner's woundedness or expand her capacity for self-love.

My exertions had only depleted me. I had exhausted my self giving **to** my partner the kind of loving I felt I needed **from** a partner, misguidedly assuming my loving would fix her enough so that she could then love me enough to fix me. It didn't work that way. It **never** does. I was filled with resentment and despair. I was bereft.

This long, excruciating journey taught me that healing into self-loving is always an **inside** job, a gift one can only give to oneself. It forced me to give up my conviction that anyone could love another being into wholeness and self-love. And, it moved me to give up my long-cherished fantasy that someday someone (outside my self) would love me so fully that I'd have to love my self.

As I worked on disentangling the many layers of psychic/emotional enmeshment with my now ex-partner, I simultaneously began what has become the most important work of my life. Over the past 30 years since I left that relationship, I've been passionately committed to the practice of treating my self as lovingly, tenderly, compassionately and unconditionally as I'd hoped some fantasized lover might. I've been becoming the fiercely loving, protective Big Momma who can love **me** into wholeness and self-loving. (See **The Little Ones Story**, page 9 and **Coming Home**, page 287 for more about this process.)

Often our voyages into darkness are ways that our pasts become present. Unresolved material from earlier times reappears in the context of our current life. As we live through this current version of the repeating story, we have an opportunity to move further both toward becoming conscious of the process and toward bringing resolution to it.

The devastating experiences with my ex-partner **were** my past become present: my partner's cold, mean treatment of me was an emotional replay of my mother's treatment of me as a child. My spiraling exertions and obsession with trying to fix my partner paralleled my years of trying to fix my mother. My despair and rageful internal ranting were also the same. This time around, I was able to go all the way through to the other side: I learned to stop trying to make someone into the mother for whom I yearned, to stop giving to another the very mothering for which I yearned and, instead, to turn that mothering toward my self.

The advice and reflections from all my caring friends asked me to abort the incomprehensible, agonizing process in my life that was being so excruciating for them to watch. Listening to my own inner knowing, I was able to choose to stay, to live fully into this long cycle of devastation. My dedication to seeing it through to its own, organic resolution opened me to the most powerful healing of my life.

May you find the courage to consider choosing to listen inwardly, especially in the most confusing times and particularly when others are having a lot to say about what they think you should be doing.

Remember, too, that when we pour loving onto someone who does not love him or her self, the person devalues and trashes both that love and the one who gives it. Groucho Marx described that person's basic attitude years ago: "Why would I ever want to join any club that would have me as a member!"

Consider being incredibly gentle with **your self.**

PLEASE, PLEASE, PLEASE if you recognize your current situation in my story, remember that the only wounded one your love can ever heal is your very own self. No matter how exquisitely you love, you cannot love an unavailable or emotionally or physically abusive partner into wholeness. Healing into wholeness is always an inside job, one best reinforced by a therapist or a support group.

If we are in a relationship with someone who treats us poorly, it is our selves that we need to love and heal, not our partners. Getting support to help us to give our selves permission to turn our unconditional loving toward our own selves is important. A good therapist and/or Al-Anon group can offer that help.

3-13. Measuring Your Self

Measuring your self by anyone else's process, achievements or life circumstances is a violation of your very own tender, delicate being... Remember, always, each of us has: different lessons we're learning, different learning styles and different inner timetables for our own unfolding... Your own way is always the best way for you... trust that!

From my fourteenth summer, the time of my first real job, having enough money has not been a problem in my life. Partly that's been because I've never been much of a consumer, hating shopping and feeling oppressed by having to manage more than a relatively small number of possessions. And, I've been blessed with an automatic balancing process inside of me. When there's less money coming in, my spending habits reset themselves accordingly, usually without any effort or thought.

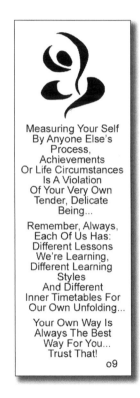

Measuring Your Self
By Anyone Else's
Process,
Achievements
Or Life Circumstances
Is A Violation
Of Your Very Own
Tender, Delicate
Being...

Remember, Always,
Each Of Us Has:
Different Lessons
We're Learning,
Different Learning
Styles
And Different
Inner Timetables For
Our Own Unfolding...

Your Own Way Is
Always The Best
Way For You...
Trust That!
o9

I've also been willing, through the years, to do almost anything (legal) to earn money when I've needed it. This willingness enabled me to find or invent work for my self whenever circumstances called for it. During my college years I did file clerking, ran the school switchboard, modeled for art classes, cleaned up art studios after classes, did ironing and childcare, delivered campus mail, cleaned typewriters, bought and sold sweaters and waited on tables.

In graduate school I had what my friends agree was the most outrageous of my willing-to-do-almost-anything jobs. I worked the night shift at The Flick, an open-all-night fancy ice cream parlor and restaurant that showed old-time movies in New York City. At 24, I was a budding feminist and a graduate student in psychology running subjects for my dissertation research project by day. Four nights a week from 8 PM till 6 AM, I worked as a poor man's version of a Playboy Bunny. The job involved wearing a leotard, cinch belt, mesh tights, high heels, white celluloid cuffs and collar with a black bow tie while serving oversized ice cream sundae specialties, espresso and after-bar-hours breakfasts.

There were free dinners and breakfasts for me at the restaurant and usually $40-$50 a night in tips (there was only a token on-the-books wage). For 1964 that was an incredible deal, never mind fending off the salacious remarks/attentions of the late night drunks. (We had a genteel bouncer watching out for us, and we learned to finesse things with quick and easy humor.) By seven in the morning I'd be back home in my fifth-floor walkup tenement apartment, soaking the imbedded chocolate syrup from body in my cast iron bathtub-in-the-kitchen. I'd sleep four hours or so and then go back to the laboratory to start my daytime life.

At 32, burned out after completing both my Ph.D. degree and seven years as a private practice psychologist in New York City, I dropped out and took to the road, heading west in a van that I'd set up as a bed-sitting room. (See **Pirouettes**, page 125 for more about that.) At that point, I thought I'd never do psychotherapy again.

A lifelong super-achiever, I spent the next 20 months committed to learning how to be comfortable doing nothing but traveling the west coast and getting a tan. After a while, I began to experiment with different ways to make a living: I baked cakes and cookies in an organic bakery. I spent several months selling my own designed and hand-crocheted clothing in a cooperative shop in a 1970s-style marketplace. For nine months, I worked as a Health Education Coordinator in a collectively run free clinic (speaking about mental and physical health issues in schools and colleges and on a weekly radio show as well as helping kids on bad acid trips at live concerts).

I cleaned houses with a woman-run contract cleaning service (I've always **loved** cleaning and making order – it's something I regularly do to ground and calm my self). I did other people's errands. For a while, I even tried being the doorperson-cum-bouncer at a women's bar. It was this connection with the women's community that opened me to the possibility of trying to do psychotherapy again – in an untraditional and experimental way.

Over the years, I've actually started four different psychotherapy practices in four different geographies. Each time, since my standard of living has always been a modest one, I've managed to be making a living within three to six months.

In the earliest years of my first private practice, whenever a client might feel done or choose to come less often, or when there was a rash of cancellations, I'd worry about my practice/business falling apart: an edgy feeling familiar to people who free lance or work for themselves. Yet, each time, new clients would appear soon after others left. It felt magical, as though some benevolent presence were watching over me, keeping me secure.

My faith in this automatic renewal of my practice grew. Gradually, I was able to trust it even when replacement clients were slower in turning up or when I had an increasing number of empty hours in my workweek for longer periods of time. I learned to see the slow periods as times for resting; they always came before cycles of accelerating growth in my personal evolution. The more I recognized this, the more I was able to relax into the rest cycles and stop filling that precious time with fears about my income disappearing.

In my work as well as in other parts of my life, my faith in the ongoing support from a benevolent Spirit presence has continued. That presence (that I now call the Grandmothers) helps me to be in the right place at the right time, it brings the right people into my life, nudges me along, opens my eyes to possibilities and sometimes, slows me down. These days I believe that, no matter how it may look or feel, everything is actually going just as it needs to for my unfolding.

Still, there are times when that belief is seriously tested. For three years starting more than eighteen years ago, my practice and income were diminishing at what seemed an alarming pace. Even as I reminded and reassured my self of what I'd easily accepted under less disturbing circumstances, I began to wonder if Spirit were nudging me out of this kind of work, forcing me to let go of it. I couldn't imagine what else I might do at this stage of my life. At 54, I was feeling much less adventurous than at 24 or 32 or 42. There were many moments of anxious edge-walking. Then, I would come back to center; knowing that, if this were truly to be the end of this cycle in my life, the new direction would reveal itself to me in a timely way.

The precariousness of my balance was complicated by what was happening in the lives of three of my closest women friends, all of them also therapists. It was, for each of them, a time of expansion and abundance professionally. Their burgeoning practices were full if not sometimes over-full. Each was experiencing a constant stream of new client referrals. Their incomes were solid and increasing. This, while I was in what looked like professional decline: very few clients, no new referrals, living close to the bone. Baffled, I worked hard to use the open time to rest and **not** to worry, to trust that this contraction had some purpose and that there wasn't something wrong with me.

Even as I **knew** not to make comparisons, knew how damaging that would be to my delicate, in-transition self, it was a huge struggle to not measure, to not compare, to not judge. My task was to hold what was happening in my life as a necessary part of my journey. My test was to resist the culture's view of this process as one of failure or collapse. It was a time of stretching, of deepening my trust, of resisting the temptation/pressure to **do** something to force this process to abort.

In the end, I felt so proud of me for staying compassionately with the frightened parts of my self through this arduous passage, proud of me for being able to do some significant resting in the middle of it. The way out lay (as always) in embracing and going **through** all of it: the feelings, the questioning and the doubt.

At some point three years later, the releasing that I needed to come to inside of me finally happened. (And that's a whole other story.) New directions emerged. My website was one of them. Now my practice (which I continue to love and enjoy) is usually as full as I want it to be. New people appear just as others come to places of closure. When things slow or contract, I'm able to welcome and enjoy the open time.

My faith in process is more profound now than ever. Still, I know that there will occasionally be other times and ways I will be challenged to sustain that trust – especially when there'll be no clue about the point of the challenge.

It helps so much to remember that each of us has different lessons we're learning, different learning styles and different inner timetables for our own journeys. It's never okay to measure our selves against anyone else's achievements or pace. Our own way is always the best way for us – we need to believe that no matter what.

Consider honoring the rightness for you of your very own path and your very own pace.

3-14. When Others Criticize You

You can love your self no matter what
anyone else thinks or says about you!

By late 1984, I'd finally managed to extricate my self from the tangled relationship that I'd struggled in for over seven years. (See **Others' Views**, page 259 for more about this.) I was, at almost 44, reclaiming my own separate life. And, at the same time, I was moving out of the relative isolation I had chosen while in that relationship.

It was a transformative time. Finding my way back to my self, I began meeting and getting to know some delightful women. It often felt like Spirit/the Grandmothers had a hand in the ways in which I met these new friends. The simple sweetness of these connections was balm to my battered psyche.

One of these new friends was a scientist/naturalist/artist that I met while meandering on my favorite canyon trail one early evening. I came upon her and her dog only moments after I'd felt a surge of longing for someone to hang out with. We walked together for a

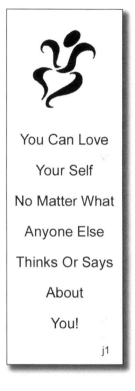

You Can Love

Your Self

No Matter What

Anyone Else

Thinks Or Says

About

You!

j1

while that night, sharing stories about our connections to wild places, to solitude and to the magic of Ojai. She was living and working in Los Angeles on weekdays. On weekends, she would come to replenish her soul in a little cottage that she was renting in the East End of Ojai. The cottage was just around the corner from the rented cottage in which I was replenishing my own soul. Both recovering from complicated long-term relationships that we'd recently ended, we each were still talking with our former partners, trying to navigate the shift from relationship to friendship. And, we were each consciously engaged with our spiritual journeys. The parallels were striking.

We began spending time together out on the trails when she came to Ojai each weekend. As we hiked, we shared tales of hope and frustration. We reflected on the differing styles with which we were approaching our struggles to disengage from compulsive attempts to save our now ex-partners from the unhappiness of their problem-filled lives. We became a support group of two for this transitioning time in which we each found (and were finding) our selves.

While we were both committed to our spiritual journeying, we had different paths and different ways of being on those paths. She was immersed in a Buddhist tradition, intensely formal in her practice and study. I was involved in a much looser intuitive approach to my spiritual evolution. I let my self be guided by the energy of the deep feminine: the voice of the Great Mother/the Grandmothers that spoke in my heart as I wandered in the wild places. These quite different approaches and the richness they held for each of us were, in the early days of our getting to know each other, a source of intriguing dialogue.

With mind and body, I was exploring the Field of the Sacred Feminine intent on discovering what the essential nature of female eroticism might be. I was captivated imagining the possibilities of a feminine erotic nature that hadn't been, for millennia, co-opted and circumscribed by male images of female sexuality. I was awed by the vibrant erotic energy I felt in my connection with the natural world. The Great Mother was my teacher. I shed my clothes wherever I felt safe to be naked in the wild places. Sitting in the little waterfalls on the river, cuddling with or napping cradled in trees, curled into or wrapped around boulders, I let their energies resonate in my body and being. I was absorbed, feeling the erotic flow connecting me with the river, the trees, the boulders; feeling the expanding openness of erotic arousal, the dissolving of boundaries, my self melting into the all-that-is.

My sharing about these experiences was part of our dialogue about spirituality, relationship and life. After a while, we ventured into experimenting together with erotic energy. At the start, this felt like a safe and natural extension of our sharing since we'd already been playing with psychic energy, trying to send and receive images with each other over distance.

Erotic play also wove in and out of another friendship I was involved in at the same time as Anita (not her real name) and I were experimenting together. I was open in both sharings about being not at all interested in creating a partnering/romantic relationship with anyone, then or possibly ever. I simply wanted to explore on as many levels as were safely available with anyone with whom I was engaging. Both women said they understood and accepted where I was coming from.

Around this time, the owners of Anita's cottage needed to reclaim that space for their own family. At the same moment, one of the other two cottages on the property where I lived became vacant. Anita, delighted with the synchronicity, readily made the move. At the start, her greater proximity felt fine with me. Our separate commitments to our solitude, my openness about where I was vis-à-vis relationship and her Ojai presence still being limited to weekends promised clear boundaries.

Not long after her move, she left her job in Los Angeles. She moved down the road to a new Ojai living space that provided her with reduced rent in exchange for caretaking the property she'd live on and found a job in her scientific field in a nearby community. As she spent more time in Ojai, she began meeting people including some of my friends. She developed her own separate connections with two of those friends.

After a while, things got complicated. On several occasions, she'd make plans for us with those friends, speaking as if we were a couple. She was taken aback by my sensitivity to something she called "insignificant" or "merely semantic." I'd explain further. She'd appear to get what I was taking exception to. Then it would happen again. I'd be furious. She'd refer to me as her girlfriend and I'd call her on that. She'd be surprised by my objections to her proprietary language. She couldn't seem to hear that it wasn't a matter of semantics for me.

She became impatient with our erotic energy play, pushing verbally for what to me felt like just plain sex. I was upset by her attitude and tried again to clarify what I was available for. She'd seem to understand. Then, just back from a trip, she actually became physically pushy about sexual touching. It felt abusive and invasive, so I left and went home, furious.

As I walked the quarter mile up the road to my cottage I finally saw that dialogue was not possible with this person: she just couldn't hear me. Despite how things had been earlier in our sharing, what was going on now was toxic, unacceptable. I was done, not open to negotiation.

Once home, shaken and outraged, I wrote a letter telling her that I recognized that she didn't or couldn't hear me in my own terms no matter how I tried to explain me and that I found her behavior abusive. And given that, I wrote, I saw no point in attempting any discussion about my decision to be done with our sharing. Still shaking with rage, I left the note in her mailbox in the middle of that night.

Late the next morning, she arrived on my doorstep in a rage of her own. Though I had nothing more to say to her, I felt I had to give her the opportunity to have her say in response to the letter. To insulate my self from her rageful energy, I stood holding one hand over my heart and one over my solar plexus. I made sure to stay far enough away from her so that my body was outside the range of her swirling energy field.

She stalked back and forth across my studio ranting at me, telling me what a "manipulative, malevolent, spiritually fraudulent, people-user" I was. One of my most vivid memories from her diatribe was of her telling me how despicable I was because I "used people and when you're no longer getting what you need from a relationship, you just callously crumple it up and throw the person away like a used candy wrapper!"

Though it was hard to listen to her condemnation of me, I felt no need to defend my self. I simply acknowledged that I could see how she experienced me. I was, amazingly, able to allow her to have her perceptions of me, though they differed from my own and even, sometimes, paralleled venomous accusations I'd occasionally heard from my inner critic.

At some point her rage was spent and she left. I was exhausted by the work of holding me safe and centered in the face of her storming. Yet, I also felt exhilarated. It was a milestone in my life. I'd stood solidly in the middle of my own reality even as I grasped how reprehensible my way of being was for her. I could accept the context of her negative perceptions, could see me through her furious eyes and still remain clear that her behavior had been abusive and unacceptable to me.

Both before and after this watershed moment, there have been friendships and relationships that I've left because they've stopped feeling right for me. Part of what Anita accused me is true about me: when an intimate connection no longer nourishes or grows me, I do leave it. Usually, I do this with grace and caring, honoring what has been. Time already shared and the depth of that sharing are not, for me, reason to stay or to continue in something that no longer feeds my soul.

In earlier days, I'd feel anguished and critical of my self when I came to the place of being done relating with someone who'd been, till then, an important part of my life. I stayed longer than I wanted to in order to postpone having to cope with the person's and my own negative opinions: about me, about the quality of my friendship, about the authenticity of my caring. I've often felt uneasy with the fact that my delight in my own solitary company makes interpersonal relationships less essential to me than they seem to be for many other people. The reality that I can and do leave when being with another ceases to offer me more than I can offer my self makes for a not always level playing field.

At the time I went through this uproar with Anita, I had already grown more accepting of the way I am in the world of relatedness with other(s). I knew that it did not matter whether it came from woundedness or wholeness; it's merely how I'm wired. I'd also realized that even when I do full disclosure about my self in the early days of a developing friendship, people do not necessarily believe or get the full implications of what I tell them. And, I'd recognized that sometimes there is nothing for it but to allow others to have their own readings of me while I stay centered in my own sense of my self.

These days, I accept that some friendships, while rich and intriguing at the start, may only be nourishing for a season of my life. Others begin in the same way but then continue to flourish through countless transformations and seasons. There's no knowing which are which at the start. I have my own permission not to stay in any connection beyond the season(s) in which it grows me, no matter what the person may think of me for letting go of our sharing.

As we practice becoming fiercely protective mothers to all of our little and big selves, we become unconditionally accepting of our whole, imperfect, still evolving, not-always-shining selves. Since our own good opinion of and love for our selves no longer depend on how anyone else sees us, we become more willing to allow others to have their own visions/versions of us. We become less susceptible to others' negating views of us. And, as Terry Cole Whittaker once wrote, we realize that "What you think of me is none of my business."

Keeping our own good opinion of our selves doesn't require that we invalidate or argue away another's less loving experience of us. But, we may choose not to be close with people whose views of us are negative or so discrepant from our own.

Consider loving and accepting your self no matter what anyone else (or your own inner critical voice) thinks or says about you.

3-15. Forgiving Before It's Time

When you "forgive" before you've gone inward to plumb the depths of your hurt and anger or, before you've acknowledged your right to your upset... You're violating your deepest self!

My mother died on Valentine's Day, 42 years ago, just three months after my 30th birthday. After several years of estrangement, I had become re-involved with her during the two years of treatments for her ultimately fatal metastatic breast cancer. And, I'd spent each of the last ten days of her life sitting beside her hospital bed as she lay in liver coma, moving toward her death. It was long before the Hospice movement, and hers was neither a conscious nor an openly acknowledged dying. Yet, I felt a compelling need to make sure she would not die alone. I tended her and crocheted quietly for hours looking out at the winter landscape in Central Park. My father came to relieve me for the evenings after his workday ended. I'd walk home, see a few clients, go to sleep and wake again each morning to another day of the deathwatch.

In the end, she did die alone, discovered at the changing of the shifts at seven in the morning, just before I was to arrive for the day. I did not grieve for her. On the morning of her death, and forever afterward, what I felt was gratitude and relief: I would never again have to deal with her as a physical presence in my life.

When You "Forgive" Before You've Gone Inward To Plumb The Depths Of Your Hurt And Anger Or, Before You've Acknowledged Your Right To Your Upset... You're Violating Your Deepest Self!

s2

It was the best Valentine gift anyone could have given me. Her death left me having to deal only with my mother's destructive presence as it lived on within me: the venomous voice of my inner-critic, the Hatchet Lady. I was also freed, at last, to feel the fullness of my rage at this woman who had so damagingly mothered me. While she lived, my rage at her had been stifled by my sense of the fragility beneath her hostility toward me. Liberated from the fear that it would destroy her, I began the journey of plumbing the depth of my fury.

From early in my life I had learned (as so many of us have) to make excuses for my mother's unremitting cruelty toward me. Typically that involved (as so often it does) blaming my self: I was not being a good enough girl, not behaving properly or, in some obscure, inadvertent way, provoking her to meanness.

From the earliest I can remember, I was constantly trying to appease her, undeterred by the fact that most of what I did seemed only to escalate her nastiness toward me. I learned independence early. Although it's probably apocryphal, there's a family tale of my walking to the corner candy store holding someone's (not her) hand, clutching my penny and asking the man there for a pretzel when I was nine months old. A similar tale has me out of diapers before I turned two.

My precociousness had to do with the fact that it was always infuriating to her when I needed anything. Getting hurt or sick petrified me. I'd react with hysterical crying. When I came to her in terror or pain, she'd yell at or ridicule me for malingering and "making such a big deal out of nothing!" As I've reflected through the years, I've considered that my terrors (or, indeed, any of my needs) might have overwhelmed and frightened her, facing her with her incapacity to cope as a parent. Perhaps it was this that stirred the rage she'd vent on my needy little self.

I can remember being paralyzed by fear at having the breath knocked out of me when, at six or seven, I'd fall while roller-skating. After the first fall, when my coming to her for comfort triggered her wrath, I'd sit on the sidewalk where I'd fallen, in a panic with only my already terrified self to try to comfort me.

I have no memories of tenderness or loving closeness with my mother. The only gentle touch I remember was her washing my hair when I was too little to do it my self. All other physical contact with her involved being yanked, pushed or slapped. But, more than contact, I remember icy distance and being ignored.

My earliest, most devastating memory of her mothering comes from when I was a little past three. It was 1944. My father had enlisted in the Navy just before he would have been drafted into the Army. Most other women with children in her position gave up their apartments, moved back in with their parents and went to work in factories. My mother, at 26, went back to the work she'd done (and loved) before her marriage, as a relatively well-paid legal secretary. She kept our apartment – living (with considerable delight) as an attractive, glamorous single workingwoman – and sent me to live with her parents.

My maternal grandparents were warm, loving non-English speaking Eastern European immigrants. They lived three blocks away from our apartment. They doted on me. During the year that I lived with them, my mother would pick me up for the day on Sundays. Occasionally she'd take me back to our apartment on a Saturday, after a half day of work, for a sleepover with her. We rarely spent time with the four of us together. (In my late teens I learned that there had been years of discord and resentment between my mother and both of her parents by the time she'd left me with them.)

The memory I have is of waking up one night on my cot in the small room off my grandparents' kitchen. I woke in anguish, crying uncontrollably. My whole body remembers the convulsive sobbing, the inconsolable longing for "my mommy." Nothing my grandparents did, no amount of holding or soothing words quieted my desperation. I had to have my mommy.

It was after dark and my grandparents had already been in bed, undressed. Still, grandpa got dressed and walked the three blocks to get my mother. (They had no telephone in those days.) I've no idea how late it might have been, or whether my mother had been asleep, or how long it actually took for him to go and come back with her. I sobbed non-stop, choking on my own mucous, curled between my Grandma and the doorjamb to my room the whole time he was gone.

I remember hearing the key in the door, then seeing my mother in the doorway. My body turned cold with panic as she stalked in and stopped, leaning back on the porcelain washtub on the far side of the room from where I stood. The fury in her hard eyes is still a powerful, visceral memory; so, too, her glacial voice as she snarled at my sobbing little self across the room, pointing a wagging finger at me. "If you **ever** do this to me and your grandfather again, I'll…."

For years, I couldn't remember with what it was that she threatened me before she turned and stalked right out of their apartment, leaving me frozen and bereft. I recalled the rest of her sentence some twenty years later, in my first therapist's office. In the middle of an almost dissociative panic state triggered by becoming aware of feeling intense neediness in his presence, I had a frightening physical experience. It felt as though invisible hypodermic needles were pulling all the strength out of my knees. In that moment, I re-heard her enraged voice snarling at me: "If you **ever** do this to me and your grandfather again, **I'll break both your legs!**"

Her endless litany of belittling words and actions (or ignorings) lacerated me throughout the first 30 years of my life. The internalized version of my mother, my vicious inner critic, the Hatchet Lady, continued the lashings for another seventeen. (Only after years of working on and with the Hatchet Lady, was I at last able to defang and transform her into an almost gentle ally.)

As I've grown into knowing my self more fully, I've understood how trapped and beleaguered my mother must have felt as a parent/wife/ woman in her times. I've felt sadness for the woundings in her life, for how damaged she must have been, for how few options were available to her. I've been able to see the grief and resentment underlying her competitiveness with me: I received from her parents and from my dad the tenderness and attention she so craved from them. How infuriating it must have been for her to watch them treat me as she yearned to be treated by them. I can understand that she would resent and want to punish me.

As I watch young mothers with young children, I know I could never in my wildest dreams have had the emotional wherewithal to cope with the 24/7, 100% attention it takes to parent in our non-tribal culture. I am filled with gratitude for the awareness, the help of Spirit/ my deep-knowing self and the willingness to tolerate considerable criticism that combined to allow me the freedom, as a young woman, to choose consciously to neither birth nor parent children. I know my mother's world was a harder one in which to see that option, much less risk choosing it.

Freeing my self from the toxic legacy left by her mothering has been my healing journey. The wounds and tangles of my relationship with her were, in a sense, the greatest gift she gave me. Without the comforts and acceptance of traditional mothering, I've had to find ways to comfort and mother my self. From the deprivation and pain I suffered, a keen awareness of what a being needs for it to grow and thrive emerged.

My years of doing the inner work to provide for my self a compassionate, unconditionally loving, fiercely protective mother-within have born lavish fruit. This fruit has nourished me, the people I work with as clients and, more lately, the people who read the tales I write from the inside of my healing process.

I would not be the woman I am, a woman I love and freely share, had I not suffered from my mother's mistreatment. It was the ground from which the me that I am was born. I've created wonder and magic from that pain. I would not trade this me for a different childhood, a different mother.

I can and do feel compassion for that seriously damaged woman, for her impossible predicament. I can and do accept that she did the very best she could within the limits of her capacities and the level of consciousness available to her. I cannot and do not, however, forgive her for the ways she wounded the delicate being that I was. I cannot imagine what would make forgiving her a possibility in me until or unless the day comes that it doesn't feel that to do so will violate the tender damaged little one inside me who was her hapless victim.

Volumes of pressure from New Age, spiritual and psychological hype all around us keeps pushing forgiveness as the singular solution, the only path to freedom/enlightenment, the ultimate goal of all healing for all of us. Over and over, through the years, I have struggled to keep wresting permission to honor my own unwillingness to forgive what feels to me unforgivable. Revisiting all of this painful history as I've written this tale has moved me again and acutely, to emphatically carve out the space for my right to hold what's so for me.

Whenever we who have been victimized or traumatized – emotionally, physically, psychically, sexually – are being pressured into forgiveness before or unless that forgiveness arises **organically** from our own depths, we are being encouraged to violate and re-victimize our wounded selves. Any philosophical system, spiritual practice, psychological theory, religion or person/healer (including any part of our selves) that would so pressure any of us needs to be challenged/ questioned/set aside in this domain. Sometimes the best we can hope for is acceptance, compassion and perhaps some sympathetic understanding of the context of the victimizer's life circumstances.

Consider being as tender as you possibly can be with your wounded, upset, hurt or angry self.

3-16. Not Rushing

Rushing keeps you from feeling the process you're in the middle of.
If the process seems too much or too hard to feel, it might well be
leading somewhere it won't be okay for you to be...
Slow down and listen-in to the deep knowing place!

It was the fall of 1990, six years and three property owners after I'd moved into my first magical, healing cottage. The cottage nestled in the East End of Ojai, a somewhat rural area of orange groves, avocado groves and horse properties with magnificent views of a range of bluffs (the Topa Topa Mountains) that are reminiscent of New Mexico vistas.

The cottage had appeared in my life in a burst of good fortune in 1984 as I was leaving a tortuous seven-year relationship. The search for a new home had also been tortuous, a bleak process during which I despaired of ever finding a right-feeling place for my self. I'd felt stymied in my search, hard up against the end of the month when my about to be ex-partner and I had to leave our shared rental. Out of the blue, a woman in one of my Giving Up Deprivation groups called to let me know of a cottage that had just become available.

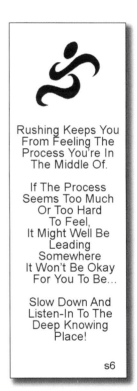

Rushing Keeps You From Feeling The Process You're In The Middle Of.

If The Process Seems Too Much Or Too Hard To Feel, It Might Well Be Leading Somewhere It Won't Be Okay For You To Be...

Slow Down And Listen-In To The Deep Knowing Place!

s6

That delightful converted two-car garage became the nest in which I came to know, love and provide for the abandoned Little One inside of me. Though I had nested before in my life, this was the first time I was consciously making a home in the world for that Little One. As I reclaimed the neglected, forlorn outdoor spaces around the house, I simultaneously reclaimed the neglected, forlorn places inside of me. I moved tons of rocks, boulders and construction debris as I moved through the tons of emotional debris buried in my broken heart. I used the strewn rocks to build meandering walls, tilled and fertilized the cleared earth and planted gardens. The landscape and I grew and transformed together. Together, the cottage and I became a nourishing home for all the emerging me's of me.

The first property owners had been essentially invisible – an address to which I sent my rent. The second owners were an exuberant couple my own age who, at first, came only on weekends. The husband reveled in construction projects, knocking down walls and extensively remodeling the main house while jovially adding a picture window and bathtub to improve on the basic perfection of my little cottage.

At some point they found a more suitable full-time home in Ojai and sold the property to their daughter and her husband. Things began to change. At first they, too, were only a weekend presence – albeit a more intense, more invasive one than their parents had been. Then, they began planning major reconstruction involving tearing down both the main house and the second small rental cottage on the property. During the construction they hoped to use what had been my cozy home as their roost on occasional weekends. Once the new expansive main house was finished, they'd move to Ojai full-time and my home would then become the husband's painting studio and the wife's home office.

It was heart wrenching to imagine giving up that womb space. The process of searching for a new space was gut wrenching. When I'd first moved to the cottage, I'd had only a few possessions, the bare bones of what I needed to be comfortable: all thrift store and garage sale stuff, nothing I couldn't easily leave behind. Now, as I searched for a new space, I was no longer traveling so lightly.

Over the six years of making a home for my self, everything had gradually been transformed. My various thrift store couches and chair had been reupholstered and slip covered in matching white canvas. I'd made and covered (and then repeatedly recovered) a sizeable collection of large and small floor and throw pillows in changing cycles of brilliant color that reflected the changes happening in me. As sounding and making art had become essential non-verbal healing pathways, first in my own healing journey and then in my work with clients, I'd gathered a collection of second-hand ethnic percussion instruments and art supplies of every description.

Along the way, I'd bought a hot tub that had provided me nightly with safe, warm embracing. I'd need private outdoor space for that in any new place. And, too, in all but rainy weather, I'd grown used to sleeping year round on the ground in a tent. I'd need private outdoor space for that as well. It was overwhelming. This time I'd have to find a place that not only felt right but could, as well, accommodate all this equipment-for-a-healing-life. A daunting prospect, it was one made more challenging by the grief I felt at having to leave the home in which the new me had been born and nourished.

I cried a lot, ranted a lot; felt sad, confused and distraught. I searched from mid-September through December and on into early January. In such a small town there weren't many things available and nothing of what was available felt workable. Demolition began in mid-December. By January first, the electrical and gas lines on the property were capped. That meant no operating refrigerator, lights or phone answering machine, no stove, no hot water or washer/dryer. Since the phone lines were left intact, an old non-portable phone that plugged directly into a wall jack allowed for phone service. I couldn't have done without that. It was all pretty rough. Yet, there was still nowhere to go.

I saw evening clients by candle light, cooked on my two-burner propane camping stove, kept my perishable food in a big Coleman ice chest, washed dishes with cold water and sponge-bathed with small amounts of propane heated water as I had in the old days of living in my van. I was camping-in at my cottage. A kindly local motel owner let me rent a room for $15 for an after check-out/before check-in hour so that, bringing my own towels, I could have a hot shower and wash my hair a couple of times a week. I patched together 500 feet of outdoor extension cords so that I could plug into electricity at the neighbors' on the next property. Besides a phone, the other thing that I couldn't live without was my phone answering machine. Having a three-socket outlet plugged in at my end provided me with the bonus of lamplight to read by at night and a clock radio for more gentle awakenings on mornings when I needed to waken at a particular time.

Over and over again, I'd be tempted to take something, anything to abort the excruciating process of looking and not finding anything that felt right, to get on with life instead of being stalled out in this not here-not there place. It was an awful time. I hated it. Often, I felt like I couldn't bear it for one more minute.

Still, deep inside I knew that I had to trust in the process. I had to stay in the middle of what I was being taken through. I had to not rush my self through it to some other place that wasn't where I really needed to be, someplace that would merely be an escape from this here that I hated being in.

In the middle of the worst of the pressure to rush to some other side, a woman in another of the Giving Up Deprivation groups told me she had an unexpectedly vacated duplex that might work for me. The inside and private yard spaces looked more workable than anything else I'd seen. But, it was in the middle of a neighborhood of tract homes. And, across a field out behind it was an elementary school. That meant loud buzzers that rang at odd times throughout the day and a playground that hosted multiple daily recess periods. It would have been a stretch after living in the quiet countryside of the East End. It felt like a close-but-no-cigar place. Still, it was hard to say a definite "no" at that desperate-feeling moment.

The woman who offered it to me had some work she wanted to do to fix the place up for whomever might be the next tenant. That meant she had room for me to stay in a "maybe, if nothing more right turns up" place for at least another ten days. I made a deal with her and with my self: if nothing more suitable appeared by January 17th I would commit to taking her place, starting February first, on a month to month basis while I continued my search. Camping in might not be workable for as long a time as it might take to get to where I was meant to go next.

On the 12th of January a friend who did house-sitting called to tell me that a house at which I'd once visited her was coming vacant on February first. I remembered the house, a sweet little cottage in the middle of a large orange grove. A converted carport, it was smaller by half than my converted two-car garage, one large room rather than two. I went by to peek in its windows and fell in love. I could see my necessaries fitting inside and outside of it, could envision letting go of what wouldn't fit into the smaller space. I was jubilant. In the complex process of locating and getting to connect with the property owners, I never doubted that they would rent to me. I knew that this was my new home, the one Spirit had in mind for me.

They were delighted with me as a prospective tenant and accepted me on the spot. (On a hunch, I'd brought before and after photos of my soon-to-be-former cottage and yards.) The move happened gently, in slow stages. The money and the contractor I needed to do the electrical work and privacy fencing for my hot tub arrived at just the right moment. The things I needed to sell, sold easily. Every step of the way went smoothly.

It felt good to get smaller again, to have less and therefore less to take care of. In the old cottage, I had expanded to the point that I needed someone to help me keep up with the yard work and someone else to help me keep up with the housework. It had become more of a life than I could handle on my own. It was comforting to downsize house and gardens to a level that I could manage on my own again. I loved having more time to be still and to rest; less time required of me to tend-the-temple. And, it was a blessing not to have helpers around when I wanted to be alone.

The months of suffering through looking-and-not-finding had given me time to grieve the loss of my cherished cottage, to do the work of letting go and of feeling all the complex mix of distresses that were involved in that process. For all my doubting that I'd ever find a place as wonderful as that first cottage, this new one felt even more magical and perfect, as though the first were the rehearsal and this one the performance.

Being slowed down by circumstances (and conscious choices to not abort the painful process) had served me well; even as I hated and ranted and wept my way through the whole of it. The journey transformed me, taught me a lot about navigating through intense and difficult times. All of it expanded my ever-burgeoning trust in Spirit. All of it prepared me for what, as I wrote this tale 14 years later, was yet another cycle of having to leave a home to which I'd become quite attached. I was again in a cycle of going through countless weeks of frustrated, disheartening searching; a cycle of despairing in the middle of simultaneously trusting that Spirit had a hand in it and would surely bring what I need when the time was right.

Everything in our it's-the-bottom-line-that-counts, get-over-it and don't-just-sit-there-do-something culture constantly presses us to keep moving forward; to keep moving away from challenging emotional processes like grief, despair and pain as quickly as possible; to take action or take a pill to get over it now. Very little around us (except Pema Chodron's work) supports or encourages our taking the risk of simply staying with our selves through all of whatever emotional process is unfolding within us until it naturally completes itself. The rushing away keeps us growing ever more fearful of such processes. We worry that, were we to give in to the feelings, we might never re-emerge from their depths. This is exactly the opposite of what is actually so about emotions.

Much of New Age cant (think here of Rhonda Byme's best-selling book, *The Secret*) would have us leap away from intense so-called negative thoughts or feelings lest they attract more such energy and lead to negative outcomes; a don't-think/feel/say-that-or-you'll-make-it-so kind of distortion of what is true. Holding the faith and feeling the upset all the way through is how we actually heal our wounds without doing the equivalent of spiritual bypass surgery.

When we slow down and listen deep in the middle of our despair, grief, terror, frustration, irritation, rage we can dare to feel, release and heal whatever is moving within us. The knowing place inside us will help to hold us safe through the storms. And, it will help us to find our way to the authentic other side, even when there is a long trajectory to reaching it.

When we run and rush away from the hard places, we don't get to know whether the hardness is a challenge that, if met, will heal us or if the hardness is a warning signal that we are moving in a direction that is ultimately not good for us. Only going slowly enough for the listening-in will let us know which is so at the time.

Consider slowing down and listening in to the deep knowing place within you whenever you're tempted to rush through something that seems too hard to feel.

Coming Home: Reclaiming and Re-Mothering the Wounded Little One(s) Inside

(In 1984, at 43 and feeling devastated, I began the process of kindling a fiercely protective, unconditionally loving Mommy-Inside. An extraordinarily powerful inner ally, she helped me to care for the long abandoned Little One Inside who had begun to capture my attention and concern. This is a chronicle of the first five years of that journey.)

As I sit down to start writing, my body seizes up in layers of contraction. Most of them start in my back, around and between my shoulder blades and also at the level of my diaphragm. They almost take my breath away. I lie down; breathing slowly and deeply, I search (by means I can neither name nor understand) to find where and how to begin the physical unwinding process for each vortex of constriction.

After several months of this, I understand that what's going on in my body is a physical manifestation of terror. I don't feel it emotionally, but some small being long locked inside me feels it intensely. Without words, images or memories, my body is responding to some threat I do not, in my grown-up self, perceive.

Curled up in bed on a heating pad, cuddled around my saddest, most forlorn-looking teddy bear under a soft fleece comforter, some of the tension releases. The heat warms the ice-at-my-core sensation that comes with the contractions and I ease into the middle of being with my body having its feelings of terror. I drift briefly into semi-consciousness, then am wrenched into wakefulness by a dream: I am driving my car when suddenly some dark fabric-like creature attacks and covers my face. I can't see where I'm going. I can't breathe. I can't pull it off my face. Suffocating and terrified, I wake in panic.

Awake, I hold and rock the teddy bear and my self. Inside me the Mommy croons lovingly to the Little One, "Oh, my little sweetie is so scared. It's such a scary time for you, Little One, but I'm right here with you. Honey, you won't be alone, I won't leave you. I'll hold you and rock you and stay right here the whole time. I won't let anyone hurt you, dear heart."

When the terror constricts my body while I'm with someone, I pay attention to it. At another time in my life I might have vaguely noticed the tightness as background and continued with the interaction as if nothing were going on in me. Now, I hear my body screaming at me to stop what I'm doing because the Little One is feeling petrified. I stop everything and go inside, melting into the pain. Sometimes that gives birth to a knowing about what stirred the emotion; other times I remain mystified. I simply stay with the pain and with the Little One until the wave passes. When I do this and talk lovingly to her, it always passes. When I try to override it or ignore her calls to me, it gets stronger and more persistent. People in my life are getting used to my doing this; my fierce determination to not abandon that frightened part of me keeps me centered and encourages others to respect my process even when they have trouble understanding it.

There are many moments these past weeks when an elephant's foot of grief lands crushingly on my chest. I feel as though I could crumble to the ground dissolved by tears and the weight of unspeakable anguish. In the middle of crossing the street, walking down a supermarket aisle, driving my car, drifting on a boulder in the canyon – whenever it comes, I sob and shake inside and speak softly to the hurting Little One. "Oh, my sweetie, I'm sorry you hurt so badly. I love you so much. Poor little honey, it's being so hard for you now." The grief expands and spreads through me as I allow my self to yield to and go with it. After a time, just as with the contractions, the waves of sorrow pass away.

When they leave I, like a child, am fresh, open to whatever is happening in the moment. There is no residue. Life feels vibrant, joyful. I am eagerly engaged in this experience of reclaiming lost parts of my self. In the midst of the pain there is joy that I am coming more fully home to my self.

I've been deepening into intimate closeness with a handful of women friends nearby and at a distance, as well as with a small circle of other women teacher-healers with whom I seasonally sit in Council. I know that these deepenings are part of what is triggering, in the littlest, nonverbal self of me, the echoes of ancient terrors I can't remember feeling. Something inside me is cracking open, falling away. As it does, my being-in-a-body is reliving all the anguish and fear the Little One felt before she long ago shut down and ceased living inside a feeling body.

Exploring Helplessness

Allowing my self to collapse into the helplessness of these experiences is something new for me. For most of my forty-eight and a half years my way has been to transform disempowering circumstances into empowering opportunities. My goal: never allowing my self to be in any situation where having my reality controlled by someone else might be a possibility. Over this past year, Spirit has nonetheless provided me with a succession of circumstances that have left me feeling helpless and out-of-control. My usually peaceful physical and emotional space has been repeatedly disrupted: by a new landlord (with no sense of boundaries and no respect for the earth) who along with troops of workers has been spending his weekends tearing out the wilderness around my house (so that he "can see" all of his property); by a pogrom of possums and gophers who've been tearing up and destroying both my tiny patch of grass and many of my grown-from-babyhood plantings; by having my car (packed full of ceremonial objects and garments, musical instruments, art supplies, camping gear and new books) vanish from a parking space in San Francisco on my way home from a Council meeting only to reappear vacuumed clean of all my treasures (including my favorite teddy bear); by having my back go into deep spasm on three different occasions, each one leaving me incapacitated and dependent for several days.

With each challenge, I consciously chose not to get into my habitual if-we-don't-fix-it-make-it-better-figure-out-the-most-empowering-way-to-tell-the-story-to-our-self-we-will-disintegrate-or-die mode. Instead, I chose to risk immersion in the not-knowing, not-doing place: to simply be with my self in the midst of the overwhelm not trying to bind the chaos into some form I could name and do something about.

As a very different sort of warrior, staying in the middle of the powerless feelings, I discover that choosing to surrender to these terrifying feelings is the most empowering commitment I've yet made to my self. I continue to find the courage and patience to stay in these moments as they intensify and then pass. As I yield to the helplessness and hang in with the worst of it, gentleness and peace enfold me. To stay with feeling the unlabelled pain and my defenselessness seems to be the only help I need these days. In surrendering to these experiences I am feeling a wholeness I've never reached with my formidable attempts to avoid being out-of-control. When I let go into the darkness, after a time, I fall through the bottom of it into a radiance and freedom far beyond anything I've ever known.

The courage for this part of my journey is sourced by the work I've been doing with my self over the past five years: growing a fierce, unconditionally loving Mommy inside of me. There is, at last, someone actually there for me. Competent and trustworthy, she protects me, holding safe space for me to risk feeling the helplessness that was buried along with the Little One who once lived in constant terror. Her presence allows me to be the child it was never before safe to be. This Mommy inside of me was birthed in a labor of self-love that began only when, in great despair, I finally abandoned the illusion that anyone outside of me could ever love me any more than I was able to love my self. (Until then, in my periodic episodes of black depression and self-decimation, I would imagine that someone else's love for me might someday love me into a fuller acceptance of my self than I seemed capable of on my own.) In abandoning that illusion, I stopped abandoning my self and began learning to accept my self all the ways that I am, unreservedly with gentleness and patience for even the most awful and disagreeable me's.

Finding A New Frame Of Reference

For most of the past five years, the journey has been primarily with and within my self, alone. It was essential to disconnect more radically than ever before from the outside world. Both the hetero-patriarchal and the New Age spiritual cultures that surround us felt toxic to me. They assault us (both through media and the so-called acceptable standards of social interaction), suppressing us into often less-than-conscious submission to values and norms that are, as far as I can see, inimical to a healthy relationship with one's self, much less with anyone else. Through a lifetime of moving consciously, steadily toward greater wholeness, self-love and nourishing self-care, intuitive messages from within have been leading me to choices that usually are the opposite of everything that I've been taught about how to encourage growth and healing. Through a succession of dropping-outs, I'd lived most of my life as an outsider, trusting and following my intuitive knowing, often paying the price of feeling very crazy. This latest, most extreme retreat from the world-at-large gave me back the energy I'd been expending to keep the constant barrage of invalidating, crazy-making messages from crushing the tender shoots of my emerging capacity to love all of my self. With this retreat came the courage and spaciousness to accept and welcome Darkness and Chaos as my teachers. I opened to the depths of my own confusion, despair, anger, rage, fear, terror, and meanness so that I might receive their teachings.

Repeatedly, I am shown that healing comes from embracing the very places in my self I had always thought it best to get-beyond. I learn to honor my fears. I learn to not push-through them, to not be afraid to acknowledge them or to acknowledge my taking them seriously. I learn to trust that what I once might have called running-away-from or avoiding behaviors are in fact important breaks that I need to take while I grow and fund the energy I'll need for later goings forth. I learn the power of giving my self my own permission both to be exactly where I am at any moment (even and especially when it's someplace I hope someday not to have to be) and to stay there forever if I need to.

I learn that when I deny or disconnect from the darkness within (my sadness, my despair, my meanness, my anger, my rage, my terror, my ungenerous feelings toward others, my wanting things my way) I am stealing my own power. There is power that comes when I can claim and speak aloud, without shame, these dark truths-of-the-moment; I and others can be in truth and clarity with each other rather than being drained by the confounding energies of suppression and disguise. From this open sharing, significant change can be born.

I learn to not be afraid to put my self and my Little One first in any considerations. I learn that this is my first responsibility to my own healing and to the healing of all beings and of the planet. I learn to dare to speak as much of my inner truth as I am aware of anywhere, anytime – no matter what agreements others seem to have made. I learn not to be afraid to admit that my own truths will be more important to me than what anyone else has to say or to offer about their experience of me when what they share doesn't resonate for me. I learn not to be afraid to give up anything that feels like compromise or sacrifice. I trust that when we come from our own deepest truths and stay with the discomfort of apparent differences until we find common ground, we will find ways to each have 100% of what we need. And, perhaps most important of all, I learn not to be afraid to lavish loving encouragement and celebration upon my self for going only as fast as the slowest, most frightened part of me needs to go in order to feel safe.

The path to these knowings and to the Mommy-Inside has been through reaching toward the abandoned child-within. It began with a teddy bear (selected with very special care), time (five days a week unplugged from the outside world), and the canyons of Ojai. I spent my days practicing caring for and nurturing my body, heart and soul. I did Reiki and yoga in the mornings (unless I didn't feel like it) and walked long hours in the canyons by day and by evening. I climbed hills, up creek beds, into the arms of trees. I curled up with boulders, melted into little waterfalls and let the streams flow through me. I felt day becoming night, dark becoming dawn. I lived with my favorite canyon through a searing fire that uncovered her bones and then through the almost immediate beginning of renewal as green sprouted out of charred stumps of what had been. I felt young, little and very safe. I played with colored pens, pastels, paints and clay. Drawing and writing in my journal with my left hand (the one that has no rules or expectations) I made space for the Little One to speak to me with images and words. I called for her and talked with her of my yearnings to know her, of my awkwardness in approaching her after for so long ignoring and abandoning her, of my intention to become ever more trustworthy and available to her. Slowly, cautiously, she began to trust my intention and commitment to learn to love her unconditionally and be an advocate for her needs. She began to speak and to share her long hidden self with me.

Embracing the Little One's Grief

Having throughout my life been comfortable with feelings of melancholy, it was easiest for me to be there for her in her sadness and despair. I would hold and rock my self and the teddy bear that would stand in for her. I would listen to her when she felt unhappy or upset and didn't want to be around certain people or to do certain things. I'd make sure we didn't ever do anything that felt scary or uncomfortable to her. We grieved together for all she'd never had the first time she was little. We grieved for the ways in which I had been as harsh, impatient and rejecting of her as the outside world had been in those early days. We grieved for the loss of the chance to feel free simply to be little and have needs. And, we grieved for the loss of the dream that anyone else could now or ever mother that part of us. We cried a lot and spent long hours feeling very sorry for our selves. Then, slowly we began to make the world safe to be little in, at least when by our self.

Watching and feeling the cycles in nature taught me that moving away is always the beginning of moving toward, if your eyes are truly open. My daily bonding with nature reminded me to remember patience, to remember that all processes have their own timing for birthing, blossoming and decaying (provided we don't interfere with or restrict that flow by imposing our notions of how it should be). Watching the slow process of new growth after the fire's devastation helped me to remember that the seed of new life is forever hidden in the ashes that become its food; that there is no hurry, only time and growing. And, too, that both the blossoming forth and the dying away are part of growing. Giving my self fully to the sadness and despair began the birth of new aliveness, though it took a long season for the light to return in its latest form.

Finding My Anger

As the Little One became more trusting and I, like the Great Mother surrounding me, became more reliably patient and accepting, a time came when strong feelings of anger (the more focused, specific version) and rage (the more amorphous, all-encompassing version) began surging into my consciousness. In situations where the old, ostensibly evolved, grown-up me would have psychologically/spiritually understood the circumstances and people involved, spiritually by-passing the feelings (the messiness and pain of feeling small-minded, mean, dark and negative), I began to stay open to the Little One as well as to the grown-up part of me. When I did that, I could understand and yet still feel all the ugly feelings, without judging my self badly for them. I gave up the belief that anger and rage are not evolved things to feel. (I had long ago given up the "nice girls don't..." rule in exchange for the equally emotionally repressive one that "enlightened beings don't...")

It was harder with these feelings than with the sadness, pain and despair but, again, I gave my self permission to be in the middle of whatever ugly hatefulness I was feeling. I gave my self permission to stay there or, in the old way of seeing it, permission to be stuck there indefinitely, until or unless some release came organically, from my deep belly place.

I found ways to move the energy of the anger and rage through my body. (A special friend, wise in the ways of rage, helped me pay attention to the way it gets caught in the body.) I banged on gongs, drums, chimes, the piano and my bed and (with battaccas – the stuffed encounter-bats) on door jams. I screamed, shouted, cursed and roared at home, in the canyon, at the ocean and often while driving around in my car with the windows rolled up and the music blaring. I stomped and flailed fists and feet on my mattress. As I allowed my self to experience my rage in the safety of my own company, without judging my self for feeling it, I could recognize the situations and circumstances that, now and in the past, stirred my anger. After a time, I began telling people how I was feeling when I was angry or enraged. Later on I became more able, without dumping or blaming, to let people know what, in what they were doing with me, was angering me. I sometimes even allowed my self to yell at them to stop when I needed to do that. I felt excitement and a sense of freedom as I permitted my self to be feeling the anger rather than just knowing that it was there.

When I first started banging and screaming out my rage (alone with my self), I experienced intense palpitations. I could barely breathe. I would have to stop after only seconds of pounding to catch my breath, to find some balance. Then, I'd go at it some more. As the energy coursed through me, I one day remembered a knowing that had come to me intuitively, years before, when I had explored with psychedelics. If you attempt to contain or control intense waves of energy/feelings rather than just allowing them to flow through you, their velocity increases to vortex proportions; you feel nauseated and terrified. When you stop resisting the powerful flow and instead surrender – letting the current carry you or wash through you and out your pores – you discover that rather than being out-of-control, you are in the middle of something that has an organismic coherence you can feel in your bones.

As I submitted, allowing my self to ride with the intense feelings, they would crest, reverberate and then diminish, receding on their own. This was as true for anger and rage as it was for grief and despair. Sometimes as I raged, old images would surface of situations in which I had been, but not felt my being, enraged. Sometimes, after I started banging, there was nothing but energy and rage. After a while, I would be spent. There might be tears, exhaustion or laughter. But, soon, a calm would come and with it, often, clear knowing of what I needed to speak of or to do to change whatever had triggered the rage.

The more I, without judgment, allowed the rage and anger to surface, the more they informed me. My feelings were healthy organismic reactions to circumstances that I experienced as noxious or invalidating to some part(s) of the me I was in that moment. This important information allowed me to move into my life in ways that were not possible before I began the practice of listening to my anger. Again, I was learning that surrendering into the dark feelings allows for one's inmost truths to emerge; that embracing those feelings could be not only safe, but also illuminating.

The coherence to be discovered in yielding to chaos is typically more substantial than any order imposed by the part of us that tries to control or dilute extreme feelings by means of our mind imposing structure. That coherence is incomprehensible, just as the chaos is threatening, to the part (our rational, logical masculine aspect) of us that sees the world as either in- or out-of-control.

With the Mommy-Inside's permission and encouragement, the Little One began to feel safe to be aware of her rage and to express it directly in her child's language of immediacy. Without efforts to translate her reactions into more suitable or seemly forms, she informed people of when she wanted to put them in the trash or bury them in the backyard for treating her badly or telling her things she didn't want to hear. She could trust that she would not be judged or abandoned for speaking her truth: the Mommy would love her and be on her side no matter what other people might say or do. The Mommy also became free to be ferocious in her protection of the Little One. Without taking time to be polite, she directly and calmly expressed her anger to anyone who either treated the Little One badly or who tried to tell or ask the Little One something that the Mommy knew neither she nor the Little One needed to hear just then. The Mommy was especially fierce about not allowing anyone to help the Little One since so often other people's ostensibly helpful gestures felt fraught with danger to the Little One and to the Mommy as well.

Much wisdom came from dancing with the depths of my own sadness, grief, despair, rage and anger. Knowing the power that flowed from moving into and through these strong feelings unimpeded by my own or anyone else's thought processes and having become more familiar and comfortable with having those feelings resonating their parallels in me, I became freer to serve as a guardian and witness for others in the midst of their chaos. I was less worried or fearful that they would not be able to get through those places without my intervention. I was less threatened by what feeling-with-them was stirring in me. Feeling safe to feel-with-them, not needing to move them prematurely through or beyond the immediacy of the energy of their chaotic intensity, I offered powerful, non-verbal support affirming the safety of the process. I was living my trust in the power of staying with the darkness until the eye (or the I) learns a new way of seeing. My confidence in my and their natural processes provided the ground for awakening/reawakening their faith in their own self-in-process. And, my sitting in witness with others through their diving into their dark places helped me fund the courage for what has become my own next step. I began opening to terror and helplessness, feelings that were, as I've earlier described, even further from my repertoire of embodied experience than the feelings of rage and anger had been.

Bringing My New Self into Relating to Others

The feelings of terror and helplessness surfacing in this newest stage of my journey seem connected with my becoming embodied and my moving into relating intimately with others from my newly emotionally and physically embodied self. Over the past two years the Little One, the Mommy and I have been practicing being the all of our selves we can be, openly, everywhere as much of the time as we can while still feeling safe inside our selves. Some days I feel like a one-woman traveling guerrilla theatre troupe as I keep giving voice to all the subterranean levels I am aware of in my interactions with others. I tell them when it feels to me as though they've disappeared behind their eyes leaving me a facsimile to relate to. Rather than continuing what feels like a charade of communication, I ask them what if anything they know about this energy shift I'm sensing. I also stop our dialogue when I feel me wandering away from listening to what they're saying. I believe that this happens in either of us for reasons that we can discover together if we look at what has just taken place. I am giving up the dark secrets I've kept in my intimate relationships (e.g., where I feel superior, when I feel emotionally stingy and resentful). And, secrets that I've kept even from my self (e.g., where I still am more giving than I truly want to be) are rising into my consciousness.

For the first time in my life, I am surrounded by a number of women who are as dedicated as I am to becoming more conscious and impeccable in all their relationships: with self, with others, with the planet. They are women who are willing, as am I, to risk and struggle to be in truth with themselves and with each other, committed to taking responsibility for doing their own emotional homework. As I come together with these women – in council, in friendships and in one more-than-a-friendship – our shared intention is to serve healing and the loving acceptance of our selves and of our selves-in-relation. We do this with the conviction that in this process we are helping to generate a powerful wave of healing on the planet.

Along with the excitement in this, there is a great deal of hard work. For me, there is also the rising into consciousness of all the terror and powerlessness that shaped the Little One's first years and the choices that her past later led me to make about trusting and relating intimately with other people. Early in the complicated, excruciating relationship with my biological mother, the Little One learned that no one outside of her self was dependable or trustworthy. My mother's responses to my needs came always with resentment. For her, mothering was not sharing a loving merging so much as it was being called upon to give away that which she most craved for herself. She birthed me (she told me before her death) to give her the affection she felt starved for in her marriage. Of course, once I was born, she was overwhelmed by the neediness of an infant. The mothering I received taught me that needing or wanting anything from outside my self was shameful and dangerous both physically and emotionally. Sharp nails, yanking hands and lots of feeling cold and wet are body memories that surfaced as I've re-embodied. To survive, the Little One disconnected from her body and, making a virtue of necessity, became adept at living richly within herself – needing or wanting very little from outside sources.

Until these past two years, the most enlivening moments of my life were those spent in only my own company. Early experiences that required keen sensitivity to subtle shifts in others and my abiding fascination with introspection opened me to an awareness of less-than-conscious processes that set me apart from most people I'd ever met. I would need to constrict, to dim the intensity of my awareness around others; it was either that or feel crazy.

In these recent relationships, I am able, for the first time in my life, to be all of my self while around others. Even more amazingly, the resonance of being in relation with others who seem as present to their inner selves and processes as I am to mine opens places that are sometimes beyond what I can provide for me by my self.

This experience of belonging, of no longer feeling so alien brings both delight and fear. With the joy of feeling part of a community of other similar beings comes the possibility that I could lose that comfort, have it suddenly taken away if I relax into having it. It is this that triggers the terror and powerlessness I feel as I open to others on such a deep level.

The depth of my friends' self-awareness and spiritual consciousness invites me to risk telling all of the truth about what I feel each moment in their presence, to risk giving up my lifelong conviction that revealing my self at this level is dangerous. The dependability of the Mommy-Inside helps me to dare being this exposed in my sharing. Because she keeps the space safe for me or else gets me out of there, I feel brave enough to risk becoming conscious of the long buried fears and paranoia stirred in the Little One when I allow my self to be all of the wonderful and awful of me in my sharing with these women. With the Mommy standing guard, I am able sometimes to allow mirroring to come through interactions with these women rather than only from the teacher within my own depths.

What comes of all this is that I am no longer dealing with the historical realities that usually confirmed my paranoid fantasy that I was being experienced as too much, too serious, too convoluted, too incomprehensible or too much bother by those with whom I sought to share my deepest feelings. Among these women I risk being exposed in the middle of the Little One's vulnerabilities and fears about what others might be thinking or feeling about me or my participation. I risk letting her name those fears and terrors as they emerge in her experience of our interactions. The Little One has me asking these others for reality checks when she feels afraid. She believes that they will answer with the truth of what they are experiencing in themselves, that they will be answering from a level of self-awareness and emotional honesty with themselves that is congruent with my own.

Because these women are willing and able to acknowledge what in them may have triggered her response of fear or uncertainty rather than merely dismissing her terror as groundless, my Little One is slowly becoming less terrified around them. I can let her speak her truths of the moment without needing to intervene and speak from my old, familiar, more comfortable place of the articulate grown-up. That grown-up has for years spoken very freely and openly about such feelings, typically long after the precipitating moment was passed. Sometimes at edges where the Mommy is not yet strong enough to hold the world safe, I still can disappear the Little One into that grown-up articulate self without realizing I've done the shift. But, this happens less often as my special friends and I practice giving and receiving feedback about the usually less than conscious shifts in level of interaction that we each do (in our own individual styles) when we are afraid without being aware that we are afraid.

I am moving into unexplored territory in me at the same time I am becoming available to experience others' responses to and reflections of me. Even as I go to the edge of what I know about my self or about my self-in-relation, having the Mommy with me helps me to know that I will recognize that which in their feedback, although new to me, does feel true for me. And, that I will be able to separate what is true for me from what feels to be more about them and their conscious or unconscious projections onto me. I believe I will, even at the edge of my knowing, continue to choose my inside-eyes view of my self over any not-resonant or critical outside-eyes view of me.

Even as we're each intending to tell the whole truth, we are all often blinded to some parts of our selves by our fears. So, when as sometimes happens, the Little One still feels uncertain after the reality check, her version of what's happening still guides my behavior; no matter what anyone says and even if they all think I'm being stubborn or crazy.

Over the past five years, being little, undeveloped, hungry for love, frightened and yearning for closeness has gradually become safe for me when I am alone. I've been able to stay with these, before now, intolerable feelings without judging my self and without feeling the shame and disgrace that would in the past attend any hint of such needfulness or insufficiency. The growing edge in my evolution is being able to carry this capacity out into the arena that has always mobilized those feelings most intensely: close relating with others.

When the others around me are willing and available either to expose themselves similarly, or simply to sit with their own little selves having feelings that resonate with mine, I am as able to stay with these feelings as I am when I'm alone with my self. I can feel the Little One's hungers and terrors increasing as her closeness with these friends intensifies her long unacknowledged (by me) yearnings to belong, to be a part of some healthy family and to have more of this magical newness of being all of me with other people.

When I feel safe enough to be with her terror of rejection and abandonment, to name it as it's happening, to stay right there in the middle of it feeling that it's okay to feel that terror, to stay embodied, to stay present because it's not here and now that's threatening her – I come home to the part of me that's been locked up and denied all my life. My safety comes both from knowing that I and the Mommy will not abandon her no matter what anyone else chooses to do and from the fact that these treasured women have proven to be honest, even when they don't like something she's doing or saying. What terrifies her most is when she feels the pretend accepting that creates total confusion in her about what's going on. In her past, that pretend-okay would usually mean there'd later be terrible consequences for her.

Because I feel safe here and now, I can let go into this process of reliving the ancient terrors locked in my body since so early in my life. That the specialness of these women stirs the Little One's longings makes it all very present for her and allows healing to happen now. I'm so grateful for this opportunity to go deeply into this old, damaged place in me.

When the Little One is immersed in terror, I am not feeling endangered; not by her terror, not by her vulnerability, not by its disclosure as she is vibrating with it and not by the people we are with. Instead, I'm feeling empowered by being able to experience that much terror, embodied, fully exposed. I feel safer and more protected than I've ever felt in my life: I have the Mommy-Inside right there and the grown-up me off to the sidelines; the Little One is no longer alone with her terror. (She's also not in hostile, dangerous territory.) I am able to feel and to reveal the vulnerability precisely because the other aspects of me are there to help and to take care of her if she needs anything more than just to feel the feelings and feel beloved and protected by the Mommy and by me. My terror and longing are loud and clear. I am able to be with them in my self. What I need from those outside of me is simply that they bear honest witness in whatever outside way they can as I dive and process and emerge.

Trying to Cope with Others' Attempts to Be "Helpful"

The biggest struggle I have these days when I'm in the midst of my terror, fear, longings, needfulness, and yearning to belong comes when others take it upon themselves to help me through my feelings. Even among my cohort of conscious women, when the Little One speaks out in the middle of fear, insecurity and vulnerability, some of them respond (albeit lovingly) by trying to fix it, fix her, help her understand it's not that way here and now, make it better, tell her what she needs to pay attention to in order to feel better, help her see where it's coming from, tell her how more safely to navigate through it, or just reassure her that it's going to be all right. When that happens, the Mommy often intervenes with controlled fury. Usually they persist and feel misunderstood by the Mommy. I feel exasperated and infuriated at being intruded upon in the middle of my process and the Mommy often has to yell at the people to get them to stop it. They feel mistreated. The next step is that the grown-up me comes in and tries again to articulate the lay of the land. All the parts of me feel drawn off course and undermined; the processing gets aborted while the explaining takes place.

From the grown-up part of me, I explain that I need people to stay out of my process, that my Little One is safe even though obviously in the midst of her terror; that if I really needed something other than witnessing from outside of my self at this moment, it wouldn't have been safe to risk this processing at all. No matter what I say, it still seems very difficult for some of my cohorts to understand.

They feel my Little One's terror, feel her yearning, feel her confusion and then, despite all my protestations to the contrary, they feel that they have to do something about her situation. It feels as though nothing I can say will counter their unshakable conviction that they're right, that underneath all of it I really do want and need help from them in order for her to make it through this scary place. Even when I go as far as to stand in three separate places, speaking with my three separate voices (Mommy, grown-up and Little One) to get them to see that there's more of me available to me than just the terrified child, they still persist in their conviction. It drives me wild.

The tenacity with which they hold to their reality despite my own clarity that I do not want or need assistance or intervention but rather its opposite – witnessing – makes it clear that something strange is going on here. What's being offered as help (as if it were for my benefit) seems to have more to do with their own unconscious projections than it has to do with my actual need. Especially since the helping words and the attempted gestures of physical comfort they persist in offering feel invasive, suppressive, undermining, disorienting and even threatening to me.

When an outside person attempts to mother or do therapy on me while I'm both in and also being with that child place of terror, that person keeps herself in her grown-up rather than in her own child space feeling the resonance with my child-terror. Her acting to "help" me feels like an invasive attempt on her part to move me out of a place that I suspect would feel very threatening to her were she actually feeling that way in her child self. Her intervention suppresses rather than promotes my processing. It feels undermining and insulting because it implies that she doesn't at all recognize the power in me that is allowing me to (safely, at last) collapse into feeling helpless. She acts from an outside-eyes view of me as incapacitated and in need of outside intervention. This message is threatening to me when I'm at the very edge of my own capacity to hold to my inside-eyes view of my self as engaged in an act of self-empowerment. As I stand precariously in this new place of consciously feeling the terror for the first time, exposing it at the very same moment, and holding my self safe in the middle of it, the outside person's intrusion disrupts me.

At this point in my healing process I am, as yet, unable to hold the space safely open for me to continue in the face of persistent attempts by others to mother or do un-requested therapy on me. Both sets of behaviors are other people's attempts to bring understanding, words and thought into this place where my greatest need is to simply surrender into the emotional storm without using my mind or my usually too-ready words to contain, shape and control the chaos. Still, each time there is strong pressure from the outside in this direction, that old familiar part of me gets mobilized and I drop out of my process and move into explaining.

I begin, as I do the work of writing this, to understand the intensity of the rage I feel at those times. When I respond to their pressure by coming out of where I am in order to deal with their manifestations of what I believe to be their own unconscious fear of my terror, I am re-experiencing what I suspect happened to me as an infant (and child) with my biological mother. I am repeating the process of disconnecting from my primary terror in order to protect my mother (or her contemporary stand-ins) from the overpowering terror my terror stirs in her. Again I wind up being mommy to the one who acts as if she is mothering me. This time around though, I seem at least to be experiencing the rage at the rip-off that I surely was not able to feel when this happened to me as a child. What I also see in this shifting is that while my own Little One's terror doesn't terrify me, the unacknowledged terror felt by those who would attend me does indeed terrify me enough for me to drop out on my self. And, against all my own intentions not to fall into knee-jerk caretaking, there I am doing it again (just as they are) and doing it out of some unacknowledged terror in my self (just as they are).

I understand, as I write this, that the next step in this processing of my Little One's terror involves me learning finally how to stay in the middle of my own process even as I become aware of another's great distress, fear or discomfort with it. Until I'm able to do that, I will continue to rob my self of my own pain in much the same way as that person's helping would rob me of it. Until I stop responding to the help by being drawn off into the explaining that tries to fix the fixer so that she won't keep trying to fix me, I continue the life-long process of robbing my self of the empowering experience of sitting with my terror or any of the other painful feelings I have even when that upsets other people. For this next step the Mommy needs to be even stronger than she is. (And we're working on that even as we write this.)

I certainly recognize the compelling need to step in, to be there to comfort, to try to make it safe or to make it better for someone in an extreme state. It's an impulse I've lived with and acted from over and over again throughout my life. In me, it's seemed to come from the fantasy that this would be what I'd want were I to be feeling as little and helpless as the other appears to be feeling. (A kind of magical thinking that if I'm there to make it okay for you when you're so helpless there will someday be someone there bigger than me to help me if and when I might feel so helpless.) My traveling into my own depths has convinced me that that kind of help is, at least for me, more crippling than truly helpful. My traveling has also convinced me that the best help I can receive from others is their willingness to sit consciously with their own fear and helplessness while I am with mine.

Some part of me continues to yearn (and perhaps is only just beginning to be fully in touch with the depth of the yearning) for someone outside to be bigger and more capable than I am. At the same time, it has become ever more apparent to me that if there wasn't such a person there for you when you actually were a child, it is never possible for anyone outside to cross the time-warp to provide that for the wounded child inside the grown-up you. All anyone outside can do is done by acknowledging and supporting the developing Mommy-Inside through whom their love can pass to that inner child. Nothing can be given directly to that wounded child but the illusion that something is being given her. That illusion, coupled with the fact that nothing can reach her through the time warp, leaves her feeling unsatisfied and not understanding why she feels so insatiable. It also draws her off the process of birthing a healing Mommy-Inside.

When others act in ways that intend to fix or help someone get through their pain, the one being helped doesn't get to experience the empowerment that comes with traveling into, through the depths of and out the other side of the pain. Instead of finding her own safety within her self, she gets to feel dependent on the outside person who provides the illusion of safety. And, she gets to remain blind to her own wholeness because someone has robbed her of the pain whose energy is the fuel for her transformation. Being heard, felt with and allowed to stay where you are until you're done being there is the truest support one can have. It's also the hardest support to come by from real people. The streams, rocks, trees and boulders, the earth itself have heard and helped me in that way.

The Gifts of this Journey

In the struggle to share my process and to be heard (the projections of those who are listening to me notwithstanding), I have grown strong and fiercely self-protective. I am becoming ever more able to stand in the midst of the primordial terror connected for me with feeling powerless, frightened or emotionally hungry and little in the presence of people who see themselves as beyond all that. I am becoming more able to stand nakedly in that place, recognizing my stance as an act of the greatest power, no matter how they may view it. My willingness to be there – feeling the power of surrendering into helplessness – becomes an act of transformation: the fierceness with which I defend my right to stay there until I'm through to the other side really forces others to reexamine their own view rather than allowing them to dismiss mine.

I will not be pressured into giving up my terror until it releases me. I will not go any faster than the slowest, most frightened part of me feels safe to go. I can live in the middle of the paradox of knowing there is nothing in the situation to fear while staying with and experiencing the old terror that rises in my child-consciousness. And slowly, as I persist, others around me begin to do the same for themselves. I will not do anything that violates or overrides my feelings or my body and I will honor the power of that stance by naming it every time I take it. And, slowly, as I persist, others begin to respect their own bodies and feelings enough not to be coerced by cultural pressure into overriding their own inner messages of truth. The more of us who openly declare our selves in this process of reclaiming the dark, the child and the feminine, the more the craziness of the world as it is will be seen as just that. I will no longer be shamed into believing that having feelings and being connected with the longings and limits of my body makes me not powerful, not evolved, not worthwhile, not worthy of respect.

Part Four:
The Magic of Rest and Going More Slowly

When we reclaim the sacredness of rest, we remember to trust and cherish the fallow seasons: those cyclical periods when new growth is gathering itself below what appears to be a barren surface. We are reconnecting our selves with the healing rhythms of the natural world.

The more-bigger-further-faster-yesterday mindset of our business-as-usual world has been leading us relentlessly toward exhausting our selves, the earth in which we grow our food and, as well, what once seemed the endless bounty of our planet's natural resources.

To consciously choose to incorporate and celebrate rest as a creative part of our lives is a way of calling our selves home to living in harmony with our deep selves and the natural world. It is part of the journey to healing our selves **and** our planet.

When we commit to going only as fast as the slowest part of us feels safe to go, we are choosing to grow and move through our lives in a gentler, more humane way. Going more slowly makes space for our feelings to surface. It allows our inner knowing to direct our doings. And, it opens the door for magic to enter our lives, for us to be able to notice where and how it does.

4-1. Reclaiming Rest

Rest is as urgent, significant, meaningful, honorable and productive as any other purposeful act!

In my mid-twenties, I rarely slept more than four or five hours a night. I was constantly busy. By day I was running subjects for my dissertation research project at graduate school. At night I was working part-time as a waitress in an all-night cafe. As part of my psychotherapy practicum, I was seeing two clients each week at the low-cost university clinic. I would have an hour a week of supervision on my work with these clients and then meet with my peers in a two and a half-hour psychotherapy practicum. I was seeing my own therapist twice a week. And, aside from all that, I was seriously involved in two romantic relationships (one with a man and one with a woman).

When I had finished the research and writing for my dissertation, I began working as a half-time clinical intern/half-time research associate. The hospital at which I did this work was an hour's commute from my apartment. The research work (in a sleep,

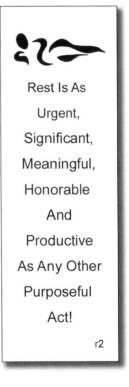

Rest Is As

Urgent,

Significant,

Meaningful,

Honorable

And

Productive

As Any Other

Purposeful

Act!

r2

dreams and ESP research project) frequently involved doing an EEG-monitored sleepover or staying up all night monitoring another sleeper at the hospital laboratory.

Throughout the year-long internship I continued with the clinic clients, the therapy practicum and the supervision hour at the university. I did, though, end my therapy and one of the two romantic relationships. Then, I began sort-of-living-with the man I'd been seeing. That involved more commuting: dragging my clothes and paperwork back and forth across Manhattan in a large carpetbag as we spent part of the time at my place, part of the time at his and part of the time separately.

In place of sleep and rest, I drank an outrageous number of cups of coffee, smoked at least two packs of cigarettes a day and dieted rigorously, regularly taking an appetite suppressor without consciously understanding that it was an upper. (Just how much of an upper became clear when a friend, who'd taken one to stay up one night to finish a paper, found herself unable to get to sleep for three whole days.)

In my late twenties, I chose to move upstate to Buffalo, New York where the man with whom I had been sort-of-living had relocated for a research position. I took a full-time job as a counseling psychologist at the State University there. And, at the same time, continued to complete my work with the practicum clients in New York City. This involved commuting by plane for part of every week during my first three months in Buffalo.

Not too long after that commute ended, it became clear that neither Buffalo nor the full-time living-with part of the relationship was working out. I moved into my own apartment in Buffalo and began rebuilding professional connections in New York City. This involved me in yet another three-month-long air-commute. Hired as a visiting professor, I was teaching two projective psychological testing courses on Friday evenings and all day Saturdays at the New School for Social Research in Manhattan.

During both of these air-commuter periods, I worked four long-hour days a week at the University counseling center. Fridays I traveled to the City to teach (or see clients) and visit with my closest women friends. Saturdays, after my late afternoon class (or client), I'd catch a ride to the airport and return to Buffalo. Sundays were spent preparing food and clothes for the week to come and spending relationship time with one or the other of the two men with whom I was then involved. I never came up for air. Rest was not in my vocabulary.

I continued to live many variations of this breakneck pace until my 31st year. That year, something inside me came undone, hit me upside the head letting me know that I couldn't go on like this and survive. Severe back pains, vivid premonitions that I would die if I didn't get to some place green and some insight into the underpinnings of my nonstop busyness all combined to catalyze a major shift in my life.

In a struck-by-a-lightning-bolt moment, I realized that all my frantic doings (being highly productive in conventional terms, pulling off superwoman feats of accomplishment) had been misguided attempts to antidote a core sense of my own unworthiness. And, I understood that, if I couldn't feel okay or worthwhile **just** for being, no amount of doing could ever make me feel any differently.

With this new consciousness, I began the practice of committing to doing less instead of more every time I felt beset by my familiar sense of not being enough. I sought ways to dismantle my overwhelmingly busy lifestyle. I collapsed my workweek to three longer days instead of five shorter ones. Then, I rented a beach house for the winter so I could spend the other four days a week hanging out there. I stopped all the running around that I had been doing in the City. Instead, and at the beach, I rested: lounged, napped, read and took long, leisurely bicycle rides around cranberry bogs. The shift slowed me enough that I could begin to feel and recognize what was going on within me.

I thought about moving to the beach community and starting a psychotherapy practice there. My partner and I even looked at houses and consulted with a builder whose work we liked. Fortunately, before we went too far down this road I realized that, unless I found a way to address the deeper issues, I would simply recreate another too-busy life in this small village. The more I listened inward, the clearer it became that my only hope for the changes I needed (to help me learn to value my self just for being) required a radical disconnection, a putting down of **all** the roles and frameworks in which I had till then been living my life. I felt pushed from deep within to find empty time and a place in which to begin nurturing whatever it was inside of me that needed to be born. In a series of gradually decelerating steps, I was able to do this putting down, this carving out of space for germinating a new way of being in my self. (See **Pirouettes**, page 125 for more of this story.)

Resting in the middle of my super-achieving life had opened a door for me. Over these next 40+ years, I've committed my self to reclaiming the significance, meaningfulness and productivity of rest as a purposeful act. I've worked diligently on learning to value, honor and love my self just for being. The two paths, not surprisingly, have been intimately interwoven.

Resting – unplugging, being unreachable for even short periods of time – provides us with the spaciousness we need for an inner life to blossom. The more in touch we are with our inner life, the more able we become to live from the inside out. We get to know who we truly are, to feel our own unique worthiness. We grow more grounded and centered, more able to act from a place of balance and self-awareness.

Yet, everything in our modern world conspires to keep us from addressing this need within us. Multi-tasking and over-full calendars have become the gold standard: the measure of a person's worth/ importance or their credentials as a good parent. Laptop computers, iPads, portable FAX machines, beepers, pagers, increasingly multifunctional iterations of smart phones and proliferating social media seduce us into believing that never being unplugged or unreachable is a wonderful rather than a crippling thing.

All the high-tech, digital, state-of-the-art, laborsaving gadgets and gismos have helped us turn our selves into hyper-stressed beings (both adults **and** children) who feel we haven't time enough for all we have to do to survive. None of us ever sees the time we're supposedly saving with all these devices; that time is filled up with more busyness and doing.

And, what once might have been leisure time has also been co-opted. High-tech, expensive-equipment-intensive and extreme sports have replaced true leisure with activities that are evaluated in terms of accomplishments and challenges conquered. We count up miles run, biked, paddled, swum; heights/degree of difficulty of slopes skied, cliffs scaled, mountains biked, rivers rafted, etc.

The more we keep doing, the further we get from (and from valuing) our true selves. The further we get from our essential selves the more daunting it is to contemplate slowing down, resting and simply being with those selves. Yet, rest is as (or perhaps even more) urgent, significant, honorable, meaningful and productive as any other purposeful act. It is in the open, quiet, just-being time that we find and reflect on what is actually so for us. And, it is this getting to know what is so for and in us that provides us with the ground of being from which a healing, creative and healthy life flows. (See **Rest is Sacred**, page 317 for more about this.)

Consider being really tender with and attentive to your super-achieving, rest-starved self.

4-2. Fallow Seasons

Cherish the fallow seasons... The ground of your being is replenishing itself... These still times are as empowering, essential and miraculous as the times of bursting forth... You have long been encouraged to forget that!

Until sometime in my 31st year, my life was typically filled with what the current me would call compulsive super-achievement and terminal busyness. In that transformative year I had a full-time private practice in psychotherapy earning an income that was in the top 2% of professional women's incomes. I (and the feminist man to whom I was then married) cooked and baked everything from scratch, including whole grain breads and desserts every week and our own fresh mayonnaise. We did (and shared on a 50-50 basis) all our own housework, laundry and errands.

Cherish The Fallow Seasons...
The Ground Of Your Being Is Replenishing Itself...
These Still Times Are As Empowering, Essential And Miraculous As The Times Of Bursting Forth...
You Have Long Been Encouraged To Forget That!

r6

I was part of a collective creating and administering the first New York Feminist Psychotherapy Referral Service. We held teas (serving trays of my own homemade cakes, cookies and pastries) during which we did group interviews of therapists applying to be on our list. Each of us did telephone shifts during which we talked with women who were seeking services (so that we could make appropriate referrals for them). We shared responsibility for weekly supervision/training seminars for peer counselors. And, as part of our outreach, we all were interviewed for newspaper features as well as local TV and radio programs.

I designed and crocheted all of my own clothing along with belts, vests, mufflers and hats for the man to whom I was married. And, I had a small side business creating custom crocheted bikinis and mail order crocheted shopping bags (once featured in the Sales and Bargains section of *New York Magazine*).

I did a daily hour-long stretching routine that I later learned was actually yoga and rode my bicycle 18-24 miles around the Central Park circumference road three days a week in good weather.

I crocheted while waiting on lines at the bank or supermarket, often read while walking on my way to shop and did handwork (crochet or embroidery) whenever I sat with my partner as he watched TV. There was never a moment (except during the few hours when I slept) that I wasn't occupied in some so-called productive enterprise.

Except for the particular activities, that 31st year was not unlike all the years gone before. Yet, it marked a turning point in my journey. An unremitting backache, a rumbling from deep inside my being and an insight about my super-achieving led me through a process that resulted in my making a remarkable series of choices. (See **Pirouettes**, page 125 and **Reclaiming Rest**, page 307 for more about this time.)

Within little more than a year, I had sold or given away most of my possessions. I'd bought a brand new, stripped Dodge Tradesman van that I, with the salvage of my former life, set up as a bed-sitting room. With grace and kindness, I took leave of my practice, my marriage, my family, my friends and the whole of my life as it was. Then, four months after my 32nd birthday, I began driving cross-country to California with no plan for what came next.

I'd spent that last year in a gradual process of slowing my life, disengaging from all the intensity and expansion of the preceding years. The pressure from within had guided me to and through launching into the yawning unknown. My inner knowing was clear: I had to get where it was green or I would die. I had to stop the compulsive doing that had long been my only way to attempt to quiet the vicious voice of my inner critic. This radical move into stillness appeared to offer the only path to my survival.

Despite the knowing, I wasn't prepared for the unstructured emptiness of the new life I'd been led to embark upon. The downshifting into so much stillness, so much open time was (in the language of those years) mind-blowing. It was edgy: scary and exciting in equal measure.

My days were framed by driving, finding camp grounds to sleep at, cooking/preparing my meals and taking walks or bike rides around the campgrounds in which I'd landed. Since, even on the southernmost route, it was unexpectedly cold that mid-March, I also spent a good deal of energy figuring out how to stay warm.

A radio hadn't been part of the package of a stripped van, so I made do with a presumably high quality portable radio. Most of the time the radio produced only country music (not a favorite of mine) or static. So, I drove surrounded in silence or while singing my way through a lengthy repertoire of love songs and show tunes from the forties and early fifties. (Until then I'd no idea how many of them I knew.)

With nothing productive to do, I spent inordinate amounts of time preparing and cleaning up from my meals, then cleaning up the van from my post-meal clean up. I obsessively examined and re-examined maps and routes. I arranged and rearranged my things in their storage units. Part of that process was a matter of fine-tuning the order I'd created before actually living in the middle of it. Still, a lot more of that re-organizing was a way to structure the wide-open timelessness and cope with my anxiety in the midst of it.

It was disorienting to have nothing to do, nowhere to have to be, nothing to juggle, no one else's sensibilities to attend. Yet, as I continued to drive westward, I began to settle into this new way of being. My body and being started unwinding and relaxing. I slowed down, breathed more deeply. The anxious edges began to melt away. I was able to do less of the make-work that had helped me, in the earliest weeks, to adjust to the absence of structure.

My mind wandered through memories, revisiting old, unresolved ambivalences and issues. I did a lot of wondering about what lay ahead. None of it was focused on figuring anything out. Instead, my psyche simply needed to touch lightly and move on, visiting rather than living into all these territories inside of me.

During the first three months I chose not to connect with anyone along the way. (Except for smiled hellos in campground ladies' rooms.) Weekly, I called back home to report in with one of the three people – my best friend/lover, my sister or my soon-to-be ex – who were my base camp for this solo journey. When I felt like it, I made tapes of my reflections and experiences. These I sent back to one or another of the three of them to share with each other. When I felt lonely I'd wander around in large drugstore-supermarkets like Long's or Walgreen's.

The loneliness was a need to simply be around other human beings rather than to get involved with them. I craved the stillness, reveled in it, wanted to slip more deeply into it. Relating with other people seemed premature. I wasn't yet ready to risk looking through outside eyes at how I was living. The new balance growing inside me, the feeling okay in and with my self while doing absolutely nothing seemed too fragile to submit to anyone else's opinions or reactions.

After I'd been traveling a while in California, I began to talk a little with some of the people I met. When and as I did (in those early days), I consciously chose not to share anything about my former life except the fact that it had given me the financial backing to be free to be doing nothing for a while. This practice of "erasing personal history" (an idea borrowed from Carlos Castanada's Don Juan books) made it safer for me to acknowledge my doing-nothing lifestyle.

I did varying degrees of nothing, living in my van on-the-road for almost a year and a half before I slowly began plugging back in to a more ordinary lifestyle. It had been a radicalizing, healing time in my life. In the middle of doing nothing productive or worthwhile by society's standards, I felt more okay about my self, more worthy as a being than I'd ever felt in my over-filled, busily super-achieving former life.

I got to know my self in new ways during this long season of fallow time. I discovered and nourished parts of my self that I'd never before been aware of; parts that had had no room to emerge in the middle of a too busy, too connected life. Eating when I was hungry, napping when I was tired, going to sleep and waking up when my body was ready for either, not relating to clock time, doing whatever the energy inside me moved me toward – I learned my own rhythms, felt the texture of my own flow.

Without my own or other people's agendas and expectations about emotional intimacy and relatedness, I discovered just how voluptuous my solitude could be, how it nourished and renewed me. Without the constant clamor of the stimulation and input that came with being so busy and so emotionally invested with others, there was time for my being to assimilate and rest.

Re-engaging with regular life – living in a particular place, finding new work, establishing my self in community, making friends – was a stepwise, careful process of exploring my new and renewed self in contexts that I had been away from for a time. There were fits and starts in that re-entry. It was easy to be co-opted by the dominant paradigm; hard to stay firmly in my own slowed down center in the midst of the powerful tide of everyone else's high-gear living.

Yet, I persisted. Unswerving in my choice of a nourishing life in the slow lane, I lived from a deep attunement with my own organic rhythm. Sometimes, seasons of high activity did and do evolve organically from my usual unhurried pace. These are a recognizably different kind of busy. Still, even these more organically based doings can sometimes feel like too much. (See **Surrendering**, page 239 for more about that.) And, the energy of the dominant paradigm can often escalate the organic busy into just-mindless-busy if we aren't paying close attention to our belly feelings.

Over the more than 38 years since my re-entry into ordinary life (albeit in the slow lane), I've learned to make retreats-into-stillness a regular part of my living. In earlier years, I'd do these once or twice a year for ten days, two weeks, or even (though rarely) a whole month. In the past few years, I've felt an increasing need to take shorter periods more often. And, most recently, I've been making the space to take a week each month to unplug and be in stillness.

These time-outs are much less radical shifts than that original one. Nevertheless, they create small islands of intentionally fallow time into which I gratefully sink. These empty, quiet times are a wonderful hedge against being unwittingly drawn into busyness.

Sometimes, Spirit hands me fallow time: several clients graduate themselves, take time out or go on vacation all at once and there's a gap of time before new people come to fill those open spaces. Other times, no writing, art or other creative process is in motion within me. Occasionally, these not-consciously-chosen fallow periods last longer than might feel comfortable or welcome. It can seem that nothing is happening inside me during them. I've learned not to be concerned about any of it. Once in a while – even after all these years of knowing better – I have a few moments of worry that nothing will ever flow again. But, then, I take a deep breath and remember, "Oh, this is a fallow season, I can choose to do deep rest instead of doing worry."

We live surrounded by a context (the dominant paradigm) in which fallow time is disparaged: seen as non-productive, slothful, to be avoided at all costs. It takes courage and persistence to claim/reclaim empty time as the essential, empowering part of juicy living that it is. Even when nothing visible seems to come from such periods, you can be assured that the ground of your being is replenishing itself all the while.

Consider giving your self (or receiving) the gift of empty, still time to rest and replenish your cherished self.

4-3. Rest is Sacred

*To rest is a sacred act of nourishment and solace
that takes courage and trust!*

Recently I first heard, then read, that in most nature-based tribal cultures, adults average between three and four hours a day doing what we might call work: tending to the provision of food, clothing and shelter. The other hours of their days are passed in individual or communal creativity and play: storytelling, song, dance, ritual, art, and **rest** – the sacred art of just **being**.

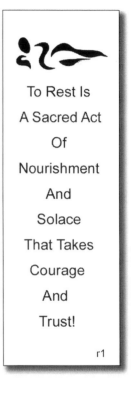

To Rest Is

A Sacred Act

Of

Nourishment

And

Solace

That Takes

Courage

And

Trust!

r1

I've spent the past more than 40 years of my life unlearning my so-called advanced culture's values and gradually finding my way to a lifestyle that honors my own wholeness. I've made a fierce commitment to listening inward to my body and my being. In my dedication to making choices that nourish the needs I uncover with this listening, I am being led to craft a life that is similar to this ancient, enduring model that I hadn't even known about till now.

When I began this conscious journey inward, I discovered a voracious hunger in me for time to be still and empty, time without talking or doing or being with other people. As I moved to create this space, I kept encountering inner and outer pressure to stay so-called normal, to continue filling up the potentially empty time. Part of me struggled with fear that it was only my doings that made me valuable, a worthwhile person.

My being and soul felt starved, my body exhausted from the adrenaline of unending stress and busyness. Even getting sick hadn't ever been a reason to interrupt the pace – I'd invariably keep going, sick or not. Still, I had a compelling sense that part of me would never get born or might actually die if I didn't make a quiet place in which it could germinate. My hunger for the nourishment and solace of stillness grew urgent enough to keep moving me out of the crazy-making, squirrel-in-a-cage **doing, doing, doing.** It helped me persevere in finding my way to the sacredness of rest.

Slowly, I started carving out empty time in which to be free to drift in whatever directions inner urgings and Spirit might move me. Free to doze, nap, daydream, watch the sky, wander aimlessly in the natural world or other places of beauty. Free to putter about my inner and outer worlds without the requirement that I accomplish anything of redeeming social value. Free from external demands and input so that I might, in leisure, digest and absorb my own experiences and come to know more of who I am and what I need in order to be whole.

I suspect that we all need some of this kind of nourishment woven into our days. When we open to valuing and incorporating rest, we are creating sacred space for magic, wonder, self-knowledge and Spirit to enter and inform our lives. Whatever enters and informs our lives moves through our lives to enter, inform and transform the world around us.

It takes great courage to choose for rest, to consciously carve out not-doing times in the midst of the constant liminal and subliminal pressures around (and within) us to stay productive in society's terms: immersed in the more conventional and, till now, more acceptable busyness of our peers.

It also takes great trust to choose for the sacred space of resting: trust that tolerating and resisting the pressures to return to busyness and business-as-usual will indeed lead to a gradual lessening of those pressures. Trust that any initial uneasiness we might feel in the open, drifting time can, with practice, give way to a growing sense of the voluptuousness of just **being**.

To inspire your practice of sacred resting: look for SARK's *Change Your Life Without Getting Out of Bed*, the ultimate nap book. Reverberate with this Spanish proverb: "How beautiful it is to do nothing and then, afterward, to rest." Explore and consider the shape rest might take for you in your everyday reality.

Gather a few friends to help you create a rest ethic, try doing heads-down, eyes-closed at your desk for five minutes every hour as a way to begin stopping-the-world.

Remember to be very gentle with your self as you practice moving away from busyness.

4-4. Going 75 mph

You are never any "where" until the slowest part of you gets there...
You can leap forward and slide back as many times as you need to...
And, you can also choose to advance by taking smaller steps!

I spent most of the first 32 years of my life constantly hurling my self forward at great speed, pushing my self mercilessly to the next step, stage or level. To that earlier me, anything less than the emotional equivalent of 75 mph looked like being stuck. My journey was full of dramatic cycles of careening forward, crashing into emotional walls of one sort or another, getting battered, winded and my knees full of gravel.

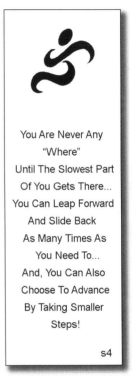

You Are Never Any
"Where"
Until The Slowest Part
Of You Gets There...
You Can Leap Forward
And Slide Back
As Many Times As
You Need To...
And, You Can Also
Choose To Advance
By Taking Smaller
Steps!

s4

After each crash, I'd be frantically busy for a time tending my wounds: metaphorically picking the gravel from my knees, bandaging cuts, wrapping bruises and sprains. By the time I'd finish this repair and regrouping process, I'd invariably look up to find that the wall I'd crashed into had, by then, disappeared. Surprised and delighted, I would be on my way again: doing 75 mph, hurtling (unawares) toward the next wall, crash, etc.

My life was full of exciting and dramatic movement (albeit often of the ten steps forward, nine step back variety). It was also pretty exhausting and often devastatingly hard on me.

Late one night, a friend and I left a board meeting at the Santa Barbara Freedom Clinic on our way to a café for a delayed dinner, she in her Volkswagen Beetle and I on my bicycle. She would get to each intersection much faster than I would. Then, every time, she'd have to stop and wait for the light to turn green, with both her motor and the car's at fast idle.

Tootling along on my slower bicycle, I'd get to each of the corners just as the lights turned from red to green. There were many such corners on our way. More than enough of them for me to get that it didn't matter how quickly or slowly we got to each intersection (threshold), neither of us could go through it until the red light turned green.

It was an "aha!" moment, a turning point in my life. I realized that the way I had been choosing to deal with the time before the red lights in my world turned green – the time before the slowest part of me arrived at the crossings/thresholds – had been the source of much of the exhausting drama in my life. Till then, it had felt too scary to move slowly, to take small or even intermittent steps. Only careen-crash-batter-regroup had ever registered as aliveness or progress to me or, it seemed, to the world around me.

It took time and living for me to fully assimilate this new understanding. But, on that night, I began choosing to look at life with different eyes, to change my scale for measuring movement. I started viewing everything through magnifying rather than usual, culturally approved, minimizing lenses. As I looked with these different eyes, I could recognize the progress in baby steps. I grew less afraid of and more able to risk moving slower and choosing smaller steps.

It has taken a whole lot of practice, (and **lots** of lovingly reminding my self that this really **is** an honorable and righteous way to live) for me to comfortably choose to go more slowly and gently along my path. These days, I'm more likely than ever to get to the thresholds of shifting in my life just as the lights are turning green, with even my slowest part right there with me. There's something comforting and comfortable about that. I love it.

There is richness and vibrancy to life lived more slowly and gently. Going slowly allows us to more fully feel both what we're moving through and how it's actually affecting us. This widening awareness allows us to know sooner and more clearly when something isn't right for us. It also allows us to need less because we're actually taking time to savor and experience whatever it is we are in the middle of rather than always zipping unfeelingly through it to get onto the next accomplishment or acquisition.

The more we risk practicing to choose the gentle path, the harder it becomes to be taken over by the cultural more-bigger-faster-yesterday trance. Yet, starting the practice without support can, in our crazy world, be scary and isolating. Think about starting to practice with a friend or two as a mutual support network.

Consider being tender and careful with your self as you explore the gentle magic of slowing down.

4-5. Cycles

*All life moves in cycles... What has been must often come apart before
what is to be can come together. Remember to honor your courage in
the midst of the coming apart times!*

After a year of leavings and reconciliations, I
finally let go of my last relationship in
September of 1984. I found a lovely cottage
on a wild, somewhat neglected piece of
property in Ojai's East End. An artistically
converted two-car garage, it was a spacious
studio with skylights, cathedral ceiling, wood
bat-and-board walls, hardwood floors and a
huge barrel of a Vermont Ironworks wood
stove. I moved in with a cozy jumble of
secondhand furniture I'd collected during
that back and forth year. And, I began, in
earnest, the journey of re-parenting my Little
One inside.

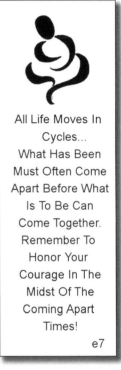

All Life Moves In
Cycles...
What Has Been
Must Often Come
Apart Before What
Is To Be Can
Come Together.
Remember To
Honor Your
Courage In The
Midst Of The
Coming Apart
Times!

e7

I saw clients two long days each week. Then,
I'd spend a day transitioning: buying vats of
flowers to arrange, doing errands, getting a
two-hour massage, cleansing, sage-smudging
and preparing my space for the Little One
and me to enter our solitary timeless world.
The first year, I spent most of my timeless
time wandering along the mountains,
canyons and streams of Ojai's backcountry. Once home, I drew and
wrote with colored pens in my journals. I painted, played with clay and
with an expanding collection of percussion instruments.

The second year I began to spend part of the timeless time creating
a real home for my Little One. I repainted, reupholstered and then
sewed all kinds of big soft pillows in bright colors. I made special nooks
for her and altars for all the bits of rocks, feathers and wood she'd gather
in the backcountry. I bought music and good stereo equipment for
playing it so that she could dance or dream (nestled in the big, soft
pillows) to wonderful sounds whenever she wanted to. I collected

drums, gongs, bells and ethnic percussion instruments so that she could make big noises or her own sort of rhythm band music (without having to practice first).

As she and I began to explore her rage and anger, big noises in the house weren't always the thing we needed to do. So, we moved outdoors to the piles of rocks, small boulders and construction debris that littered the neglected back and side yards around our house. Shoving and pitching those rocks over the hill into the wild place was exciting. Getting knee and elbow deep in the dirt, pushing boulders out of the way with our back and our feet felt delicious.

One day we stopped flinging the rocks and started using them to build rock walls and pathways and a platform for a hot tub. Then, rock gardens felt exciting so we got lots of flowers and green things to plant (something we had never done before in our life). Later on, we even put down a tiny patch of sod-grass so she could roll naked in the sun in our own, now very beautiful, backyard.

We made a fire circle and poured rings of black and then white lava stones around it. After that, we discovered a neglected vegetable patch on the far side of the property and started planting things to eat. Everything grew and flourished. For quite a while it was delightful for my Little One and me to tend the temple we had built together.

One day, late in the fourth year, we woke up feeling it had become too much like work to take care of all that we had so lovingly built. The flowers that used to be fun to arrange sat in the vats for days while we avoided them. Hiring people to help made for less physical work but, then, we had people around when we wanted to be alone. It was a **very** cranky time. We wished for a big vacuum cleaner to come and empty everything away so we could again simply be little with more open time for doing nothing or more of what felt like play.

Not too long after I made that wish, my car – filled with instruments, cassette tapes, both ordinary and ceremonial clothes and jewelry, art materials and camping gear from a trip to sit in circle with my women's lodge – was stolen from in front of a friend's house in San Francisco. It was found two days later, intact but literally vacuumed clean of all my possessions. It turned out, in the aftermath, to be an easy matter to let go of it all, as long as my beloved little two-year-old car was back with me.

It was much harder to continue the letting go process with the rest of the life I had built at home. Giving up doing twelve vases of flowers every week was just what I needed. But, the disappearance of those flower-filled vases felt like failure. As I struggled with cutting back on what had become too much to do, my outside (critical) eyes would see the enterprise as a falling apart, going backwards or letting things go (in the negative sense of the phrase). It was hard to dismantle my once again too-big-for-me life without getting caught in seeing this movement toward a simpler life as a shameful, defeated thing. I would get caught even though, in my bones, I desperately hungered for a simpler life.

It was a difficult course to acknowledge, much less encourage or celebrate in my self. Daily I wrestled with the ingrained cultural definition of progress/growth/success as linear, constantly expanding. Over and over again I looked to the natural world for support for this different progression I was living: this coming apart of what had been that, once again, was happening in my life. In the natural world, the growing cycle includes both expansion **and** decay. Blossoming/ripening is always followed by the dying away that makes compost for germinating the next cycle of growth. The roses in the garden unfold and expand only so far before the petals fall and die. The leaves on the peach tree last only so long before falling. We don't see these as signs that the rosebush or the peach tree is failing.

It takes lots of courage to honor, to not resist this cyclic process in our own lives. We have to break away from the cultural programming, the messages that daily bombard us. We have to risk trusting what comes from within our being. Life lived in harmony our inner self opens out in naturally repeating cycles.

In the coming apart/unraveling times we, like the snake, are shedding a skin that has become constraining, a way of living our life that no longer has room in it for newness and growth. When the familiar shape of our life comes apart, the pieces of it become available to reassemble in fresh ways. We get to see which elements are enduring and which were part of our journey for only a season. During the unraveling time we feel agitated, disoriented by the upheaval. We feel grief for what is passing away. Skinless, we feel vulnerable and touchy. We fear that all is lost, that nothing will ever feel solid again.

As we start to move through these times supported by the consciousness that they are healthy, important and inevitable, we recognize their arrival as signs that we are beginning a time of significant growth. We can comfort our fears in the coming apart seasons by warmly reminding our selves of all the coming together times that (sooner or later) followed all the past coming apart cycles. We can gently remind our selves how courageous we are for moving in ways that are so unsupported by our culture. We can try to move as slowly as possible. We can practice being kind and protective with our skinless selves. And we can, in calmer moments, gather a circle of friends who will, together, honor the sacredness of cyclical processes in each other's lives.

Consider being tenderly patient with and embracing of your vulnerable self in the coming apart times.

4-6. Feeling Stuck

In the "feeling stuck" times: when it's no longer possible to be as you were and not yet possible to be as you will be... Berating and badgering your self only make the between-time more trying. Remember to ease up, be patient and tender with your self, rest and trust that, deep within, the new growth is germinating! The next step always unfolds when you're fully ready for it!

So often along the journey of my unfolding, I've come to a place where I could actually see/recognize an old self-defeating pattern at the very instant that it was playing through me. Newly able to watch my self doing something that, not long ago, would have gone by without any conscious notice, I'd be aware that it was leading me somewhere that was no longer acceptable to me. Yet, despite this awareness, I'd be unable to stop or change the behavior.

It was excruciatingly painful knowing that I needed to not be doing this to my self again while feeling powerless to interrupt the behavior. For many years, these were occasions for having at my self: berating, criticizing and generally beating up on my self. "How can you be so dense, stupid, slow, screwed-up, perverse?!" and "What is wrong with you?!" were the sort of nastiness that I'd hurl at my self.

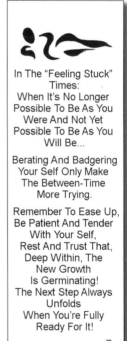

In The "Feeling Stuck" Times:
When It's No Longer Possible To Be As You Were And Not Yet Possible To Be As You Will Be...

Berating And Badgering Your Self Only Make The Between-Time More Trying.

Remember To Ease Up, Be Patient And Tender With Your Self, Rest And Trust That, Deep Within, The New Growth Is Germinating! The Next Step Always Unfolds When You're Fully Ready For It!

r7

Already in pain, the relentless litany of my inner-critic (the Hatchet Lady) would further flay me. Yet, no matter how brutally she or I treated my self, it would never move me forward any faster. I would feel stuck, furious with my self for knowing what needed to change and yet being unable to change it.

As I've worked with my self and with others over the years, I've watched this cycle repeatedly recur along the way of everyone's journey.

Gradually, I've learned to hold these times more spaciously, to hold my self and others caught this way with more gentle generosity. These feeling stuck places are actually times of growing and transitioning, even though that process may be invisible to us or to any outside observer.

We need, in these difficult and painful times, to lovingly remind our selves that being able to witness our patterns unfolding is in itself a significant accomplishment. As we witness, we become more than just the part of our selves playing out the pattern. We are both that self and a larger, watching self: the witness. As we continue repeating the old patterns with the witness self present and watching, we are able to gather more and more understanding of the steps in the old dance. We begin to see what the triggers and conventions are. We become more and more separate from the energy field of that dance. It is not the same-old, same-old when we are conscious, awake and watching. It becomes more like research, like cultural anthropology.

The more tender and generous we can be with our selves, the less critical and judgmental, the more we will be able to see and learn in our researches. We cannot, by any pressuring or goading, hasten the moment of the birth of the next step, of the next who that we are becoming. It always emerges just exactly when we're fully ready for it. Yet, how we are with our selves during the between-time, the period of transition to that moment, **is** something about which we do have options and choice.

When we allow the natural world to be our teacher and guide, we understand that growth is not always visible: unfoldings and blossomings have their own seasons. We remember that when things are the bleakest and most barren above ground, there **is** a gathering of energy proceeding, slowly, deep underground.

Using this frame of reference instead of the more-bigger-faster-yesterday yardstick of the ambient culture, we can choose to be gentle and patient with our selves. We can let our selves rest in the trust that the new growth **is** germinating even as we do our researches.

Consider the practice of being patient and generous with your self in the feeling stuck times.

4-7. Change Moving Quickly

When change is moving quickly in your life, it's best not to look much beyond right where you are in this moment... The "you-that-you-are-now" is likely to feel overwhelmed when it anticipates circumstances that the "you-that-you-are-becoming" will be well prepared to meet when they actually arrive... At such times of great acceleration, try living in the thinnest slice of now you can define!

In late January 1973, just two months past my 32nd birthday, I was slowly winding down all of my soon-to-be-former-life in New York City: Closing my private practice as a clinical psychologist by helping twenty or so clients make their way to new therapists. Having special times with my friends and family as we said our farewells. Selling off or giving away most of my possessions in a sometimes hilarious Manhattan luxury hi-rise version of a yard sale.

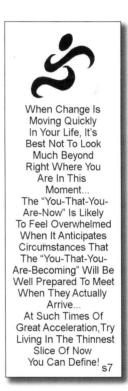

When Change Is Moving Quickly In Your Life, It's Best Not To Look Much Beyond Right Where You Are In This Moment... The "You-That-You-Are-Now" Is Likely To Feel Overwhelmed When It Anticipates Circumstances That The "You-That-You-Are-Becoming" Will Be Well Prepared To Meet When They Actually Arrive... At Such Times Of Great Acceleration, Try Living In The Thinnest Slice Of Now You Can Define! s7

Heeding a powerful urging from a voice deep inside me, I was beginning a voyage into a beckoning unknown. Preparing to go on the road, planning to wend my way toward California but being otherwise clueless about where the journey would lead, I was propelled by an inner knowing that "I would die if I didn't get to someplace green." (See **Pirouettes**, page 125 for more about this time.)

I had moved through a series of stages in the process of translating this urging. The first approximation had been a well-explored vision of relocating to a rural seaside town at the tip of Long Island. That version included moving with my partner of seven years and building a practice as a therapist in this new area. Over the course of almost six months, the plan kept shifting and redefining itself.

After a while, it became apparent that I needed to let go of my profession – the idea of starting another practice felt wrong, even suffocating. Sometime further along, the idea of staying on the East Coast – even at the very rural edge of it – felt not right. And, as the vision slowly reconfigured into a road trip to California, the notion of going with a partner in tow felt stifling and wide of the mark.

Gradually I understood that what I needed was to take leave from everything: partner, profession, friends, family, possessions and my East Coast roots. Some of the leave-taking felt like it might be permanent. Some of it felt like it might be only for an as yet unknowable period of time.

The plan became one of going forth on this open-ended trip like a turtle – with my house on my back as it were. Here, too, the translation kept refining. First I looked at mini-motor homes, then professional van-conversions. Ultimately, I knew I that I needed to buy a simple, empty commercial van and set it up my self as a bed-sitting room, creating my new living space using salvage gleaned from the life I was leaving.

Having the van as a mobile, self-contained base provided me with some primal security. I would always have my home with me; a home that would provide the safety of a familiar, comforting womb for my rebirthing process, a base camp out of which I might venture as my journey unfolded. This felt essential to the adventure of heading into the unknown and unknowable.

It was an outrageous shift for the ambitious super-achiever I had been until then. Yet, the times allowed for and even encouraged the possibility of such a radical dropping out. In the so-called real world, many different kinds of people were engaged in intense questioning, in re-examining their values and the direction of their lives. In those still-hippie days, lots of folks were going on the road, slipping out of formerly conventional trajectories.

Attentive to the inner voice that was speaking to me so insistently, I followed wherever it led. Baby-step-by-baby-step, things fell into place. I was completing my life as it had been. I felt surprisingly comfortable, without trepidation or fear as I approached the final leave-taking; unfazed by not knowing what was in store for me after I would leave.

As I moved through my preparations, I was learning a powerful lesson about navigating the seas of radical, rapidly moving change. My focus was narrowed to very thin slices of now, doing and processing just one tiny step at a time; not thinking about what was next, what might be waiting further down the path or where I might in fact be heading. The how of it all revealed itself to me in small, timely glimpses as I proceeded.

Carried by the energy moving me through the transition, I was building the confidence and emotional capacities I needed for this major shift. Each step changed me and by doing that, readied me for the next step. I was taught not to scare my self by looking beyond exactly where I was in the moment. When I reached places that might have scared the who I had been just days ago, the who I'd become by this new moment was not at all frightened.

Through the more than 40 years since that time in my life, I've held onto that powerful lesson. Whenever I find my self moving through periods of accelerated change, the knowing place inside me reminds me to keep my focus on the thinnest slices of now that I can define.

Slowing things way down is usually the best first approach to any intensity that threatens to unsettle one's balance. When that doesn't work, the practice of slicing now very thinly is the next best bet.

Focusing on the thinnest slice of now that we can define keeps us from swamping our selves with anticipations of what we're not yet equipped to handle. This narrowing of our focus helps us to not overwhelm our selves trying to encompass the sheer volume of the changes careening toward us. It's a practice that also works to calm us whenever we're feeling inundated by too many projects, too many tasks or too much obsessive worrying.

Whenever you feel overwhelmed and unable to slow the process of change to a more manageable pace, consider living in the thinnest slice of now that you can define.

4-8. Belly Feelings

Your body and "belly" feelings always tell you exactly what's so for you right now... Pay attention to these messages about your safety no matter what your own mind, or anyone else, says to dismiss or to invalidate them!

In my 31st year, at the pinnacle of my career as a consummate super-achiever, I was busily creating a perfect life. (See **Pirouettes**, page 125 for more about that.) One morning I woke with a severe backache. I couldn't sit through the length of an ordinary therapy session with any of my clients. Undaunted, for the next several weeks I stood, walked around or lay on the couch while my clients sat and shared their lives.

Your Body And "Belly" Feelings Always Tell You Exactly What's So For You Right Now... Pay Attention To These Messages About Your Safety No Matter What Your Own Mind, Or Anyone Else, Says To Dismiss Or To Invalidate Them!

o6

In those days, like many East Coast Jewish intellectuals, I considered my body (if at all) as a conveyance for carrying my head/brain around in the world. I fed, exercised and tended my body to keep it looking good and in good running order – in much the same way as I tended my car. My mind was the valued center of my identity.

I remember feeling irritated with my body for being unreliable, for creating so much inconvenience in the middle of my intense and busy life. Still, I spent extra time each morning and evening soaking in hot baths and doing gentle stretches to relieve the tightness. (I hadn't yet discovered massage or chiropractic.)

Some weeks later, I began waking each day with a profound sense of dread. Deep in my belly, there was a sense that I would die if I couldn't get away from New York City's dirt and noise, if I didn't get to some place where I could be surrounded by green growing things. **That** got my attention. I recognized that something about my life had become toxic to me; that I **had** to make changes, soon. Only years later did I realize that the backache was my body's first attempt to give me that very same message.

I was 42, in the midst of a very fraught year of working on ending a long, difficult relationship, when my body again called emphatically for my attention. During repeated, arduous and devastating conversations with my ex, pains deep in my left shoulder would grow so extreme as to literally take my breath away. I'd shrug, shake and massage my shoulder while we continued to talk, trying to ease the pain. By then I knew about bodywork. I scheduled massage, Rolfing and energy work sessions to help unravel the mess in my shoulder. It never occurred to me to hear the pain as my body's message that something in those conversations was toxic for me.

Some time later in that challenging period, I would – during those conversations – suddenly find my self off in the bathroom, having gone there without a conscious decision right in the middle of my ex's angry diatribe. **That** got my attention. I understood then that my body was taking care of me, removing me from a bad-for-me place **even** when I hadn't the conscious sense to know that that was what I needed.

It was a turning point in my journey. I realized that I needed to listen more closely to my body and to start taking my body's messages seriously. I had been overriding or ignoring those body feelings for most of my life. These feelings/messages were my natural animal-being's direct responses to what might be going on around and within me. Heeding my body's messages would, I could see, help me to take better care of my self and keep my self safer.

In my 50s, I had several experiences with body and energy workers during which I became extremely nauseated and agitated as they worked on certain areas of my body. I'd report this and ask them to stop what they were doing just then. Most listened and stopped instantly. Two of the practitioners, however, encouraged me to "stay with the discomfort." One wanted me to stay with it because she said she "was being guided" to do what she was doing and I was "interfering with the guided process." The other wanted me to see that "staying with the discomfort would lead to its dissolving."

It didn't matter to me what these experts thought. I knew that I needed to listen to my inner expert, my own body. And, my body was telling me that the energy being stirred in it was either toxic or just more than it felt safe to let in right then. I honored its message and stopped the work both times, despite the practitioners' considerations. (I actually stopped doing any further sessions with the worker who was irritated by my choice.)

There's an awful lot that pressures us to ignore our bodies' messages. Those of us who have histories of psychic or physical trauma or neglect in our childhoods have learned, early on in our lives, to cope with overwhelming circumstances by disconnecting from our body's responses. The culture in which we live persistently encourages us to override our bodies' natural warning systems. The "no pain, no gain" attitude, the enormous market for over-the-counter and prescription medications to mask pain so we can "get on with life," the widespread use of caffeine, energy drinks and other uppers to allow us to "get over" our body's natural fatigue – all these reflect that encouragement.

Still, our body and gut/belly feelings **are** always the best barometers of what's so for us in any moment. Our minds can all too often beguile us with stories about why we shouldn't (or don't really) feel those feelings. But, the truth is that we betray or dismiss our body and belly feelings only at great peril to our mental and physical health and wellbeing.

Developing our capacity to attend to these feelings and our commitment to take them seriously enough to act on their information is essential to our healing. As we develop our practice of respecting our body and belly messages, we become resistant to pressures to override or undermine these signals, whether they come from our own minds or anyone else, no matter their expertise

Consider listening more attentively and carefully to your body and belly feelings.

4-9. Not-Knowing Times

"Not-Knowing" times are an essential part of the growing cycle.
Trying to "figure it out" before it's time for knowing is exhausting,
frustrating and gets in the way of "being-in-the-process."
Talk lovingly and gently to the frightened part of you who's
fearful of not having the answer now!

In the early 1970s, responding to a compelling inner urging, I extricated my self from what had been a highly successful, accomplished life in New York City. (See **Pirouettes**, page 125 for more about that time.) I knew in my bones that going on with that life was damaging my body and being. I had no idea of where I might be heading. All I had was the certainty that I needed to leave, needed to travel to California on my own.

"Not-Knowing" Times Are An Essential Part Of The Growing Cycle.

Trying To "Figure It Out" Before It's Time For Knowing Is Exhausting, Frustrating And Gets In The Way Of "Being-In-The-Process."

Talk Lovingly And Gently To The Frightened Part Of You Who's Fearful Of Not Having The Answer Now!

e8

Though it wasn't an uncommon behavior for those times, I was older than most of the people who were dropping out of their lives. Nothing in my compulsively super-achieving history would have suggested that I'd ever choose such a path, that I would be drawn to launching my self into an unstructured, yawning unknown. But there I was, at just such a threshold.

During my years of being in private practice as a psychologist, quite unaware of it, I had regularly been stashing away a good bit of money. Some less than conscious part of my being seemed to have been preparing the way for me to walk out of my life into the not-knowing with some cushion. I was able to leave with enough money to be adrift for a considerable chunk of time.

It took close to six months to prepare for my departure. Those months were filled with closing a full-time practice; buying a stripped commercial van, transforming it into a turtle-like womb-shell in which

I could always be at home; saying my good-byes to spouse, lover, friends and family; winnowing my possessions down to what I would carry with me into my new life. During that transitioning time, I realized that an essential part of the journey I was embarking on involved having no plans or goals.

For the whole of my life before then, I'd always been heading somewhere particular, intent on accomplishing or achieving whatever it was that felt important at the time. This journey called me to be unfettered by those usual commitments. I was excited and eager to begin living in the not-knowing-anything place. I had no fear, no anxiety about the lack of structure ahead. Instead, I itched and ached for the openness that had never been a part of my ordinary life.

During the earliest days of driving cross-country, having nothing-whatever-to-do proved to be challenging. I handled the edgy transition with a kind of obsessive busyness in the van when I wasn't driving. There were endless things to fuss with in preparing or cleaning up from my meals and refining the organization of my little space. Gradually, and particularly once I got to warmer geographies, the fussing and busyness calmed. I relaxed and began to luxuriate in the gentle, flowing sense of drift.

Over the next 20 months while I lived in and traveled the western coast in my little van-womb, I found comfort in the remarkable stillness and peace of the not-knowing place. A lot of old, unfinished inner material could and would surface in that empty space. Some of that was quite intense. Some of it was painful and taxing. But, there was time and open space in which to practice just being with it all. I wrote in my journal, walked, rode my bicycle and crocheted a lot. I hung out on beaches. I watched the sky and the sea. After some three months of keeping mostly to my self I started meeting new people and exploring how the me that I was becoming would relate to other beings.

I wandered into trying different kinds of work for brief periods of time. Then, after those 20 months, I was prompted to move indoors and to try a job as the health education coordinator in a radical, free-health-care clinic. Nothing about any of this felt like it was the new where-I-was-going. Rather, it seemed part of the adventure of being a passenger on a magical, mystery ride. I was interested, amused and somewhat surprised by where I was being taken.

After less than a year, though, I had managed to recreate much of what I had separated from when I'd left my New York life. The deadening super-achieving, over-committed, over-involved habits had resurfaced. The forms they took were different. Still, the messages from my body/belly grew increasingly clamorous. I needed to disengage, to go back to the drawing board. There was more inner work to be done, more need for uncommitted time and space in which to continue unraveling what inside of me still drove these damaging habits. With a good deal of struggle (see **Feeling Confused**, page 69 for this tale) I was able to find my way out of these newer entanglements. Once again, I went eagerly into the uncluttered spaciousness of not-knowing.

At first there was great relief. The not-knowing space felt comforting. It was welcoming and peaceful. I began to examine the troublesome habits, to uncover more about the woundedness out of which they were again rising. But, fairly shortly, everything shifted. Feelings of uneasiness and fearfulness began to swirl in me. I worried that I would never again be fit for anything but a life adrift in not-knowing, that I would only be able to hold my self centered in my new ways of being if I was alone and unconnected to work of any sort. The prospect was frightening to contemplate. There were no calming clues or clear messages from Spirit/my inmost self to direct me.

In my discomfort and anxiety with the not-knowing, I started trying to figure things out. My mind convinced me that no new direction could or would emerge until I had used up all of the money stash that had been my stake for this new life. There was over $11,000 (a lot of money in late 1976) still left after three years. I chose to split the stash with my sister who, at that time was making a significant career change, going back to school for a new degree.

It was odd to be acting on a decision that came from thinking and figuring after having felt so completely (and willingly) led by Spirit/intuition/deep self for so long. Not surprisingly (at least in retrospect) that decision, in short order, hurled me into more rather than less anxiety and confusion. I felt desperate, in and out of feeling frantic, up against the wire. I became totally preoccupied with making my now smaller stash of money last as long as possible.

I began taking odd (in both senses of the word) jobs. I joined a woman I knew in her contract housecleaning business. At least there was no danger of becoming enmeshed in super-achieving there. Then I worked weekend evenings as the doorperson-cum-bouncer at a local women's bar. Most of the Santa Barbara women in the then new wave of feminists-coming-out-as-lesbians went there regularly to hang out, drink juice and dance. It was more like a community center than a bar. And, many of these women were my new friends. The job offered me a way to be at the bar and (comfortably) a little removed at the same time.

In the midst of the uneasiness, I also became involved in a relationship that challenged every bit of the self I'd thought I was at the time. My partner's workaholism (80+ hours a week) exaggerated the discomfort and worry that continued to plague me. Rather than staying with my agitation and going deeper with it, I became more and more busily, co-dependently enmeshed in taking up the slack left in her life by my partner's overworking. From the moment my figuring-it-out self had taken the reins, my slide into chaos and despair kept accelerating.

And then, magic found a way to happen despite all that I was doing to get in the way of it. Those were the early days of non-monogamy as the path of political correctness in the Southern California lesbian community. (That was the 1970s version of what has more recently resurfaced incarnated as "polyamory.") Several women in the Santa Barbara community had begun exploring this path. A few were getting painfully tangled in the emotional messes it could easily provoke. My past as both a feminist psychotherapist and a woman who had lived bisexually in an open marriage was, by then, fairly well known in the community. Several weekends in a row, some of the distressed women and their caring friends came over to me as I sat at the door of the bar reading my book while serving as doorperson/bouncer. In many variations, they implored and cajoled me to consider doing counseling or psychotherapy again. They felt I would be the perfect person to be a resource for our community in the middle of this upheaval.

I felt sympathy and concern for the women involved. I remembered what hard work it had been to stay sane, to be compassionate and honest in the midst of the open relationship through which I had lived. Still, at first, I couldn't begin to fathom putting on the therapist hat again. The whole idea had me feeling vaguely nauseated. The women persisted and pressed. Someone (I no longer remember who it was) asked me to at least think about under what circumstances I might possibly be open to doing the work, even for a brief while.

So, one day as on hands and knees I scrubbed someone's tiled kitchen floor, I actually started thinking about what I would need to make it possible to do therapy again, probably as a brief experiment. I thought about all the things that had made me need to stop doing the work.

I remembered the claustrophobic feeling of being confined for so many hours a day to an office – even though it was beautiful, comfortable and in my own home. I remembered how it had felt: clients brought, worked on and left their pains in the air and walls of that room. By the time I stopped seeing people there, it had felt as though the layers of pain absorbed into those walls were thick and suffocating.

I remembered the 50-minute hour that I (to my great professional chagrin) had so much trouble sticking to. It had been frustrating for me to interrupt people in the middle of their process because "that's all our time for today." Of course, what that line really meant was that there was someone else in the waiting room ready for their appointment with me.

I remembered how much I was left hanging – feeling just as unfinished as my clients were feeling when they were interrupted by the clock. I remembered how that lack of completion left me mulling over and over what had gone on in each client's life. How, because of the lack of closure, I often felt as though I was engaged in living not only my own but twenty other lives simultaneously.

I remembered how locked into the work I felt. Once I began working with someone, I was committed to going the distance with them, a distance about which I would have little say despite its impact on my life. And, I remembered all the paperwork, billing and keeping track of accounts receivable that ate up so much of my non-client time.

As I remembered, I thought about the blessings of my California life. The nourishment of hours spent at the beaches, in the mountains, in green and open spaces; the joys of timelessness, of being more off the clock than on it. Of the specialness of a life that allowed me to hang out with a friend until we were organically ready to end a conversation, not having tight schedules aborting our time together. The blessedness of having space and freedom to move anytime in any direction that Spirit/ my deep self led me.

Out of that hands-and-knees reverie, came a seed of possibility. If I could meet the people I might work with outdoors or in **their** own spaces. If we could meet each time as if it were just this once that we were going to work together. If we could sit or walk and work together in that meeting however long was needed for the person to come to some closure about the issues we were addressing. If I could, as a one-time consultant to each person, help them – as part of their coming to closure – design a plan of how to go forward with their own work on the problem(s) they'd brought to our time together. If people could complete the session by paying (pro-rated) for the actual amount of time they'd used as we finished. Then, I could make the space inside of me to try doing the work of a therapist again. If it didn't work for me, if I needed to stop, I wouldn't have made commitments I couldn't keep.

From that seed grew a practice I called Catalyst that worked in exactly those ways. It started with me serving the women who had entreated me to come back to doing counseling/therapy. It lasted many more years in the one-time-at-a-time form, even though people could always call back the very next week if they needed/wanted another one-time.

This new (to me at least) way of doing therapy/consultation was Spirit's gift to me. It was born out of the willingness (all the trying-to-figure-it-out notwithstanding) to live in the middle of a long season of not-knowing; a willingness to see not-knowing as a valuable part of the growing cycle in which much could be germinating. Not-knowing times seem to be a kind of neutral or idling gear through which we must pass every time we prepare for a major shifting of our inner/outer gears.

Over the years the shape of my practice/work has continued to transform as I've transformed. It's refashioned itself into some amalgam of Catalyst and my returning willingness to be committed to ongoing availability to the people who use me as their consultant. Having learned to use sage and prayer to cleanse my space, I feel freer to see people in my studio. Still, I often do house calls or outdoor sessions when people would prefer that. And, most recently, I do a lot of my work by phone with people who live at distances from Ojai.

These two long cycles of not-knowing taught me trust, patience and the importance of keeping my figuring-it-out hands off the controls when other (these days much less major) cycles of not-knowing arrive. I practice talking compassionately and reassuringly to the sometimes disquieted, antsy parts of me who may feel upset or challenged by the not-knowing. (It usually calms the agitation when I do that.) And, I continue to be amazed at what comes into being at the far sides of even the most interminable seeming seasons of not-knowing.

In our crazy out-of-balance culture, we feel compelled to rush our selves to come up with answers before we've let our selves live into the questions. We feel pushed to make **any** decision rather than risk the criticism we fear for quietly waiting for direction to emerge organically from our inner-knowing places. I think here of the demeaning pejoratives like "passive," "not being proactive," "wishy-washy," "indecisive" thrown at us when we choose to hang out and wait on our own inner timing.

Claiming not-knowing times as honorable, empowering seasons of germinating and inner preparation seems essential to living more compassionately with our selves and other beings.

Consider tenderly reassuring the parts of you who are fearful of embracing not-knowing times, of not-having-all-the-answers-right-now.

4-10. Going More Slowly

Remember to go more slowly when you feel scared or anxious!

When, at 43, I started hiking the trails in Ojai, I joined an aging English woman who was leading informal explorations of the local canyons and mountains. A veteran of Sierra Club hikes, she was interested in gathering smaller-than-Sierra-Club groups of Ojai locals so that she could share with us her knowledge of the surrounding wilds.

Remember To

Go More

Slowly

When You Feel

Scared

Or

Anxious!

e1

It was an odd choice for me given my usual inclination to venture into nature on my own; odd also because it involved getting up every Sunday at what was for me – night owl that I am – a rather ungodly hour. Still, it was a great way to become familiar with the trails and their challenges before I went out on them by my self. Each week I trekked with groups of eight or ten other novice trail-walkers. As we went ranging around the front-country, I discovered a terror I hadn't known was in me. Whenever the trails had steep drop-offs without even some low chaparral between me and the drop, I would experience almost paralyzing terror.

Walking in the middle of a line of hikers along a narrow trail and coming to one of these edgy places was quite alarming. Surprised by the scary passage in front of me, I'd feel petrified and also acutely aware of the people behind me. There'd be no space either to let them pass me or for me to turn around, pass them and go back.

The pressure to keep moving ahead was intense. So was the anxious paralysis in my body. That no one else seemed the least bit affected by this edge that so frightened me left me feeling isolated and as if I were over-reacting. Used to seeing my self as a courageous, fearless warrior-woman – at least on emotional and intellectual terrain – I felt embarrassed by my anxiety. And, even more, I felt terrified that I was terrified.

This was the legacy of childhood experiences of having a mother who responded to my frightened need for support and comfort with angry impatience and ridicule. Very early on, I became terrified of feeling terror because all I had to help me cope with such towering fear were the limited resources of my petrified little self.

Fortunately at 43, my recently kindled unconditionally loving Mommy-Inside-me was available as my protector. At each such edgy physical place, she would speak to and advocate for me. She would whisper that it was okay to be scared, that I wasn't being a sissy, over-reacting or being melodramatic: that I was simply feeling what was so for me. She let me know that she was here with me now and forever more, that she would care for and help me in the scary times and that I would never again have to be alone with and overwhelmed by my fears.

All of it was whispered in my heart in an instant. Her presence gave me the permission and courage to matter-of-factly tell the hikers behind me that this was an edgy crossing for me, that I was sorry to hold them up but that I needed to go very slowly in order to get across it. Hearing this, hikers ahead of me would turn around to offer encouragement and even extend a hand for me to grab onto. They were solicitous and patient. Their kindness moved me to tears.

I would breathe slowly and deeply to calm and center my self. I'd lean into the side of the mountain, hold onto rocks or chaparral, take tiny baby steps and gradually make my way across the frightening interval. Sometimes the hikers I was with would cheer me at the end of such a crossing. I felt seen and supported. I felt very brave and well acknowledged for my bravery.

In earlier seasons of my healing, I would have been both afraid of and embarrassed about revealing my fearfulness. I'd have expected to be ridiculed, scoffed at or, at best, mercilessly teased for being "such-a-girl." In the face of trepidation about revealing my trepidation, I would force my self into doing whatever it might be while acting as if I weren't at all anxious. I would move as quickly as I could, racing to get through whatever it might be that was scaring me. I never saw any alternative way to approach these awful moments.

Acting as if I weren't scared when I was usually led to stomachaches and nausea. When, at last, I'd be on the far side of the experience and away from other people, I would collapse, exhausted. Holding my self together when I felt like falling apart was utterly draining.

As I started the work of kindling the ferociously protective, unconditionally loving Mommy-Inside (see **Coming Home**, page 287 for more about this) I was able to be with my fearfulness in new ways. For the first time in my life, there was a connected, loving Mommy whose tender and care-filled voice I could hear within me all the time. I could hear the voices of the frightened little selves in me as separate both from the grown-up me and from this loving Mommy voice. I could separate all of these from the nasty, belittling voice of my internalized mean mommy (the critical Hatchet Lady). And I was learning that what the mean mommy voice was telling me was never the truth.

All these years and all this hiking later, those edgy trail places and the patches of slippery shale still scare me. I still go across them very slowly, holding onto the side of the mountain and using a lightweight bamboo walking stick to give me more confidence and support as I go.

Almost 30 years later, I'm open about and respectful of my fears and anxieties regardless of whether they're about things physical or emotional or interpersonal. Whenever and wherever they're stirred, I advocate for my self, carving the space – no matter what the circumstances or what anyone else has to say about it – to go very slowly and care-fully. I have my own permission to take as many breaks as I need to calm and re-center my self as I move through the fearfulness. Sometimes, I even give my self permission to completely opt out of doing whatever it might be that's so anxiety-provoking at that moment.

We live in a culture that's filled with messages that make it unacceptable to honor our fearfulness or to respond to our scared selves with compassion and kindness. Certainly we've all heard the myriad variations: "we have nothing to fear but fear itself," "bite-the-bullet," "feel-the-fear-and-do-it-anyway." And "be man/woman enough to just do it."

It takes courage, fierceness and lots of intentional practice to give our selves permission to feel scared or anxious; to name what we're feeling out loud, as if it truly is acceptable and respectable to feel this way; to go more slowly and carefully as we protect our frightened selves and to not allow anyone (including the self in us that may be afraid of being openly afraid) to shame or push or ridicule us as we take such good care of our selves.

We're surrounded with rhetoric that warns us about the danger of "giving in to our fears." The message: doing so will only make us more and more incapacitated and paralyzed. As is so very often the case, the cultural message is a complete reversal of the being-level truth. If we are gentle, encouraging and protective of our fearful selves, they gradually feel safe enough to trust our concern and to experiment with venturing beyond where before they had had to stop.

Consider tenderly allowing your self to go more slowly in any circumstances in which you feel scared or anxious.

4-11. When You're Tired

When you're tired, rest... Even when "There's no reason to be tired," and, especially when "There's no time for rest!"

More times in my life than I could hope to count, despite the fact that I seemed to be doing nothing any outside eye could see, I've felt exhausted. The kind of exhausted that makes it hard to find the energy to get out of bed in the first place. And, once you've managed to do that, it's the kind of exhausted that then makes you feel like collapsing for a lengthy nap after you've barely brushed your teeth, made your chai and set out your vitamins for the day.

When I'd first notice this kind of total tiredness, I'd put my self through a long inventory of probing questions. The self-interview was meant to uncover what I might be depressed about. Because, of course, given our cultural mindset, not having the energy to get out bed and wanting to sleep a lot were both automatically readable as signs of depression.

When You're
Tired,
Rest...
Even When
"There's
No ReasonTo Be
Tired,"
And, Especially
When "There's
No Time For
Rest!"
r3

Finding no signs of depression, I (like any not-yet-recovering super-achiever or any self-respecting member of our compulsively super-achieving society) would then move on to caustically challenging my right to feel the way I did. "You're not **even** doing anything! What have **you** got to be so tired about!" After these demeaning interchanges with my self, I would of course be **even more** ready for a nap, a really long one.

Over these past more than 40 years of traveling in the slow lane of life, I've been learning to accept my tiredness and exhaustion when they come. It's become apparent that it's ridiculous to argue with my body, to require it to explain itself to me or to require it to prove that it's not in fact feeling what it feels.

I've been learning, as well, not to take in messages suggesting that I should feel shamed by or inadequate about my feeling tired for no apparent reason. As I've gotten older (at this writing I'm on my way to my 73rd birthday) there have been increasing challenges to my acceptance of my occasional tiredness or need for rest. In our youth-obsessed media/culture, tiredness and low energy are portrayed as shameful signs of aging, of being less valuable, of not being able to keep up/be vibrant/be youthful. Certainly (the media would have it) these signs are meant to be hidden/masked/medicated or herbal elixired away. Boundless, unflagging energy as the Holy Grail, sigh. Oh, Spare me! I hold and value a very different image of juicy aliveness.

The thing about acknowledging my body's needs for rest and naps is that, when I give it what it craves, I feel so much better. If I lie (or stay) down when the first waves of tiredness hit, it usually doesn't take very much stopping to rejuvenate and re-energize. When it does require more than a little bit of stopping, I've taken to lavishing my body and being with just as much resting as it needs. These days, I can allow my self to luxuriate in the voluptuous sensuality of resting, napping and lolling about doing nothing. It's taken a lot of practice to get to this. But, it's been a very satisfying journey. And, I get to feel like such a radical revolutionary.

One of the important revelations along the way of this practice and commitment has been understanding that tiredness that doesn't seem to have an external cause is almost always a sign that significant emotional or consciousness shifts are happening below the level of my awareness. (These typically do, after a while, reveal their substance to my conscious mind.)

It's no surprise that we rarely consider how energetically taxing conscious and less-than-conscious emotional work can be. We live in a culture that gives little value or credibility to inner work or the emotional side of our experiences. How we deal with grief and loss – being strong, stoic, getting on with life quickly (the Jackie Kennedy model) or taking anti-depressant medications to "get back on one's feet again" – is a case in point, revealing the crazy, devastating disregard we generally have for emotional processes/processing.

I've seen that my tiredness and exhaustion also come from unacknowledged internal demands I've lived with. I've been run, most of my life, by a pressing need to come to completion or closure in anything I was doing before I could have my own permission to take a break or rest. It never seemed to matter whether it was something significant (like a paper or report) or something fairly inconsequential (like the dishes after company for dinner or cleaning my house). I'd keep pushing through till every last "t" was crossed, the last dish dried and put away or the last mat shaken out before I could let my self take a break or unplug.

On top of it all, I was a dedicated list maker. Resting and taking breaks were always postponed till I'd finished whatever was on the current list. Of course, by the time I'd get near the end of the original list, a secondary follow-up list had already been generated; still more to keep pushing through. The moment when the reward of rest was finally earned or appropriate never seemed to arrive.

I find my self apologizing to my poor body for all the times I have, over the years, forced her to push through her tiredness. This pushing usually involved combinations of coffee, chocolate, food, diet-pills and tuning out on my body. Pushing through always costs. (Even as it is **so** positively reinforced in our culture.) It requires using up some of one's core energy, the non-replaceable energy that doesn't fully replenish with the resting that's been delayed till much later than when it was needed.

I feel sad that it's taken so long for me to stop these socially approved of ways of mistreating my body. But, I'm grateful that I don't and won't do that to my self any more. I've had to work diligently at letting go of the insidious imperative of needing completion in order to deserve rest. Part of the work has been experimenting with defining smaller bits-of-completion that I could reward with breaks. Some of it (**very** brave and edgy) has involved just going ahead to risk taking breaks smack in the middle of the activity. And, a good deal of it has been the delightful outcome of my evolving commitment to the revolutionary notion of rest and rewards **first**, work second.

I've also experimented with limiting my list making to grocery lists, errand lists just for a particular day's travels out in the world and occasional lists of clothing, etc. to be gathered for a trip. Every once in a while, the old urge overtakes these limits and I feel pressed to write things down because they're noisily circling in my head. I've learned not to take those getting-things-out–of-my-head lists as imperatives. For the rest, I practice surrendering into the faith that Spirit/my inner self will lead me to whatever needs doing or remembering. This actually works amazingly well and in the **most** magical ways.

As I've moved further into the habit of taking unearned breaks before or without completions, I've realized something about those over-the-edge periods when we're feeling the crunch of time pressure, constantly watching the clock and whipping our selves into an hysterical frenzy over how what needs doing can't possibly be done in the time available. These are interludes when rest and breaks are more essential and productive than ever.

During these times, our bodies and psyches are screaming for some moments of heads-down, stop-the-world, take a few deep belly breaths, stand up and do some stretching, stretch out (even on the floor) for ten minutes, walk outside to get some fresh air, read a few pages of an unrelated book, space out. And, the strange truth is that in these crunch times, even the most minimalist rest-breaks actually help us to be more efficient. When we are faithful to the practice of bringing them into the picture, these breaks interrupt the momentum of the tension and frenzy. They unknot our brains and our energy, allowing us to flow more freely in our tasks.

I'm suspicious of all messages, no matter from where they originate, that tell us that there's no time for rest. Telling our selves that or telling our selves that there isn't time enough to do what has to be done are both ways that we shoot our selves in the foot. When we instead decide to tell our selves that we have enough time, that we in fact have all the time we actually need – these messages open up our psychic space and become the truth of the matter.

Coming out-of-the-closet about our tiredness, honoring it, our need for rest and the sacredness of rest are – in our more-bigger-faster-yesterday culture – radical, insurrectionist acts. It helps things along when we can consider turning off cell and regular phones and going off-line for even some small bits of time. Being always accessible adds significantly to our exhaustion and makes resting/down-time much harder to come by.

Part of being a revolutionary for rest is speaking out, loudly and proudly for the time-out that one is taking. As more of us value rest and openly acknowledge the acceptability of our feeling tired, we help subvert the dominant paradigm of whirling super-achieving as the epitome of worthwhile humanness. I love it when someone I haven't seen for ages or someone new to me asks what I'm up to these days. It tickles me so to watch their disconcerted reaction to my exhilarated "As little as possible!" response.

It's important to for us to gather as much support as we can while we move to reclaim the sacredness of rest and the righteousness of feeling tired. Two of my favorite writers are Rest Radicals who speak out loud about resting. Susan Kennedy, better known as SARK, has written the ultimate nap book: *Change Your Life without Getting Out of Bed.* Most of her other truly delightful books are full of insurrectionary rest messages as well (do visit www.planetsark.com). Anne Lamott's columns in back issues of *Salon* (the on-line magazine at www.salon.com) are often liberally laced with rest radicalism. Her *Traveling Mercies, Plan B* and *Grace, Eventually* essay collections are wonderfully counter-the-dominant-paradigm in this and other self-care domains.

Consider the possibility of resting whenever you're tired (what a concept) and consider celebrating your courageous self whenever you do just that.

4-12. Being Different

When it gets hard, remember to remind your self that it's okay to be different!

I've been marching to a different rhythm from nearly everyone around me for most of my life. In my earliest days, though, I didn't notice or know that this was what was so for me. Others' reactions to or comments about me over the years gradually made me conscious of my differentness. With that consciousness, feeling good about my self sometimes became a daunting prospect.

When It Gets

Hard,

Remember To

Remind Your

Self That

It's Okay To

Be Different!

j3

I felt confused by my differentness; upset by the teasing and snubbing to which I was subject. Often I felt odd, out-of-place and even crazy compared to my peers. Yet, I couldn't find other ways to be that felt any better to me. When I tried to copy normal behavior – what everyone else was doing – I felt even crazier, completely off balance. And, most of the time I wasn't particularly good at the business of passing for normal. Turning to my own company gave me the solace and comfort absent for me in the society of my cohort.

In part, my being a loner was simply how I came into the world. It was, as well, the way I learned to survive the inadequate, often hostile mothering that I received as a little person. After my early experiences of not fitting in with others my age, I became even more invested in being my own best company. Of course, the more time I spent with my self, separate from others my age, the wider the gap between us became. I was old-for-my-age, wondering and feeling about things that were of little concern to my peers. The more I wondered, the more out-of-sync with them I became.

My fascination with inner landscapes started in those years and expanded as I read my way across the library's shelves. I identified with and lived in the worlds that I read about or listened to on the radio. Everything evoked vivid visuals in my mind's eye and empathy in my emotional being. I traveled far and wide, back in time and across many geographies as I explored fairy tales from around the world and the myths and legends of many other cultures. Inspired, I wrote poems and stories of my own, drew pictures and created my own fantasy worlds. In summers in the mountains, I played in imaginary worlds among the trees and tall grasses. And, I watched and listened intently (and secretly) to the adult world around me, always more captivated by that world than the world of my age group.

For a brief two-year period in high school, I was part of a cohort of Honor Society students that did a lot of theater and musical projects together. It was a fleeting season of feeling part of a group of people my own age. We were a fringe-y group – what would probably be called nerds these days. And, as might be expected, I teetered at the fringe of the fringe.

In my early mid-thirties I hung out with and seemed, for a time, part of another small fringe-y cohort. In that season the group was one of social activist feminists-coming-out-as-political-lesbians.

Except for those two periods in my life, I've rarely fit in with the norms of my age peers, my professional peers or my cultural/socio-economic peers. Through the years my differentness has felt like one of the most significant aspects of my being-in-the-world. In my lower-middle-class-aspiring, actually working class family, it was cause for others' consternation, dubious commentary and perplexed questioning.

I was sexually active much earlier than my friends and living on my own when nice-Jewish-girls of my age/class didn't do that. Then I lived, unmarried, with a man well before that was considered acceptable behavior for young women my age. Once I married, keeping my own name, choosing not to have children, living in an open marriage and having a woman lover continued to place me at the fringe. Dropping out of my highly successful private practice in psychotherapy and my open marriage to live alone in a van traveling to and around the West Coast made my oddness even more notable.

Devoting my self to recovering from a lifetime of super-achieving, committing my self to self-nurture, living in the slow lane with lots of timeless resting, choosing the richness of empty time over the riches of high income in a culture that measures our value by how busy we are and how much money we make at our busyness – all this placed me beyond the pale in newer ways.

Owning my voracious hunger for solitude, respecting my abiding inclination to have only my self as significant-other and choosing to live in a primary relationship with my Self rather than with another person in a culture whose gold standard is a two-by-two socially outgoing existence – has continued to mark me as outsider.

Through all these years of being on the fringes of my culture, of following my own inner urgings rather than doing what was expected of me, I've had both wonderful and excruciating times. The wonderfulness has come from and with living in harmony with my true nature: standing firmly in and acting from the truths at the center of my being.

The excruciating times have come at moments of inner upheaval or transition. In these times the ground under me grows unstable. I'm no longer who I've been and not yet clear about who I'm becoming. The truths at my center are wobbly. Until fairly recently, I could be swept up in agonizing self-doubt and self-criticism during these transitioning periods. The stinging voice of my now mostly defanged inner-critic can still, even these days, rise briefly to the surface when I'm on such shaky ground.

When life is calm, I feel quite okay about my differentness, my out-of-pattern choices. I no longer have the need (as I earlier did) to see my differentness as my being superior in order to feel at peace with it. When I'm hanging out in the between-place and feeling disoriented, uneasiness about my differentness comes up and my inner critic often snidely insinuates that I choose the ways I do because I can't handle real life, that I'm too damaged/too screwed up/too vested in being different for its own sake to handle living "like a normal person."

I'm more likely, lately, to recognize that voice/those nasty insinuations as a signal that I need to attend to parts of me that are frightened by the bigness or uncertainties of the changing that's taking place. I'm able, then, to avoid getting caught up in going for the whole awful ride that the critic used to take me on. Instead, I gather the little scared parts to me and work to help them feel more safe with the shakiness of the transition process.

I remind my self that it doesn't matter why I choose what I do, only that I keep on choosing what feels right to me. I remind my self that in these times of turmoil I inevitably feel uncertain about my choices, more vulnerable to my own or others' outside-eyes challenges about my process. I remind my frightened self that there's nothing wrong with us or with our path. I remind my self that it's all right to be different **even** in times when being different feels scary and difficult.

I move more slowly and gently than usual during these unsteady periods. When I'm feeling so vulnerable and un-jelled, I'm particularly careful about where or around whom I'm putting my self. I stay away from situations and people who might intentionally (out of fear) or inadvertently (out of caring) press me to opt for what they see as the comfort/safety of conventional choices. Gradually, as I come more solidly into the next me-that-I-am-becoming, the shakiness quiets down. I again feel centered and comfortable with all of the who(s) that I am.

Living in a world where difference and living from one's own personal ethic are viewed with suspicion, it's essential to keep reminding our selves that being different and choosing differently than the herd is an acceptable option. It helps to remind our selves that being different is merely that – not being better or being worse than; that even though being different can be hard out-there, it's a perfectly fine way to be, particularly when it's our basic nature.

When we're feeling intense pressure to be like everyone else, to not honor all of whom we each are – it's important to remember that, no matter what **anybody** (including our own inner critical voice) says, it's actually essential for us each to be all of whom we are, to live from the center of our own truths. No one else carries our particular thread into the tapestry of all life. If we don't honor it and carry it with integrity and commitment, it will (as Martha Graham pointed out) forever be lost from the whole.

The words of e.e. cummings speak to the intensity of that commitment: "being nobody but your self – in a world which is doing its best, night and day, to make you like everybody else – means to fight the hardest battle any human being can fight, and never stop fighting."

When life gets hard, remember how important it is to lovingly remind your self that it really **is** okay to be different.

The Sacred Feminine

*(This piece was written in 1996 during a season when
I was collaborating with a close friend creating women's
craft shows, drumming events and shared booth spaces
at many west coast women's gatherings.)*

Twenty-four [now, in 2012, almost forty] years ago at 32, I was in a successful feminist marriage, working as a psychologist in a full-time private practice in New York City, doing a thousand and one productive activities in a thousand and one creditable domains. (See **Pirouettes**, page 125 for more of those details.) No matter how well I did all that I took on, I usually still felt horrible about my self. I felt like an imposter: always in imminent danger of being exposed as worthless, either never-enough or else too-much.

A severe backache compounded my low-level chronic depression at the same time I realized there was nothing more I could think of to do to prove my worth to the relentless critic inside my head. At that moment I went over the edge. I had one of those 1970s "CLICKS!" I realized that if all I was doing and accomplishing wasn't enough to make me feel okay, no amount of more doings could ever do it any better. In that blindingly clear moment, I saw the swindle I'd been sold over and over again all through my life: the belief that worthiness and lovableness were not intrinsic, not my birthright; that they had to be earned by deeds; that love received just-for-being was valueless. The critic-in-my-head had bought that bill of goods and daily re-sold it to me from the inside of my very own being.

In that moment, I felt, in my belly, a profound realization: if I couldn't feel worthy just-for-being, no amount of doing could ever be enough to give me a dependable sense of value. Underneath all the achievements, accomplishments and applause I would always know and feel a deep sense that any false step could reveal the empty, worthless core of me.

In that moment, (although I would not fully understand it for many years) I took a powerful, empowering leap into an alternate reality. I began by practicing a different response to the periodically recurring sense that I wasn't enough. Each time, I risked doing **less** (rather than more) of what I was already doing at the moment I had the feeling of being not-enough.

That practice began the process of refusing to accept the whole crazy-making framework that kept telling me that only more, bigger, faster, yesterday was valuable or okay. That practice began (just barely) the process of learning to listen to the deep (yet faint) voice of the Sacred Feminine (the Great Mother/The Grandmothers) re-emerging in my consciousness.

Over the years since that luminous moment, I have been listening more and more closely to the now not-so-faint voice of the Sacred Feminine as it speaks through my inmost self. I am coming to live and move more and more of the time in that parallel, sometimes invisible, universe where woman-centered values, ethics and inner-knowing guide my choices. I remember to love my self no matter what anyone else thinks or says about me. I go only as fast as the slowest part of me feels safe to go. I am compassionate, gentle and tender with my self. I remember that rest is a sacred act: as significant, productive and meaningful as any other activity. I remember to listen inward when I feel confused, trusting my body and my belly to let me know what is so for me. And, I keep letting go of all the rules and forms I've been taught when they conflict with what my inner knowing tells me.

In work a close friend and I have been doing together over the past few years we have been taking what we each have learned from our separate experiences of listening inward to our deep selves and begun the exciting process of exploring how collaboration unfolds in the field of the Sacred Feminine. We repeatedly discover that old forms and ways (even those that are much honored) feel confining and deadening. It seems almost impossible to have new things happen through the old forms. We are constantly being taught to create only loose and permeable containers for the work; to be willing to let go even of provisional form if what comes to fill it takes us somewhere else. We are taught to stay with intentions rather than to be limited by more focused goals, to stay unattached to outcome and to be willing to range where the energy in the moment takes us.

We learn to follow the lead of Spirit/our inmost selves taking the first steps as they come to us, believing that the unfolding energy will shape and refine us as we move along with it. We trust that we do not need to see where we are going, only the step that asks to be taken next. We learn to stop all forward motion whenever either of us feels uncomfortable (even when we are barely able to articulate the nature of the discomfort). We have faith that the discomfort in our feelings or in our bodies is an important message about what is or isn't going on in the sharing. We accept that what becomes manifest in either of us has significance for both of us in the shared field.

We talk about what has words, we listen inward and we listen to each other. We sit in silence, we ask Spirit for help and guidance. Sometimes we rant about our frustration, sometimes we cry. Sometimes we just slow down and breathe. We are clear about our differences when they emerge. We do not require that we agree, or that we do things similarly, only that we clearly hear each other's view/concern/need. Rather than homogenizing our selves or compromising the best of what we each hope for, we risk sitting with the edges and discomfort of our differences until we see the way that honors the essence of what both of us need.

Sometimes it's excruciating, this process, this waiting. We stay long past the threshold at which the discomfort might in the past have caused us to cave in. We stay because we believe it **is** possible for each of us to have 100% of what we need in the shared space. Sometimes the path to resolution reveals itself easily and magically.

Sometimes when it's hard, we each give our selves permission to walk away from it all for a time (or even to entertain the possibility that we might just let it go forever). Then the magic creeps up behind us and happens anyway. And, what looked like an ending or a detour instead opens a whole new path.

Opening to the energy of the Sacred Feminine Field (and our deep selves) has kept us both moving beyond our limited earlier visions: of our selves, of our collaboration and of the work we are being asked to do each moment.

In the Sacred Field of the Feminine we remember that we can be loving, compassionate and tender with our selves in every moment no matter how imperfect we may believe we are. We remember the magic of going slowly, the voluptuousness of resting, the extraordinary strength of vulnerability, the wisdom of not-knowing, the pregnant richness of empty places within and around us, the lavish healing gifts of the natural world, the soothing balm of silliness and the numberless other wonders that we, in our inner knowing places, can't help recognizing as familiar, even if long forgotten.

May we all keep learning to ever better hear the voice of our inner knowing selves, and may we always walk and dance in the wisdom and beauty of the Sacred Feminine as She lives within us.

Afterword

In each of us, often deeply buried and inaccessible, lives a vibrant, inviolable creature self, the pure essence of who we truly are. When not interfered with, this deep self – our wise and knowing simple animal being – unerringly, instinctively moves us toward that which grows and nurtures us. Just as unfailingly, it moves us away from all that endangers us on any level.

The whole process of socialization in our so-called modern western culture is a relentless curriculum that surrounds and embeds us in values and prescriptions that undermine and contradict the credibility of these inner urgings.

So much of what ails us and causes us intense grief and struggle in our lives comes from our being cut off, alienated from the knowings of this essential self. The pain of this alienation is further compounded by the myriad liminal and subliminal messages that threaten us with the loss of the love, care and relationship with all who matter to us should we choose to turn inward to make connection with our deep self a priority. We are warned that self-ishness is always unacceptable, reprehensible.

We have come to be frightened of authenticity, of strong emotions of any sort: joy, sorrow, anger, grief, fullness-of-self. We have learned to fear and override the need for slowness, the need for rest: for empty time and space to be inward, quietly reflective.

The healing journey of finding our way home, of making peace with all the parts of our selves is one of un-layering, of shedding and separating our selves from the misguided beliefs and requirements by which society has disconnected us from the place of wholeness within us. It is the slow, careful process of uncovering and exploring the depths of who we truly are, of our wild authentic selves.

Gently and lovingly we create a safe oasis in which first to observe and then to begin suspending the self-undermining ways we have been taught to live. In this oasis, away from the clamor of things as they are out-there, we allow the truth within us to surface, to be heard. Over time, with great care and patience, we begin the practice of living from the center of our selves, from our deepest truths.

Some Loving Reminders
for the Practice

The loving acceptance you so deeply hunger for can never reach you until you've learned to give that gift to your self.

You **are** entitled to love your self just exactly as you are right now.

You are always doing the best you can in this moment. If you could do better, you would do better.

Practice being as gentle with your self as you would be with anyone else you truly cared about.

Listen in to your body and your belly feelings, they will always tell you what's so for you.

Practice making room and safe space to feel **all** of your feelings.

Speak kindly and lovingly to your self as much of the time as possible.

When you feel sad, depressed or in grief, take time and space to fold inward to be with the aching and the tears until they're done. (They **will** be done, sometime.)

Listen to your angry, nasty, mean-spirited feelings, they tell you when something not-good-for-you is going on.

When you feel scared or anxious, move more slowly, ask the frightened part what it would need in order to feel safe.

Go only as fast as the slowest part of you feels safe to go.

Remember that growth is a process, not an achievement. When you feel discouraged, take time to lovingly acknowledge how far you've already come...there is **always** further yet to go.

Remember, too, that all life moves in cycles...what has been must often come apart before what is to be can come together.

When you're tired, rest, **especially** when there's no-time-to-rest.

Remember that rest is a sacred act – as significant, meaningful, productive and honorable as any other purposeful act.

When it gets hard, remind your self that it's okay to be different.

Applaud all the baby steps along the way of your journey. Acknowledge the wonder of your persistence in the difficult times. Marvel at the miracle of your courage and your trust-in-the-process.

Delight in your self at every possible opportunity: you are a magnificent work-in-progress!

Appendix I:

Finding the Story/Essay for Any
Rememberings and Celebrations Card

In the Table of Contents – in parentheses after each story/essay title – you'll see a lower case letter and number combination. These same combinations appear in the bottom right corner of each card illustration. This is my way of organizing the cards according to their images.

It allows one, when randomly choosing a card from a hard copy deck of 64 Rememberings and Celebrations Cards, to locate the story connected with that particular card. The images, named for the energy they embody, provide a basis for grouping the cards.

Using the code below and the details on the following pages, you should easily be led to the page where the card's story begins.

 Bursting – cards with this image have a b + a number

 Cherishing – cards with this image have a c + a number

 Enfolding – cards with this image have an e + a number

 Jumping – cards with this image have a j + a number

 Opening – cards with this image have an o + a number

Resting – cards with this image have an r + a number

 Soaring – cards with this image have an s + a number

Pages on Which a Particular Story/Essay Appears:

Appendix II

Ordering information

Compassionate Ink is the publishing imprint through which Robyn offers her nourishing collection of resources celebrating going slowly, compassionately embracing all of our feelings, nurturing the Little Ones Inside and honoring the Sacred Feminine.

The forthelittleonesinside.com and the compassionateink.com websites host the words, images and tales Robyn has been creating over the years. These have all emerged from her dedicated life-long journey of healing (and helping others heal) from the harshness that our crazy-making world visits upon all of us, especially women. (Robyn L. Posin, Ph.D. is a licensed psychologist in private practice in Ojai, California.)

Go Only as Fast as Your Slowest Part Feels Safe to Go: Tales to Kindle Gentleness and Compassion for Our Exhausted Selves is also available in Kindle, iBook and Nook formats. After a first read of these emotionally uncensored, autobiographical healing tales, many open the book randomly in moments of unease, confusion or doubt and read the chapter to which they've opened as a message from Spirit/their Deep Self.

Tenderly Embracing All the Ways that I Feel and Am: Journaling to Kindle Gentleness and Compassion for Our Precious Selves is a natural extension of and companion to *Go Only as Fast as Your Slowest Part Feels Safe to Go*. A bound 8.5" x 11" journal, its otherwise blank pages are edged with words and images to inspire and invite you to kindle gentleness and compassion for your precious self as you write, draw, explore and reflect on your journey.

Choosing Gentleness: Opening Our Hearts to All the Ways We Feel and Are In Every Moment, is a collection of short essays and poems-with-drawings that encourage us to give our selves permission to be exactly how we are in every moment—to honor and embrace wherever we are in our process without criticism and to treat all of our feelings with tenderness and compassion.

Catalog of Treasures

Ordering information for the Remembering and Celebrations Cards, the deck of 64 bookmark-size cards that you've seen, paired with their tales, in *Go Only as*

Fast as Your Slowest Part Feels Safe to Go: Tales to Kindle Gentleness and Compassion for Our Exhausted Selves can be found at www.compassionateink.com/catalog-of-treasuresalt. There you'll also find ordering information for Robyn's collection of healing note cards, postcards, poster cards and amulets.

Appendix III:

Robyn's Availability

A California Licensed Psychologist, I have been working with clients since 1964. I'm available for open-ended, one-time or ongoing individual consultations by phone or in person in Ojai, California.

My commitment is to creating safe space in which to help people (re)connect with and honor the wisdom of their own inner knowing: the wisdom that can guide us to living life more in harmony with who we truly are, even in this crazy-making, invalidating world.

I work interactively, dedicated, as far as I'm able, to working in your personal idiom rather than pushing you to work in mine. My approach is eclectic, influenced by a strong feminist consciousness: I think it's important to note when and where noxious cultural influences are contributing to what ails us. A deep spiritual consciousness (not about God/Goddess or any particular religion or ism) is another element that I bring to the work: I believe we come into a body to do soul work and that we can experience our selves as more than merely victims if/when we see the challenges we're facing as opportunities to grow our selves/ our souls.

Part of helping you (re)connect with your inner knowing involves having you be in charge both of how long we meet in any session and how often you choose to return. Each time we meet, we work until you reach some closure around the issue(s) you've brought to the session. Usually this comes when you have some clear ideas of what you might focus on as you continue the work on your own. The option of such organic closure allows your work to progress more efficiently. Some people use as little as 35 minutes each time while others use as much as three hours. At the end of each session, you pay/send a check for the time you've used, pro-rated at my current hourly fee.

If you'd like to talk about the possibility of arranging an individual consultation and check on my current fee, you can drop me an email at Robyn@compassionateink.com.

About the Author

Robyn spent her first 32 years as a hyper-self-critical, super-achiever never at peace with her self. Just past her 32nd birthday, at the urging of a voice deep within her, she dropped out of that life, took to the road in a self-contained van and began the journey of uncovering who she might be without the overlay of all her driven excelling.

Now in her mid 70s, she lives life in the slow lane, at peace (at last) with all the ways she is and isn't. With two affectionate, quirky kitties, in a small rented cottage surrounded by a private meadow, she grows food and flowers in containers, feeds myriad seed-feeding and humming-birds, spends endless hours reading in her hammock, floating in her hot tub, aimlessly puttering around the house and garden, walking about town and on the local trails, seeing therapy clients a few hours on two days every other week, occasionally hosting free and for-donation women's wisdom circles, writing almost-monthly columns for her website and sleeping in a windowed tent in her meadow year round but for rainy or windy days.

Writing and making art weave randomly through her days and this (her first) book has been birthed in a seven-year process of going only as fast as her slowest part felt safe to go.